CHRISTIAN TRAINING P

CW00835787

ENGLISH BAPTIST HISTORY AND HERITAGE

A Christian Training Programme Course

by Rev Roger Hayden

Secretary of the Baptist Historical Society

Illustrations by Jane Gascoigne

Published by
The Baptist Union of Great Britain
April 1990

© Author and The Baptist Union of Great Britain 1990

ISBN 0 901472 13 1

Designed, typeset and produced for the Baptist Union of Great Britain by
Gem Publishing Company, Brightwell, Wallingford, Oxfordshire.

Printed in Great Britain by Pike Printers, Kettering, Northamptonshire.

Contents

Preface

This CTP manual on Baptist History and Heritage has been prepared with several aims.

BAPTIST UNION EXAM

The material provides the basic text-book for those preparing to take the BU exams in Baptist History and Baptist Principles. The examination questions will be based on material in the book, but in addition the following books should also be carefully read: B.R. White, *The English Baptists of the Seventeenth Century* and Raymond Brown, *The English Baptists of the Eighteenth Century*. Both these books are published by the Baptist Historical Society, in 1983 and 1986 respectively. E.A. Payne's *The Baptist Union: A Short History* will provide further material on the nineteenth and twentieth centuries. Dr. Payne's book is available from BU Publications in Didcot.

Throughout this present volume there are frequent occasions when you are invited TO THINK ABOUT the material you are reading and its application to Christian discipleship and church life today. If you are preparing for the BU exams then these questions point in the direction of issues you will be asked to discuss.

BAPTIST IDENTITY

The material might also be of use in ministers' fraternals or church study groups. In these contexts the TO THINK ABOUT questions will be of special value and will, we hope, contribute to the contemporary discussions relating to Baptist identity. To understand their heritage will help Baptists today make a considered and constructive contribution to discussions about both inter-church relations and the place of the historic denominations in the overall Christian scene in this country.

PERSONAL INTEREST AND STUDY

Our hope is that this volume will also find its way into the hands of many folk, both in Baptist churches and those of other persuasions, who simply enjoy discovering the thought and practice of God's people in previous generations. For some it may be an introduction to their understanding of the people called Baptists.

ACKNOWLEDGEMENTS

Several people have either supplied photographic material for reproduction in this volume or granted permission for material to be copied. We gladly acknowledge the co-operation of the *British Library*; the *Baptist Historical Society*; the *Baptist Missionary Society*; *Churchman's Publishing Limited* to reproduce material from John Caffyn's *Sussex believers: Baptist marriage in the 17th and 18th Centuries*; the *East Midlands Baptist Association*; *Bristol Baptist College*; *Regent's Park College, Oxford*; *Broadmead Baptist Church, Bristol*; *Arnesby Baptist Church*; *Haven Green Baptist Church* and *Horsham Unitarian Church*.

Paul Mortimore
Editor

Author's Preface

The writing of a Christian Training Programme script on this theme puts the author under great stress. It requires a general knowledge covering a long period of history. Inevitably it is highly selective and has to leave out so much that could properly have appeared within it. In the end there will be some emphases which are not quite in tune with reality. For this I apologise, and especially if I have misrepresented some of my friends. There is only one proper remedy. Get hold of the primary documentation and read it for yourself, and enjoy its thrill as you get a glimpse of what other Christians have discovered by the Holy Spirit in times past.

The errors are all mine; but I thank a wide range of friends who have shared this project with me, not least the present CTP Secretary, who has worked so hard to present a lively, illustrated text, which is a tremendous help to learning.

Roger Hayden

UNIT 1

History and Baptist Historians
A brief over-view of Baptist origins

WHAT IS HISTORY?

A study of Baptist history of necessity begins with a fundamental question: What is history?

History, it has been claimed, is concerned with the 'resurrection of that which happened once' (G.J. Renier). Historians are those who use knowledge, imagination and mastery of the available evidence to cry: 'Lazarus come forth'. This is a distinctly different approach from that of the scientist who seeks by knowledge to repeat in the present, again and again, that which happened once in the past. The historian's task is to discover all the traces left by unique, unrepeatable events and so determine what actually happened once or who said what, where, and when? And through it all comes the insistent question: Why?

In the laboratory the scientist can speak of tracks or 'traces' as an invisible particle leaves bubbles in a liquid. The historian has a host of 'trace' items to call on in his task of resurrecting that which happened once. An item of

clothing, a coin of the realm, a picture, a published work, a building, a map, are all such 'trace' elements. There is also such non-material evidence as the conviction of people called Christians that Jesus is alive.

The natural world is mysterious, hiding its secrets cleverly, and is unwilling to reveal them – but it has no forgeries, and it does not lie. Not so the people who make history, nor even, sometimes, those who write it! Lies and forgeries are occasionally part of the history. Documents from the past must be evaluated in respect of authenticity. If they are genuine, are their contents true or false? To what extent has the writer's involvement in the events blinded him to some facts and coloured his judgment about others?

WRITING HISTORY

When all the available evidence has been assembled, and its worth evaluated, how is 'history' to be written? Usually it is presented as a description of political, economic, social and religious factors which interact and mingle together as part of a 'period' of history. A few have tried presenting history 'in the round', ignoring the usual sub-divisions in the interests of presenting the life of the period as a complex yet unified whole. Many historians only write about a specific, very limited, area of concern, yet it would be wrong to judge that one type is more historical than another.

History writing can be painted on a considerably broader canvas. The attempt is made to put the human story of centuries in a single perspective. The concern is to uncover the forces at work in history, to reveal the rhythm or pattern of history.

The Decline of the West (1918) by Oswald Spengler presented the human story in terms of organisms which passed through a recognisable life cycle. The early, creative period derives from a rural society, and this moves through urbanisation to decay and death, just as the seasons of the year pass from Spring through to Winter. The demise of civilisation has little to do with human frailty and everything to do with the inevitable death which falls on society in its winter season. Humanity has no choice in the matter.

For Arnold Toynbee history comprised twenty-one complete and five 'arrested' civilisations. Each civilisation is faced with a challenge which varies in form from place to place, and its future depends on the response. It can react positively, and make new growth; or it can fail to respond and then disintegration follows. It is the human beings in each civilisation who have the qualities which can move society forward, but they do not always use them properly. Such a cyclical view of history, in which the human race moves the wheel of history towards its final goal, provides another alternative for interpreting events.

THE IMPORTANCE OF HISTORY FOR CHRISTIANS

Even such a skirmish into the nature of history and the attitudes of historians brings awareness of the importance of history for the Christian community. The Church preaches a Gospel which is rooted in history. The moment when 'the Word became flesh and dwelt among us', within a nation which had spent thousands of years looking for God's anointed one, is a crucial moment for those who are concerned with the resurrection of Christ as the foundation of their faith.

A Baptist Old Testament scholar, who enlivened his chosen area of study with conundrums, once posed the question to his class: 'Why is an Old Testament prophet like the

winner of the Diamond Sculls at Henley?' J.N. Schofield's answer revealed the theological implications of an historical faith succinctly: 'They both move forwards by looking backwards.'

There is great wisdom in Christians taking Isaiah's words to heart, 'Look to the rock from which you were hewn, to the quarry from which you were dug, look to your father Abraham, and to Sarah who gave you birth.' (Isaiah 51:1–2.) Denominational history, as well as that on a much broader canvas, is properly viewed from this perspective, and it is always worth remembering that 'the fate of those who forget their past is to have to relive it'.

> **TO THINK ABOUT . . .**
> We each have a personal history – the story of our lives so far. Recall examples of where you have failed to learn the lessons of your past.

BAPTIST HISTORIANS – THEIR WORKS AND AIMS

It is important to remember that those Baptists who have written about the Baptist heritage prior to the present century have all too often been motivated by very distinct polemical intentions.

1. THOMAS CROSBY (1685–1752)

Crosby published the first ever *History of The Baptists* between 1738 and 1740. He was concerned to show the biblical, theological and historical correctness of believer's baptism. He countered the claim that Baptists were all illiterate labourers and mechanics. He dissociated English Baptists from the continental Anabaptists two centuries earlier. He also promulgated the view that General and Particular Baptists were essentially the same, in the interests of greater denominational unity.

2. JOSEPH IVIMEY (1773–1834)

Ivimey published a four volume *History of the English Baptists* over an eighteen-year period, between 1811–1830. Unlike Crosby, who was a mathematics teacher in Southwark, Ivimey was minister of the Eagle Street Church, London. He regarded himself as both an apologist for and a critic of the Baptists. He was not afraid to expose what he believed to be contemporary Baptist weaknesses – open communion, ignorant ministers, and tyrannical deacons! Positively, he told the Baptist story as one which was concerned with the centrality of Scripture for the life and work of the churches.

He emphasised particularly religious liberty as originating in the Baptist community. He argued the view that infant baptism had its origin in Roman Catholic practice.

> **TO THINK ABOUT . . .**
> If *you* were writing about Baptist life in the 1980s, what three features would you emphasise as weaknesses and what three as strengths of contemporary Baptist churches?

3. WILLIAM J. WHITLEY (1861–1947)

A century later Whitley was the first to apply modern historical methods to English Baptist history. His *History of British Baptists* (Revised Edition, 1932) is a book of substance, and few have equalled his breadth of knowledge. Unfortunately, although he was meticulous in using source materials, he did not provide footnote references! He was the founder, in 1908, and first Secretary of the Baptist Historical Society, and from his pen flowed a host of articles and finely edited source books of Baptist history.

4. A.C. UNDERWOOD (1885–1948)

Underwood relied greatly on Whitley in producing his *History of the English Baptists* (1947). It was the first denominational history to use insights gained by the sociological study of religion. He gave prominence to John Smyth, the first General Baptist, but was uninformed about Calvinistic Baptists especially in the eighteenth century. His use of biographical material was excessive and blurred the real developments among Baptists.

5. ERNEST A. PAYNE (1902–1980)

Payne was the undoubted doyen of English Baptist historians in the twentieth century. His two most influential books were *The Fellowship of Believers* (1944, Rev. Edn, 1952) and *The Baptist Union: A Short History* (1958). The former drew on a wide understanding of Baptist polity over the centuries to answer the question: 'What is the Church?' It demonstrated how locally independent churches are related to each other as a fellowship of believers. The second book chronicled the growth, development and advance of Baptist churches into a national union of churches after 1812. The two volumes bring together a single concern, the desire to understand and re-interpret the meaning of the Church for Baptists in an ecumenical age. Ernest Payne's other major contribution was to the understanding of the modern missionary movement. He wrote a considerable number of articles and books about the Baptist Missionary Society. He set this story within an ecumenical context in his two books *The Free Church Tradition in the Life of England* (1944) and *The Growth of the World Church* (1955).

6. CONTEMPORARY WRITERS

The Baptist Historical Society is at the moment producing a new history of English Baptists under the editorship of its President, Dr B.R. White, who has written the first volume on the seventeenth century. The Society has published the eighteenth-century volume by Dr Raymond Brown. In addition, two further volumes on the nineteenth and twentieth centuries are being prepared (1990). Dr David Bebbington has edited a major book, *The Baptists in Scotland: A History* (1988). Dr Brian Stanley is preparing a new history of the Baptist Missionary Society for the bi-centenary of the Society in 1992.

A BRIEF OVER-VIEW OF BAPTIST ORIGINS

Who was the first Baptist? The question is easily posed but the answer is by no means simple, brief or straightforward. It raises other questions. When and where was the first Baptist church formed and by whom? What factors most properly account for Baptist origins? Without doubt Baptists were the children of the Reformation, and their origins are best determined from within that context. However, we begin with some broad strokes of the brush on the canvas of Baptist history, and then we shall return to fill in the details.

TO THINK ABOUT . . .
In what ways, would we be poorer for not having access to our past.

EARLY BAPTISTS ON THE CONTINENT

Modern Baptist Christians emerged in early seventeenth-century England and Holland. They were part of the radical movement produced by the Reformation in Europe. They were people who were influenced by the life and work of Martin Luther, Ulrich Zwingli and John Calvin, as they sought a spiritual reformation of their lives and a renewal of the Church of Christ. The English Bible was a significant factor in their search. They would have understood the young student Linacre in Cambridge who, when Erasmus's New Testament was published, is reputed to have said: 'Either this is not the Gospel, or we are not Christians.' It was the Bible that brought these Christians to radical faith.

They created churches which were 'separate' from the established church; churches which

The development of printing brought the Bible to the people.

comprised believers only; and churches which sought a 'pure' form of worship, work and witness. Among other dissenters from the establishment, who eventually became Congregationalists, Presbyterian, and Quakers, were those who practised the baptism of believers by immersion in water in the name of the Trinity. They were nicknamed 'Anabaptists' because they baptised people a second time. It was a name which linked them with a very extreme group which had emerged in Munster in 1533–34, under the leadership of the Dutchman Jan Matthys and his successor John of Leyden. After a lengthy siege the apocalyptic community was put to the sword by the Catholic mercenaries surrounding the city, and Munster and Anabaptist became by-words of religious abuse to Catholic and Protestant alike. It was the matter of re-baptism which led people to identify the two groups – but the link was tenuous.

EARLY BAPTISTS IN ENGLAND

Two major groups of Baptists emerged in England in the early 1600s.

a) *The General Baptists*

The first group, chronologically, were the General Baptists, so named because they understood the work of Christ at the cross to have a 'general' application: that is, anyone who voluntarily puts faith in Christ will be saved. They were influenced by the Dutch theologian Jacob Arminius, whose theology was Calvinist in origin but made allowance for the freedom of the will in matters of salvation. The General Baptists also taught, as did Arminius, that it was possible for a Christian to 'fall from grace' – a view that Calvin specifically repudiated, speaking of the 'perseverance of the saints'. In terms of church structure the General Baptists allowed limited congregational autonomy, and gave much more power to Associations and the General Assembly. The originator of the General Baptists was John Smyth (?1570–1612), an Anglican clergyman become separatist, assisted by a wealthy layman, Thomas Helwys. Together they formed the first English Baptist church, on Dutch soil, in 1609.

b) *The Particular Baptists*

Another Baptist group emerged by the late 1630s, led by Henry Jessey, William Kiffin and John Spilsbury. They were Calvinist in theology and separatist in outlook. The Baptist congregation emerged as a result of members of an existing Congregational church advocating believer's baptism as the only right and proper form of the sacrament. They taught a view of the atonement which claimed that Christ did not die for all mankind but only for 'particular' individuals, elect by God's grace from eternity. It was this which gave them their title of Particular Baptists. Like Calvin they believed God had elected only some to salvation and that the elect would persevere and be saved. The earliest church of this persuasion can be dated 1638, though some would put it five years earlier, 1633. Their church structure gave each local fellowship complete church power, while Associations and Assemblies had only advisory powers. Though originating a generation later, they were destined to become the larger of the two groups.

By 1650 both groups were flourishing in England. The General Baptists were very strong in the Midlands and Kent, as well as London, with at least 47 churches sharing in local Associations, and a General Assembly which issued Confessions of Faith. The Particulars had a London-based national organisation by 1645, which issued a Confession of Faith and engaged in evangelistic work in the Midlands, North and West of England, in Wales and Ireland.

TO THINK ABOUT . . .

If you were preparing a discipleship course for new Christians, what key points would you want to stress about where Baptists have come from?

The space below is provided for you, if you wish, to make brief notes about the main features of the early General and Particular Baptists. To understand these now will help as the story unfolds in following units.

GENERAL BAPTISTS   **PARTICULAR BAPTISTS**

Radical Origins of Baptist Churches

> The Reformation sprang fundamentally from the recognition of the urgent necessity for reform of the Church in head and members, and its outward circumstances were determined by the failure of previous attempts to effect reformation through the existing constitutional organs of the Church.
>
> (**N. Sykes,** *Crisis of the Reformation, p*1)

It was the corruption of the Roman Church which brought Luther to add his voice to others that were calling for reformation in 1517. He identified the administrative and financial abuses in the Church. Worldliness and laxity were prevalent in religious communities. Theologians were failing to meet the challenge of the so-called 'Renaissance' scholars who emphasised the difference between Christ's words and example and current practice in the Church.

POINTERS TO THE REFORMATION

Erasmus, the leading scholar of the Renaissance in northern Europe, published the first Greek New Testament in England in 1516. In subsequent writings he did not hesitate to contrast the Catholic and Apostolic Church with the New Testament picture to the detriment of the former. To this he added the Old Testament, with its examples of the King in control of the state, priests and people. This scriptural warrant was welcomed not only by Henry VIII in England, but also by German Princes seeking authority to put down a peasants' revolt in 1525. It would be impossible to over-estimate the influence of the Old Testament precedents for the 'godly prince' in the Reformers' cause. The new power of the press which the development of printing brought to Europe made the results of Biblical and historical studies, pursued with scholarly detachment in universities, the common talk of the market place, where moderation and restraint were less highly prized.

At the heart of medieval Catholicism was the mass. It was believed to be automatic, independent of the faith of either the celebrant or the congregation. This encouraged the saying of masses for their own sake, and they were believed to help those in purgatory gain heaven. Many clergy only said the Latin Mass, spending a lifetime doing that in the various chantry chapels. This mechanistic view of religion led to a remarkable growth of mysticism. Its finest expression was in the work of Thomas a Kempis' (1380–1471) *Imitatio Christi*. Other Christian groups were seeking 'immediacy' in Christian living, and of these 'The Brethren of the Common Life' in southern Germany were a typical example. They contrasted their contact with God, which resulted in an experience of forgiveness and peace, with the empty, repetitive sacramental life of the Church. This experience would give strength later to the insistence on justification by faith alone.

TO THINK ABOUT . . .
Down through Christian history, the Old Testament has been cited to justify various practices and doctrines. Think of some examples from contemporary church life in Britain to illustrate this. What are your own feelings about this tendency?

CONTINENTAL LEADERS OF THE REFORMATION

MARTIN LUTHER (1483–1546)

Martin Luther was a German Roman Catholic priest – an Austin Friar – who spent his teaching life at Wittenberg, a small town 'perched on the edge of beyond'. He went to the heart of things only three times, when he went to Rome, Augsburg and Worms. More than most he let history come to him. However, from his pen flowed books that filled the Christian world with a desire for reformation.

By 1512 the one-time lawyer had become a doctor of theology and he succeeded his friend, John Staupitz, as Professor at Wittenberg. He lectured on *Psalms* between 1513 and 1515; on *Romans* between 1516 and 1517; in 1517 he dealt with *Galations* and in 1518 *Hebrews*. By 1520 Luther had made Wittenberg a centre for the 'new theology' of 'justification by faith alone'. He noted how he personally 'hated this just God who punishes sinners' and through his Biblical studies realised the justice of God was to be interpreted passively. It was 'that whereby the merciful God justifies us by faith . . . at this I felt myself to be born anew, and to enter through open gates into paradise itself.' Luther had this experience before the indulgence controversy.

Penance was a long established practice in the Roman Church. In the Middle Ages the church authorities introduced a secular notion whereby it was agreed that moral offences could be forgiven by a monetary payment. The money raised was used to finance crusades to the Holy Land. The idea behind penance was that Christ had acquired a treasury of merit for the Church on earth which the Pope could dispense as he pleased. By Luther's day the selling of indulgences to raise Papal finances was part of the Catholic way of life. Luther was deeply offended by the way Tetzel came offering an indulgence to finance the building of St Peter's in Rome.

Luther published his objections in the usual academic manner, nailing his ninety-five points (called theses) to the Cathedral door. What he did not foresee was the local printer translating them into German, printing, and then selling them locally. The Reformation had begun. Luther's action led to his excommunication by the Pope. Frederick, Elector of Saxony, saved Luther by having him ambushed while on a journey and taking him into protective custody. Luther worked furiously, and soon his tracts were selling all over Europe, including England.

TO THINK ABOUT . . .
Think of other examples in Christian history of vigorous, influential writing coming from people who were in prison or otherwise confined. Why should this be?

ULRICH ZWINGLI (1484–1531)

At much the same time Ulrich Zwingli, after studying classics at Berne, Basel and Vienna, was appointed priest at Glarus, where he joined Erasmus and other Renaissance scholars. In 1518 he was appointed 'people's priest' in Zurich. Zwingli resolved to preach through Matthew's Gospel exegetically with his congregation. 'His reformation', wrote Professor Rupp, 'was begun, continued, and ended through the agency of prophetic preaching.' It was a unique experiment in which each day the Bible was related to the needs of a small community who knew each other well, and among whom were the city fathers of Zurich. He came near to death in 1519, an experience which brought him close to Scripture. 'I came to the conclusion that you must leave all the rest and learn God's meaning out of his simple word. Then I asked God for light and light came.'

> **TO THINK ABOUT . . .**
> Think of other examples when preaching has played a critical role in renewals and reformations in the church's history. Will our own age be recalled as a period when expository preaching was central?

Zwingli introduced various reforms. He banned images, pictures and music from public worship. In 1525 he introduced a new form of the Lord's Supper. He presided at a table, with wooden beakers and plates, while the congregation remained seated. The congregation took the bread and wine first, the minister last, and it was understood to be a commemorative rite of great simplicity. Prophesyings – which were Biblical exposition followed by congregational comment – became a regular part of worship.

> **TO THINK ABOUT . . .**
> Zwingli's hostile attitude to images and pictures in worship can be explained as a reaction to their emphasis in Catholic worship. Baptists stand in a tradition which similarly is suspicious of them. But what explains our aversion and our fears? To whom might visual aids in worship be helpful?

JOHN CALVIN (1509–1564)

John Calvin, a lawyer trained at the Sorbonne in Paris, was also a great classical scholar. He studied the writings of Luther and other contemporary theologians. He underwent a spiritual experience in 1532 about which he wrote, 'God subdued my heart to docility by a sudden conversion.' His conversion forced him into hiding, and it was while he was passing through Geneva that he was persuaded to become the city's 'reader in Holy Scripture'. His first edition of *Institutes of the Christian Religion* had been published in Basel in 1536.

He did not get on well in Geneva, refusing to be controlled by the city authorities, and was expelled in 1538 to Strasbourg, where he met Martin Bucer. From Bucer Calvin learnt a scriptural doctrine of the Church, including a ministry which involved pastors, elders and deacons. Calvin eventually returned to Geneva and went on to develop these insights in further editions of his *Institutes*, where he accepted reluctantly a quarterly observance of the eucharist, and dropping the laying on of hands in ordination. He proposed a church court which had the right to discipline and excommunicate unrepentant members. In Geneva people could see a theocratic state in action, and many Englishmen thought it the best reformed church.

> Protestantism had been slowing down, its initial impetus spent, it was divided, tired, disheartened. After Calvin it was once more on the move, singing on the march, ready to strike new blows for liberty. He restored the exhilaration of Christian comradeship. He renewed the brave vision of the Word going forth conquering and to conquer. (Rupp, *Cambridge New Modern History*, Vol. vi, *p*119.)

THE RADICAL REFORMATION

The radical reformation comprised those usually categorised by a single word – Anabaptist.

Anabaptist was a term:

> covering a motley collection of beliefs and behaviour which range from mad millenarianism to pietism, from the reckless use of force to pacifism, from the extremes of personal egoism to humble piety and devotion. All these men and women have one thing in common: they do not fit in with any of the established religions and thus offend the principle of uniformity wherever they go . . . The fact that Anabaptism drew its following from the underprivileged is significant enough. (*Cambridge New Modern History*, Vol. vi, *p6*.)

Anabaptism had the unique privilege of uniting both Protestant and Catholic in their opposition to any manifestation of it. A major reason for such united antagonism was the Anabaptist denial of a fundamental medieval conviction, inherited by the Reformers, that church and state are indissoluble. Baptism not only admitted to the church, it also admitted the person to the secular community. To remove this rite from children was not only a spiritual disaster but a revolutionary political statement.

TO THINK ABOUT . . .
Why do you think that today's Free Church people are not more vocal in their opposition to links between church and state?

THE BEGINNINGS OF ANABAPTISM

The re-baptising movement began in Germany and Switzerland. In 1521 three 'prophets' visited Wittenberg from Zwickau. Thomas Müntzer, a Zwickau preacher, proposed a radical reformation of church and society which went far beyond anything suggested by other reformers. The purification of the church must be accompanied, claimed Muntzer, by radical social change. He supported the peasants in their revolt against the established regime and eventually lost his life in the tragic aftermath. Luther was away from Wittenberg when the 'prophets' came. His colleague Carlstadt was greatly influenced by them, but Luther soon changed that and adopted a strong defence of infant baptism.

In Zurich two friends of Zwingli, Conrad Grebel and Felix Manz, both keen for reformation, believed that Zwingli was too cautious in respect of new forms of church life. By June 1524 they were pressing for a 'confessing' church, in which all members would personally testify to faith in Christ and receive baptism on account of that faith. Grebel rejected the idea of a church for 'everybody' and advocated that baptism, signifying cleansing from sin, should be administered only to believing adults. The Lord's Supper he described as a simple meal in the home of the believer, when only the words of institution would be read. Here, in fact, was one of the earliest expositions of what came to be called 'the fellowship of believers'.

In December 1524 Manz wrote to Zwingli arguing that infant baptism was invalid. A disputation was arranged for January 17, 1525, but this was pre-empted by the Zurich town council passing a law forbidding the meeting of those who opposed infant baptism. A few days later, on January 30, a group of friends met with George Blaurock and Conrad Grebel at Zollikon, three miles from Zurich. Blaurock invited Grebel to baptise him by affusion, which he did, and then Blaurock baptised the others. Over the next seven days there were 39 more baptisms. The idea of a confessing, separated church, linked with believer's baptism, was first established in Zurich in 1525. A year later the Zurich town council responded by legislating for the drowning of Anabaptists!

TO THINK ABOUT . . .

This incident, with many other similar stories from Christian history, concentrates the mind on the cost of standing for deeply held principles. If it came to it, for what aspects of your Christian faith would you be prepared to defy the law or become a martyr?

The Mennonite writer, H.S. Bender, described the Anabaptist vision as having three new conceptions:

- that the essence of Christianity is discipleship;
- that the church is to be understood as a brotherhood;
- that it offers a new ethic of love and non-resistance.

The movement spread to Strassbourg, the Tyrol and into Moravia.

Among its leadership were people like Balthazar Hubmaier who wrote a fine defence of toleration in matters of religion, *Concerning Heretics and Those Who Burn Them*. His argument turned on the point that to put a heretic to death did not honour Christ but denied him, since his purpose in coming was to give life. In fact, persecution was an invention of the devil. Hans Denck, who was a considerable Biblical scholar, propounded a doctrine of the 'inner light' in his pamphlet *To Those Who Really Love the Truth*. It was a belief which played a substantial part in English seventeenth-century

religious life and was eventually embodied in the Society of Friends. In the Low Countries and Germany the Anabaptist leader was Melchior Hoffman. He had a docetic view of Christ, teaching that Jesus was born out of Mary, but not of Mary. He was a millenarian who believed the end of the world would be in Strassbourg in 1537 and that he was Elijah, one of the witnesses who would appear before Christ's coming again. His views of the person of Christ affected English General Baptist thought when Matthew Caffyn promulgated them a century later.

Matthew Sattler was the probable author of the earliest Anabaptist Confession of Faith, a document of some significance known as the Schleitheim Articles. The Articles made seven points:

i. Baptism ought to be administered only to those 'who have been taught repentance and a change of life and in truth believe their sins to have been blotted out through Christ, and wholly wish to be buried with him into death that they may be able to rise again'.

ii. This article deals with church discipline, an important aspect of the 'gathered church' concept with its emphasis on holy living.

iii. It is stated that only baptised believers are able to share fellowship at the Lord's Table.

iv. The necessity of separating the 'true' from the 'false' church is established.

v. This article deals with the qualifications and functions of a pastor.

vi. 'The sword is an ordinance of God outside the perfection of Christ, by which the evil man is punished . . . but the good man defended.' For this reason a Christian should not accept the office of magistrate since it would involve using the power of the sword.

vii. It is forbidden to swear oaths, on the basis of Matthew 5: 34. This stand made a deep impression on society which had for centuries rested on the oath as a basis for establishing truth and justice in the courts of the land.

TO THINK ABOUT . . .

Which of these principles would you want to endorse? How 'radical' would they be considered in today's church scene in Britain?

TYPES OF ANABAPTISTS

Just who the Anabaptists were is difficult to answer, but the distinctions of Ernest Troeltsch are useful. He writes of Evangelical, Spiritualist and Anti-Trinitarian Anabaptists.

The **Evangelical** Anabaptists took the Bible very literally, believing it to be God's Word, authoritative for mankind and capable of interpretation by the Holy Spirit's work. This led to a belief in the visible church as a fellowship of believers, who alone shared the benefits of the Lord's Table. Grebel (1489–1526), Felix Manz (d.1527), Blaurock (d.1529) and Balthasar Hubmaier (1481–1528) were among their gifted leaders.

The **Spiritualists** set the direct inspiration of the Holy Spirit above the Word of God, although they were not averse to checking the revelation against the revealed Word of Scripture. They owed much to medieval mystics, played down the 'visible church' concept, and had no great interest in the sacraments. Thomas Muntzer (1490–1561), Andreas Carlstadt (1481–1541) and Caspar Schwenkfeld (1489–1561) belonged to this group.

The **Anti-Trinitarian** Anabaptists, as their name suggests, were those who denied the Trinitarian understanding of God's person. Their two most famous leaders were Michael Servetus (1510–1553) and Faustus Socinus (1534–1604) whose ideas persisted in Europe throughout the next two centuries.

The Anabaptist movement was large numerically, drawing many thousands to follow them because they were, as Henry Bullinger wrote, 'living saints'. The reason for their small influence in the Reformation period is their complete lack of organisation and state support; the violent persecution of their leaders by various state authorities in the 1530s; the total rejection of their ideas by reformers such as Luther, Zwingli and Calvin; and the 'lunatic fringe' which carried some Anabaptists into political extremes thought to herald the coming of Christ. Anabaptism was a child of the Reformation, and of Zurich in particular. Its thought forms were entirely religious but its challenge to church–state relationships had political implications which no state authority could tolerate at that period.

> **TO THINK ABOUT . . .**
> Is the expression 'lunatic fringe' emotive and subjective? Not long ago, some might have described those in the ecology movement as being on the 'lunatic fringe', but today 'ecology' is a respectable term. How do you discern between misguided fanatics and minorities who may be prophets before their time?

ANABAPTIST PRINCIPLES

It would be misleading to suggest that Anabaptists produced clear ecclesiological structures for the churches to adopt, but some clear principles emerge from a wealth of written materials, which have been summarized by Dr W.M.S. West in *Christian Baptism* (1961).

1. **The Bible is the Word of God** and therefore absolutely authoritative. Only practices specifically mentioned in the New Testament should be followed. The New Testament was the final

court of appeal, the new covenant having abrogated the old. They were Bible Christians of a precise kind. When opponents claimed they had Zwingli's word on a situation, their reply was that they had God's Word on it!

They had two weaknesses. They jumped from Scripture to their own time as if the Holy Spirit had not been active in the intervening period. They failed to distinguish between Biblical practices which were essential because they arose out of the Gospel and those which were only a response to a first-century custom.

TO THINK ABOUT . . .

This is a perennial matter for Christians to debate. What are some issues in today's church which focus the same problems in defining the right use of Scripture?

2. They advocated **a church model which was free from any state control** and known as a fellowship of believers. They claimed that the Roman model of the church, when measured against Scripture, was entirely false. They were convinced that the reformers' models also fell far short of the New Testament. They taught that the church required restitution, not reformation. They put considerable blame for all this on the Emperor Constantine, and thought the reformers only 'half-way' men. They understood themselves to be a covenanted people, with baptism a covenant sign of a good conscience with God.

3. For Anabaptists the New Testament taught only **the baptism of believers** upon a confession of personal faith in and allegiance to Christ: a concept which opposed the medieval church–state relationship and brought the charge of anarchy on the Anabaptists. Zwingli opposed abuses of the medieval system. Anabaptists opposed the fundamental concept of the system.

4. They were convinced that **Christianity was a way of life** rather than a series of beliefs. They applied Christian principles to themselves as individuals and administered a strict moral discipline within the church. They were aggressively evangelistic, working as missionaries to win people for Christian faith out of a sinful world. The Christian way meant embodying the principles of Christ's life and teaching. It was not that they believed that after baptism a person could do no sin but that he or she *should* not. Knowing they were on a collision course with the world at large, they developed a 'theology of martyrdom' which encouraged most of them towards pacifisim, a refusal to swear oaths, and an unwillingness to hold the office of magistrate.

5. These aspects of Anabaptist life meant that they were deeply **committed to religious toleration**. This was on four grounds.

(a) The example of Christ and the Apostles showed no compulsion in bringing people to faith.
(b) They had an obligation as Christians to love all people, even their enemies, which led them into pacifism as well as toleration.
(c) They adopted freedom in the church membership, believing it should be on a voluntary principle. They urged freedom from state control and a church where people joined only by a conscious step of faith.
(d) They believed faith was a gift from God, and so the burning of a heretic might prematurely uproot a soul that God planned to harvest tomorrow.

TO THINK ABOUT . . .

How closely do these Anabaptist principles coincide with your own?

MÜNSTER

The continental Anabaptists were not an homogeneous group, and in Holland the movement's apocalyptic element introduced the necessity of setting up the Kingdom of God by force of arms. One such group captured and held the city of Munster from 1533–34. Catholic mercenaries surrounded the city. To leave the city meant being killed, to stay meant being baptized, and there were wholesale baptisms in the market place. There followed an enforced community of goods.

In April 1533 Jan Matthys, the leader, was killed and responsibility passed to Jan Bockelson, known as John of Leyden. He proclaimed himself king, officially advocated polygamy on the basis of Old Testament precedent and waited for the coming of Christ.

The end came when a deserter betrayed the city's defences, which allowed the besieging army to enter. The slaughter was total. The notoriety of Münster swept across Europe, putting an end to Anabaptists as an effective force. Some of those who escaped persecution gathered around a former Roman Catholic priest, Menno Simons, whose brother had been killed in the Münster affair. The origin of the Mennonite communities is to be found in this event.

Some Anabaptists fled to England and there is evidence of their presence in Kent and Essex. Twenty-five Dutch Anabaptists were taken into custody and examined in St Paul's. From their evidence it is clear that they denied infant baptism, accepted a Hoffmanite theology, and held a Zwinglian view of the Lord's Supper. Fourteen of them were burnt as heretics, two at Smithfield, the others in various places – a policy which suggested that the authorities felt a need to make an example of them.

> **TO THINK ABOUT . . .**
> What aspects of Anabaptist thought and life-style challenge contemporary Christians and Baptists in particular? What features of their thought and life-style do you think should be avoided?

BAPTIST ROOTS AND THE ANABAPTISTS

It has been a constant matter for discussion between Baptist historians as to just how far Baptist roots are in the Anabaptist movement. W.T. Whitley sharply separated the Anabaptists from Baptists in England. In this he was followed by A.C. Underwood. It is clear that John Smyth inherited some Mennonite ideas, among them that Christians ought not to take oaths, should not be magistrates, should marry within the church family, and should be pacifist, but the first English Baptist church in England was founded by Thomas Helwys. Helwys and Smyth disagreed on a number of matters. Helwys rejected the Hoffmanite theology of the Dutch group, supported Christians taking oaths and accepted the magistracy. In this he was at one with other early English Baptist congregations who were in correspondence with the Mennonite Waterlander community in 1626.

These views have been stated by Winthrop Hudson, an American Baptist professor, who argued that early English Baptists specifically repudiated the 'Anabaptist' tag and condemned several Anabaptist ideas. He was convinced that English Baptist tradition is much more properly allied with those who emerged from Puritanism and Congregational dissent, and who theologically aligned themselves with Calvinism.

E.A. Payne argued that this ignored the complex nature of Anabaptist belief. Although some Baptists repudiated some Anabaptist views, they did not reject all the distinctive doctrines. He noted that 'separatism was treading a similar path to that trodden earlier by many in Switzerland and Germany'. Payne also argued that ideas had legs in the sixteenth and seventeenth centuries. The name was rejected, but not ideas like the 'gathered church', believer's baptism, Scriptural authority and religious toleration. Hudson ignored the General Baptist tradition, but the fact is that not all English Baptists were Calvinist by any means.

Gunnar Westin has joined in this debate, pointing out that the Dutch Mennonite refugees in exile in England also denied the Anabaptist title. The relationship was not one of identity or succession. The pilgrimage of the Puritans into the Baptist camp did not take place till the Separatists had settled in Holland, where Anabaptists had been active for 70 years.

Dr Barrie White, in *The English Separatist Tradition* (1971), *pp*12–13, claims there is little connection between the European and the first English Baptist groups.

> It is difficult to demonstrate any direct debt to the continental Anabaptists, except in the case of John Smyth and even in his case it may seem, upon closer reflection, somewhat insubstantial. Rather do the Separatists appear to have been the most important embodiment of Elizabethan and Jacobean Puritanism; similarities between the forms of English Puritanism and continental Anabaptism seem to derive more from a similar type of appeal to the norm of the church in apostolic times than to any observable sixteenth-century cross-fertilisation. At most it may be claimed that somewhat parallel developments did take place, but that, given the original New Testament source material and the nature of the Protestant appeal to it, such developments need not imply, and without clear evidence ought not to be taken to imply, any direct borrowing.

Dr White maintains that the onus of proof is on those who would assert that European Anabaptists had any measurable influence on English Separatism. He is convinced there is no explicit testimony for such a view, and therefore rejects it.

Use this space to summarise what you see as central features in the thought of the Anabaptists and the English Separatists. What conclusions do *you* draw about the roots of the English Baptists?

ANABAPTISTS	SEPARATISTS

UNIT 3

The English General Baptists

REFORMATION ORIGINS

HENRY VIII AND SEPARATION FROM ROME

The English Reformation smouldered into life with the refusal of the Pope to annul the marriage between Henry VIII and Katharine of Aragon. This eventually led to the separation of church and state from the Roman Church, and the diversion of taxes into the royal coffers, along with the revenue from the dissolution of the monasteries. The 1534 Act of Supremacy declared: 'The King's majesty justly and rightly is, and ought to be and shall be, reputed the only supreme head in earth of the Church of England called Anglicana Ecclesia.'

The *Ten Articles* (1536) were drawn up to include references to the authority of the Scriptures, justification attained by contrition and faith joined with charity. The Bible in English, built on Tyndale's translation work, was provided in every parish church and a lectionary of readings established. But the marks of the old religion were still evident. Henry himself approved the use of images, invocations to departed saints, the concept of purgatory, transubstantiation with communion in one kind only, and the celibacy of the clergy.

What Henry began was developed by Renaissance studies of the Bible, the influence from continental universities, and the far reaching measures of the advisors of Edward VI, Henry's son and successor. It was Cranmer who secured the Reformation position of the Church of England. The two editions of the *Book of Common Prayer* of 1549 and 1552 were greatly influenced by refugee theologians. These editions removed the ceremony and liturgical practice of the Roman Church from England. Rome was declared to be in the wrong, transubstantiation was decisively rejected, celibacy abolished, and communion offered in both kinds.

PROTESTANTS UNDER MARY AND ELIZABETH

This revolutionary programme was completely reversed when Mary succeeded Edward VI. Her attempt to re-establish Roman Catholicism eventually failed, but not before Cranmer and others were burnt. Many other English exiles imbibed deeply at the wells of Geneva and Strasbourg. This is the root of Calvinistic Puritanism and the Protestant principles of later Dissent.

> **TO THINK ABOUT . . .**
> Britain is an island and, it is sometimes claimed, too insular. But history illustrates that we have often been influenced by currents of thought from abroad. What such influences are shaping contemporary Christian thought in this country?

When Elizabeth I came to the throne in 1558 she was determined to have peace in the land. She detested Calvinism almost as much as she abhorred Catholicism. Nobody ever knew her real religious convictions. At the opening of her reign she was declared 'Supreme Governor of the Church' and a revised Cranmerian Prayer Book was re-instated. All the clergy were required to subscribe to the *Thirty-Nine* Articles. The Romanizing bishops of Mary were deposed, and the Pope replied by excommunicating Elizabeth, which effectively put the new Queen's life in danger from Popish plots.

THE PURITANS

The Puritans, many of them in the first instance returned Marian exiles, came to prominence in Elizabeth's reign. They felt it was imperative to establish a pattern of church life which was in accordance with the Scriptures. Initially they campaigned for the removal of bishops, but unsuccessfully. They sought to establish a covenanted church on the basis of the Calvinistic Presbyterians.

At first a 'shadow' church was attempted. Organised on Presbyterian lines, it would be ready to take over the state church when the opportunity was ripe. Puritans were well represented in Elizabeth's Parliaments and among her bishops and clergy. Taking full advantage of the anti-Roman feeling, many of the Puritans campaigned for their objectives through a variety of pamphlets. In 1572 Elizabeth made a determined but ineffective attempt to silence such pressure.

Thomas Cartwright, of Cambridge University, proposed a purified church. A Gospel church should mirror New Testament patterns. He advocated the abolition of archbishops; wanted bishops to have only spiritual power; and believed bishops should be elected by ministers and presbyters. He still gave a considerable place to temporal power in church affairs, arguing that the state should enforce church attendance, test congregations on what they had learnt in worship, and if people were found wanting provide appropriate punishments!

Cartwright was prepared to give the Church of England time to put its own house in order, but many of his contemporaries were not so minded. Another Cambridge man, Robert Browne, published a tract titled *A Treatise of Reformation without Tarrying for Anie* (1582) which aptly described the urgency of the situation for many. Browne and his friend Harrison gathered a church of forty members in Norwich. They were soon in trouble with the authorities and fled to Middelburg on the continent. There the congregation developed a doctrine of the Church as a covenanted community, members being bound to God and each other in obedience to Christ, whose will was known through Scripture.

> ### TO THINK ABOUT . . .
> In what issues in church life today do you believe the principle of 'reformation without tarrying for anie' (i.e. separation from existing church structures) should be applied over and above the principle of loyalty to other believers from whom you differ?

In London during the 1590s another Separatist church formed under the leadership of John Penry. He advocated a covenanted church membership. The text of crucial importance was Matthew 18: 17, 'Tell it to the church.' But who comprised 'the church'? Henry Ainsworth stated the church meant all its covenanted members. Another leader, Francis Johnson, claimed it meant only the eldership. This congregation emigrated to Holland, where the issues were further discussed with other exiled groups. One of these was led by John Robinson who eventually settled in Leyden. It was from his group that some members departed for America, first on the 'Speedwell' and then on the 'Mayflower' to become the American 'Pilgrim Fathers' in June 1620.

One group which stayed in Amsterdam came from Gainsborough, Lincolnshire, led by a one time Fellow of Christ's College, Cambridge, an Anglican clergyman, John Smyth. In his own person he epitomizes the emergence of Baptists from Elizabethan Separatism. His own words for this pilgrimage describe his journey from 'the profession of Puritanism to Brownism, and from Brownism to true Christian baptism'.

EARLY BAPTIST SEPARATISTS

JOHN SMYTH

Smyth's date of birth has never been established, but is usually agreed as 1570. He studied at Christ's College, Cambridge, from 1586 and among his tutors was Francis Johnson. It was undoubtedly from Johnson that Smyth first received Puritan teaching. In 1594 Smyth was ordained by the Bishop of Lincoln and elected a Fellow at Christ's College.

While in Cambridge Smyth was in trouble with the authorities for objections which he made to the burial service, the churching of women and the wearing of the surplice. No evidence remains of Smyth's activity between 1598, when he vacated his fellowship, and his appointment as a City Lecturer at Lincoln in 1600. It was at this time that he preached some sermons on Psalm 122, later published as *The Bright Morning Star* (1603). They reveal him as a loyal Puritan member of the Church of England, well aware of Separatist criticisms, particularly as they related to set prayers being used in worship. Smyth upset some at Lincoln and in October 1602 he was described as a 'factious man', and his appointment was terminated.

There was a legal dispute over his dismissal and what was called his 'personal preaching'. He published the substance of this in *A Paterne of True Prayer* (1605). 'While he drew nourishment from Geneva,' writes Dr White, 'there is no sign at this point that Smyth had any desire to abandon the fleshpots of Canterbury for the ideals of Amsterdam.' (B.R. White, *The English Separatist Tradition*, 1971, p118.) Smyth was again in trouble with the Archdeacon's court for preaching in Lincoln without proper authority. After his dismissal 'factious doctrine' was added as a further irregularity. While the dispute was in progress Smyth received from Archbishop Whitgift permission to preach in any part of the province of Canterbury, which included Lincoln. When the Bishop of Lincoln protested, Whitgift withdrew his authority. Smyth moved to Gainsborough and was in trouble with the Archdeacon's court again when, at the visitation of August 23, 1605, he was found to be preaching in that parish.

Smyth appeared before the Archdeacon's court held at Huntingdon on March 26, 1606 charged with preaching without a licence in Gainsborough on March 2. Apparently he had stepped in to take a service when the minister appointed had not arrived. Judgement was given against him and in November 1606 he faced a new charge of 'practising physic without licence'.

Gainsborough, on the borders of Nottinghamshire, was a gathering place for a number of ministers who had been in trouble with the authorities for their Puritanism. Writing to Richard Bernard, Vicar of Worksop, Smyth styles himself pastor of the Gainsborough church. Among those involved with Smyth at this time were Richard Clifton, rector of Babworth (1586–1605), who went to Amsterdam in 1608; Wiliam Brewster who went to Leyden; and Thomas Helwys and his cousin Gervase.

THOMAS HELWYS

Thomas Helwys' father, Edmund, had legal training, was a staunch Protestant and lived at Broxtowe Hall, in the parish of Bilborough, near Nottingham. Edmund died in 1590. Thomas spent three years in London securing a legal training at Grays' Inn before returning to Nottinghamshire in 1595, when he married Joan Ashmore at the Bilborough parish church. They settled at Broxtowe Hall. Though little is known of Helwys in the next few years, Broxtowe Hall

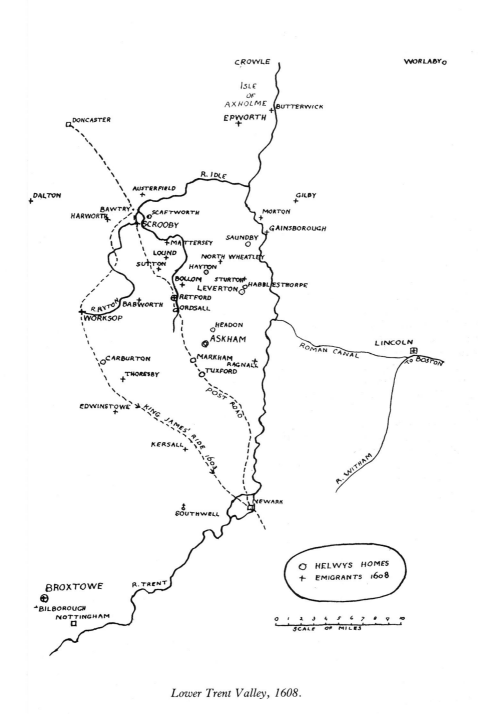

Lower Trent Valley, 1608.

Broxtowe Hall.   *Reproduced by permission of the East Midland Baptist Association archivist.*

became a place for known sympathisers with the Puritan cause. Among those who came were Richard Bernard of Worksop, John Robinson of nearby Scrooby, and of course John Smyth.

A group of Christians had formed a covenanted church at Gainsborough, and 'as the Lord's free people, joined themselves (by a covenant of the Lord) into a church determined in the fellowship of the Gospel, to walk in all his ways, made known or to be made known unto them (according to their best endeavours) whatsoever it should cost them, the Lord assisting them' (William Bradford).

> ### TO THINK ABOUT . . .
> **Do you think this principle of a local church as a 'covenanted' community, together with its implications, is important for Baptists to stress today?**

Smyth developed his separatist position over many years. He believed 'the visible Church of the New Testament with all the ordinances thereof, is the chief and principal part of the Gospel'. Smyth's writings reveal his indebtedness to Francis Johnson, particularly in his understanding of the use of set prayers in worship. At a conference in the Coventry home of Sir William Bowes, in 1606, Francis Johnson's views were the centre of discussion. Smyth's own *Principles and Inferences Concerning the Visible Church* provides the documentary evidence that he was a willing heir to the Separatist tradition. Point by point he insisted on the outline of the visible church's structure and practice which owed almost everything to Johnson and Barrow.

In January 1604 Puritan hopes were dashed by the approval of a new set of canons and discipline for the government of the Church of England. It provided Archbishop Whitgift with the means of enforcing obedience to his policies regarding the Puritans. The effects were felt in Gainsborough, and the leadership decided that they should leave for Holland, a land of religious toleration, as quickly as possible. The emigration took place in small parties, with Thomas Helwys playing a leading part in making the arrangements for Smyth's congregation.

The relationship which developed between Helwys and Smyth was very deep. Reflecting on having left his wife and children in Broxtowe Hall, Helwys wrote in 1611, 'have we not neglected ourselves, our wives, our children and all we had and respected him? And we confess we had good cause to do so in respect of those most excellent gifts and graces of God that did abound in him.' Even when Helwys and Smyth parted, Helwys could write: 'All our love was too little for him and not worthy him.'

BAPTIST PRINCIPLES EMERGE IN HOLLAND

When the party arrived in Amsterdam, a haven for seventeenth-century prisoners of conscience, they were housed in the great bakehouse of the Mennonite Jan Munter. Here they were free to worship according to the dictates of their consciences as guided by the New Testament, and, as Underwood rightly says, they were also free to experience 'all the evils of overcrowding, from exacerbated tempers to the plague' (A.C. Underwood, *The History of the English Baptists*, 1947, *p*35).

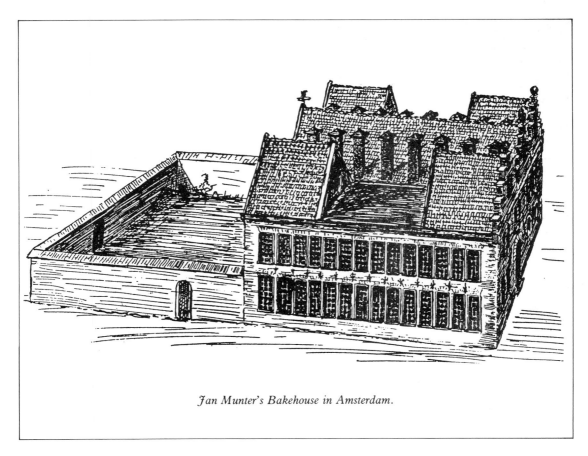

Jan Munter's Bakehouse in Amsterdam.

SMYTH'S THOUGHT

The fundamental question which concerned them was the nature of the Church, its officers, and its mission. Smyth claimed three specific issues on which he was indebted to earlier Separatists like Francis Johnson:

> Herein therefore especially are those ancient brethren (of the separation) to be honoured, that they have reduced the Church to the true primitive apostolic constitution which consisteth in these three things.
> 1. The true matter which are saints only.
> 2. The true form which is the uniting of them together in the covenant.
> 3. The true property which is communion in all holy things, and the power of the Lord Jesus Christ, for the maintaining of that communion.
> (W.T. Whitley, (ed.) *The Works of John Smyth*, i, p270.)

TO THINK ABOUT . . .
Contemporary believers often seek 'the true primitive apostolic constitution'. How would you define it in three statements which are relevant for today's church?

In Amsterdam Smyth knew that the crucial issue to be faced was the nature of the Church and its relationship to covenant theology. In 1607 he had defined the visible church as 'two, three, or more saints joined together by covenant with God and themselves . . . for their mutual edification and God's glory.' On the one side God covenanted to be their God, 'to give Christ' and 'with Christ all things else'. On the other, the faithful covenanted 'to obey all the commandments of God' (*Works*, i, p252). There was also a 'horizontal' responsibility, as Dr White terms it, accepted by the faithful for each other which 'mutually containeth all the duties of love whatsoever'.

Such ideas moved beyond Johnson and Robinson. Smyth also argued at length for all books of prayer, even the Scriptures themselves, to be removed not just during the time of prayer, but during the 'time of prophesying and singing'. Within the congregation he insisted that the 'brethren jointly have all power both of the kingdom and priesthood immediately from Christ'. Such a church had power to administer the 'seals of the covenant', baptism and the Lord's Supper, and also the right to remove the elders' power 'upon just cause'. Whereas Johnson's congregation would receive help from outside for needy members, Smyth insisted that the church should take full responsibility for its own. 'In the covenant promise of the local congregation the eternal covenant of grace became contemporary and man's acceptance of it was actualised in history'. (White, *op. cit. p128*.)

TO THINK ABOUT . . .
In what ways would Smyth's model of the church outlined here be helpful for an understanding of the church today?

HARD QUESTIONS – PARTING OF THE WAYS

When Smyth advocated believer's baptism it was the final breaking point with other Separatists. *The Character of the Beast* is the work in which change is evident. As a result, the group disbanded themselves from their church state on the view that they had not been validly baptised. Smyth then baptised himself, by affusion, then the rest of the group, beginning with Helwys.

A chorus of shocked horror swept round the English refugees in Amsterdam. Why had not Smyth approached the Mennonites for baptism? Apparently it was their heretical Christological views which repelled him. Later he decided that perhaps he had been wrong to baptise himself. He argued:

> Baptism is not washing with water: but it is the baptism of the Spirit, the confession of the mouth and the washing with water: how then can any man without great folly wash with water which is the least and last of baptism, one that is not baptised with the Spirit, and cannot confess with the mouth. (*Works*, i. p567.)

TO THINK ABOUT . . .
Does Smyth's statement on baptism remain a helpful summary of where Baptists stand, or is it an inadequate position?

If the church is built on a covenant, Smyth's opponents asked, why are children excluded? Were not Abraham's seed all sealed? Smyth replied that two covenants were made with Abraham. One was respecting his children who were his physical heirs, and the covenant seal was circumcision. The other was with his spiritual children of which the Holy Spirit, not baptism, was the seal.

> The status of baptism, in Smyth's view, had changed from being a seal of God's grace to being the means which 'doth visibly declare' a promise which has been inwardly received, and the existence of a covenant which had already been entered. (White, *op. cit.*, *p*135.)

Smyth's convictions concerning infants, who obviously could not exercise faith for themselves, was either that they are all saved, 'or that they are one of the Lord's secrets, not to be searched into'. (*Works*, ii, *p*634.)

TO THINK ABOUT . . .
The challenge made to those who today practise believer's baptism is similar to that in Smyth's time. 'What about your children and their place within the covenant community'? How do you respond? Is Smyth a help?

Baptism had become for Smyth an entry into a contract or covenant with God. It was at this stage that 'Christ was visibly put on'. His own self-baptism was possible because all believed themselves to be re-constituting the church as in apostolic times. It meant a total repudiation of any idea of 'apostolic succession'. It led Smyth to claim that 'all power ecclesiastical or ministerial is derived from Christ to the Church, and then through the Church to elders'. For Smyth, ministry was firmly subordinated to the church and the church was led by the Spirit of Christ. No Separatist had as yet placed the final seat of authority in the church so clearly.

TO THINK ABOUT . . .
In what sense ought a local church to be regarded as the final seat of authority?

One other factor was determinative for the congregation before it divided. Arminianism was gaining a foothold in Dutch churches. Arminians believed that Christ's redemption 'stretcheth to all men' and that any person was capable of faith. Baptists who held this view of a general redemption were called General Baptists, and on this issue English Baptists originating from the group in Holland were sharply distinct from the Particular (Calvinistic) Baptists who emerged in England in the late 1630s.

BAPTISTS AND MENNONITES

In February 1610 John Smyth and about thirty-one others sought membership with the Mennonites, now convinced that they had been wrong to baptise themselves. They were not immediately accepted. Within a year Thomas Helwys and those who had not sought union with the Mennonite congregation became a distinct church.

In 1611 Helwys shared in the production of three pamphlets. *A Declaration of the faith of English People Remaining at Amsterdam in Holland* was the earliest English Baptist Confession of Faith, in twenty-seven articles. The second was a forthright attack on Calvinism, *A Short and Plain Proof by the Word and Work of God, that God's decree is not the cause of man's sin or Condemnation*. The third was an *Admonition* in which Helwys dealt with the main points of difference between himself and the Mennonites.

In the *Admonition* he affirmed he had separated from his former leader because he believed 'there is no succession or privilege in holy things'. His congregation maintained that church officers may hold office only in the church where they have been ordained to that office. Helwys also differed from Smyth and the Mennonites by defending the taking of oaths. He maintained that the magistracy was a holy ordinance of God which debarred no man from membership in the Church of Christ. Against the Hoffmanite views of the Mennonites he contended that 'Christ took his flesh of Mary, having a truly earthly natural body'. (Underwood, *op. cit.*, *p*47.)

PLEA FOR FREEDOM OF CONSCIENCE

Helwys published in Amsterdam in 1612 *A Short Declaration of the Mistery of Iniquity*. It was the first claim for freedom of worship to be published in English, declaring that the Church must bear witness to the truth whatever the cost. On the copy of this book which Helwys sent to King James I, he wrote on the fly-leaf:

> Hear, O King, and despise not the counsel of the poor . . . The King is a mortal man and not God: therefore he hath no power over the immortal souls of his subjects, to make laws and ordinances for them, and to set spiritual Lords over them.

General Baptists persistently argued this point of religious freedom. They did not believe that anyone was destined by a divine decree to damnation, but that all people had the possibility of repenting and believing the Gospel. They argued most strongly that nobody should be killed for his mistaken beliefs. This might defeat God's purposes in salvation. People must be able to hear spiritual truth and receive it without coercion of any kind.

A SHORT
DECLARATION
of the miftery of iniquity.

Ier. 51. 6.

Flee out of the midft of Babell , and deliver every man his foule , be not deftroyed in hir iniquity, for this is the time or the lords vengeance, he vvill render vnto hir a recompenfe.

Hofea 10. 12.

Sovv to your felves in right eoufnes reape after the meafure of mercie, breake vp your fallovv ground, for it is time to feeke the lord , till he come & raine righteoufnes vpon you.

Anno 1612.

The title page from Helwys' influential publication.

of the mistery of iniquity. 69

But these Lords Bs. Cannot in anie wise endure one, that doth faithfully seeke for reformation, because such are onely adversaries to their kingdome. Wee still pray our lord the King that wee may be free from suspect, for habeing anie thoughts of provoking evill against them of the Romish religion, in regard of their profession, if they be true & faithfull subiects to the King for wee do freely professe, that our lord the King hath no more power over their consciences then over ours, and that is none at all: for our lord the King is but an earthly King, and he hath no auctthority as a King but in earthly causes, and if the Kings people be obedient & true subiects, obeying all humane lawes made by the King, our lord the King can require no more: for mens religion to God, is betwixt God and themselves; the King shall not answere for it, neither may the King be iudg betwene God and man. Let them be heretikes, Turcks, Iewes, or what soever it apperteynes not to the earthly power to punish them in the least measure. This is made evident to our lord the King by the scriptures. When Paul was brought before Gallio deputie of Achaia, and accused of the Iewes for persuading men to worship God contrary to the law. Gallio said unto the Iewes, if it were a matter of wronge or an evill deed, o ye Iewes, I would according to right mainteyne you, & he drave them from the iudgment seat Act. 18. 12. 17. shewing them that matters of wrong and evill deeds, which were betwixt man & man apperteyned onely to the iudgment seat, and not questions of religion. The like is shewed by the towne clerke of Ephesus in Act. 19. 38. 19. And further Paul being in like case accused of mame thinges Act. 24. in the 25. chap. he appeales to Cesars iudgment seat, where he saith he ought to be
iudged,
ij

see below

TO THINK ABOUT . . .

Consider this passage from p69 of *The Mistery of Iniquity*.

. . . for men's religion to God, is betwixt God and themselves; the King shall not answer for it, neither may the King be judge between God and man. Let them be heretics, Turks, Jews, or whatsoever it appertains not to the earthly power to punish them in the least measure. This is made evident to our lord the King by the scriptures.

What are the implications for Christians in this country of according to others the same freedom of conscience and liberty to practise their religion which we enjoy?

RETURN TO ENGLAND

Helwys was now convinced that he had been wrong to leave England. Though parting with Smyth caused him personal pain, Helwys was convinced that 'the days of great tribulation spoken of by Christ' had now arrived. He must get back to England and appeal to James I to stop persecuting the faithful.

Helwys' own family position entitled him to think he might gain access to the King. His uncle Geoffrey was a City of London alderman, living in Walbrook. His cousin, Gervase, had been knighted and was soon to be Lieutenant of the Tower of London. Helwys and the small group with him established themselves at Spitalfields.

Thomas Helwys' signed copy of *The Mistery of Iniquity* was presented to James I, though we do not know if he did this personally. The King's reaction was swift. Helwys was lodged in the Newgate Prison where he died sometime before 1616.

Thomas Helwys' autograph. Inscription of his book to James I.

THE ENGLISH GENERAL BAPTISTS

Helwys was succeeded by John Murton, a Gainsborough furrier who went to Amsterdam with Smyth's group in 1608. In that year he married another group member from Worksop, Jane Hodgkin. They returned with Helwys in 1612, but Murton too was soon in prison. He led the small church for twelve years, writing a number of tracts. *Objections Answered* (1615) was a bold plea that no man should be persecuted just for his religious belief. *Truth's Champion* (1617) defended the Arminian view of redemption against Calvin's teaching. In 1620 he addressed an appeal to King James I on behalf of those who were being persecuted for the sake of their religion.

Also within the church at this time was Leonard Busher who in 1614 published *Religious Peace*, suggesting it:

> be lawful for every person or persons, yea, Jews or Papists, to write, dispute, confer and reason, print and publish any matter touching religion, either for or against whomsoever; always provided they allege no further proofs for any point of religion, but only the Holy Scriptures (1846 edition, *p*51).

> **TO THINK ABOUT . . .**
> We live in an age when in Britain Buscher's plea is honoured. If you could be called by Buscher to support his case, what would you say?

Helwys, Murton and Busher made plain both their Arminian theology and their concern for religious liberty. They were the founders of the General Baptist tradition in England.

Other General Baptist churches were known to exist by about 1620 in Lincoln, Coventry, Salisbury and Tiverton. A few years later there was correspondence between them and the Dutch Mennonites. By 1618 the Spitalfields church had moved to Crosby House; in 1625 Elias Tookey and a splinter group established a new church which met at Southwark; and by 1639 the church met in two sections. One, led by Thomas Lambe, a soap-boiler, met in North Folgate, London. The other, led by Edward Barber, an upholsterer, met in Bell Alley, London.

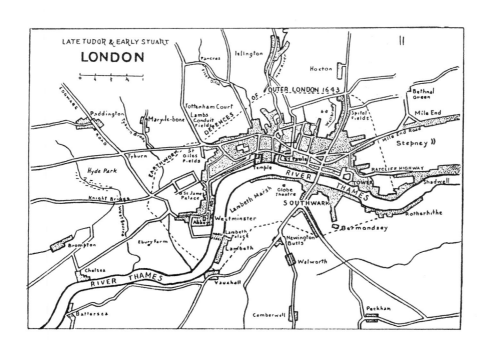

Late Tudor and Early Stuart London.

By permission of Messrs. Longmans, Green and Co.

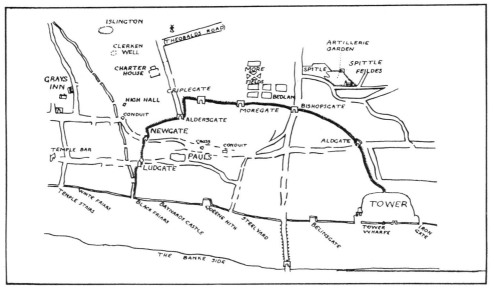

London, 1620.

THE DEVELOPMENT OF GENERAL BAPTIST CHURCHES

General Baptist churches in this period developed through a number of factors. A significant number of Anglican clergy were influenced by the wide-ranging discussions of Cromwellian England and came to Baptist convictions.

THE WESTMINSTER ASSEMBLY

When King Charles I left Whitehall in January 1642, Parliament believed it was in a position to effect a thorough-going reform of religion. The first move was to abolish episcopacy. But parliamentarians could not agree which form of church government should be adopted in its place. In June 1643 an 'Assembly of Godly Divines' was called to advise Westminster on the best solution of the matter. The discussion of the *Thirty-nine Articles* was so slow that the Assembly turned its attention to matters of liturgy and church order. There was considerable dissension. Eventually a Presbyterian form of government was advocated. *A Directory of Worship* was produced to replace the *Book of Common Prayer*, together with a Confession of Faith which was thoroughly Calvinistic. Though

Baptists were not directly involved in these discussions, it was in this atmosphere the denomination emerged.

INFLUENCE THROUGH PREACHING

Francis Cornwell was a vicar of Marden, Kent, whose Puritan views had led to his imprisonment by Archbishop Laud. His own study of the situation, particularly as it related to baptism, led him to accept baptism as a believer at the hands of the General Baptist Messenger, William Jeffery, and thereafter he gathered his own baptised congregation in Marden. On one occasion Francis Cornwell was invited to address the Kent clergy nearby, and he took the opportunity to commend a General Baptist position. Among those who went away to consider his claims was Christopher Blackwood, a Cambridge graduate, who was vicar of Staplehurst. Eventually he too accepted General Baptist ideas and founded the Spillshill church in Kent. In 1653 he moved to Ireland, where he was a preacher at Dublin Cathedral for six years, and responsible for the founding of Baptist congregations. This brief cameo typifies what was happening all over the country in Cromwellian times.

PUBLIC DISPUTATIONS

Another aspect of Baptist growth at this time was the developments which followed public disputations. These were common in this period and often resulted in the formation of Baptist churches. Between 1641 and 1700 there were at least 109 such public disputations, with most occurring in Cromwellian times. A quarter of them were held in London, the rest took place throughout the British Isles. Baptists welcomed such opportunities as occasions for preaching the Gospel, refuting slanders about so-called 'Anabaptists', and recruiting new members like Francis Cornwell and Christopher Blackwood.

Each side wanted to put their case before a wider public through the printed word. For example, the vicar of Leominster, John Tombes, debated baptism publicly no less than nine times in these years, but was not a Baptist! Yet through these debates, and the published accounts, he made a major contribution to the growth of both General and Particular Baptist churches.

CONFESSIONS OF FAITH

The desire to know where Baptist Christians stood, not only in regard to baptism, but on other matters of doctrine and church practice, led the General Baptists to issue a series of *Confessions of Faith*. John Smyth had issued a personal statement of his faith in 1608 and again in 1611. Thomas Helwys did the same. Further General Baptist Confessions were issued in 1651, 1660, 1679, 1691 and 1704. The dates have significance in that each one was making the General Baptist position clear at a critical time.

Thirty congregations in the Midlands put out the 1651 statement of faith in 75 articles, adding a postscript in which they said that the government of England must be determined in a 'just parliamentary way', an interesting comment at the time when Cromwell was contemplating taking the title 'Lord Protector'.

The 1660 statement was published as all Dissenters were having to adjust to the reintroduction of monarchy and the established church in Britain. A copy was presented to King Charles II, protesting Baptist loyalty to the crown and denying that General Baptists had been involved in armed insurrection.

TO THINK ABOUT . . .
In what ways would such public disputations over doctrine and practice enhance or damage Christian witness and influence today?

The 1679 *Orthodox Confession* was by far the most substantial statement of General Baptist beliefs. It was issued at a time when all dissenters were being persecuted ruthlessly by the state and Anglican authorities. The full title indicates its purpose: *AN ORTHODOX CREED or a Protestant Confession of Faith being an Essay to Unite and Confirm all true Protestants in the Fundamental Articles of the Christian Religion, against the Errors and Heresies of Rome.* It holds that the Apostles', Nicene and Athanasian creeds ought to be both received and believed. The Confession reflects on the attributes of God, relationships between the persons of the Trinity, the nature and office of our Lord, predestination, reprobation, justification and sanctification. The doctrinal emphasis within the Confession defended 'the fundamental Christian doctrines of the Trinity, the Incarnation, and the Atonement against those within their own fold who would have replaced the common faith of Christendom by a cobweb of private fantasies and ultimately a barren Unitarianism' (A.J. Baines, *The Signatories of the Orthodox Confession of 1679, p3*).

> **TO THINK ABOUT . . .**
> What positive value or negative dangers do you think Confessions of Faith have in our ecumenical age?

SIGNIFICANT GENERAL BAPTIST MINISTERS AND CHURCHES

THOMAS LAMBE

The life of Thomas Lambe, a native of Colchester and who by 1645 was pastor of the Bell Alley church in Coleman Street, London, typifies General Baptist life in this period.

Lambe spent much of his time in evangelistic activity, developing a whole range of techniques which matched the times. His roving missionary tours through large parts of England were a precursor of the Quaker journeys made by Fox and his companions. He welcomed public disputes with the clergy, and claimed his right to enter parish pulpits as an ordained pastor of a Christian congregation.

> **TO THINK ABOUT . . .**
> What examples can you offer of Baptists today, at local church or Union level, developing in evangelistic activity 'a whole range of techniques which matched the times'?

His church was unique in that his meetings attracted the public. M Tolmie says:

> It rivalled the theatre in its capacity to draw crowds, especially 'young youths and wenches'

and on Sundays 'many people, some of other separate churches, and some of (our) parish churches', wrote the Presbyterian Edwards, 'will go to this Lambe's church for novelty, because of the disputes or wranglings that will be there upon questions, all kinds of things started and vented almost, and several companies in the same room, some speaking in one part, some in another.' It was the custom of the congregation for two or three men to preach successively, and, when 'one hath done, there's sometimes difference in the church who shall exercise next, 'tis put to the vote, some for one, some for another . . . and strangers who come thither will make a cry, for whom they like best as well as the church'. . . . Sometimes the meeting broke apart in sections, and there was 'such confusion and noise, as if it were at a play; and some will be speaking here, some there'. (*The Triumph of the Saints, p76 ff.*)

The General Baptists had several itinerant evangelists in the 1640s. Lambe's church attracted and trained some of the most effective. Henry Denne, a former Anglican clergyman, Samuel Oates, a Norwich weaver, and Jeremiah Ives, a cheesemonger and boxmaker of London, were all baptized by Lambe and retained strong links with the London church. Between 1641 and 1646 Lambe can be traced, usually with a companion, 'in Gloucestershire (with Clement

Wrighter, who was briefly a member of Lambe's church before achieving notoriety as one of the leading sceptics of London), in Norfolk, in Essex (with Timothy Batt), in Surrey and Hampshire (with Samuel Oates), in Kent (with Henry Denne) and in Wiltshire (with Jeremiah Ives)' (*Ibid.* p77).

EDWARD BARBER

A very different London General Baptist church was that led by Edward Barber in a house in Bishopsgate. A Presbyterian minister named Edwards gave a significant and interesting account of this church, dated November 12, 1645:

> When the company was met together they began with prayer; after prayer, everyone of the company kneeled down apart; and Barber, with another of their way, went to each of them one after another, and laid both their hands upon every particular head, women as well as men, and either in a way of prayer, prayed they might receive the Holy Ghost; or else barely to every one of them used these words, Receive the Holy Ghost.

After this meeting the church sat down to a supper, 'which was dressed for them by a cook'. When the meal was over, and before the cloth was removed, the Lord's Supper was administered. Then a question was proposed, whether Christ died for all men, and the meeting was discussing this when Edwards' informant left the meeting at 11 pm.

The ceremony involving the laying on of hands marked a new departure for Edward Barber's congregation, and introduced a matter which would divide General Baptists for several decades. Some members of Lambe's church took up the same stance, under the leadership of John Griffith, and eventually formed a separate church, requiring laying on of hands of all members. Lambe and his associated evangelists opposed it, but they were in the minority, and eventually Griffith persuaded all General Baptist churches to make this a distinctive mark of the church.

> ### TO THINK ABOUT . . .
> Think through your own attitude to the laying on of hands; its place in the churches' life; its meaning; its value.

HENRY DENNE

Henry Denne offers another cameo of General Baptist life. The Anglican curate of Pyrton, Hertfordshire, for most of the 1630s, he was baptized by Lambe at Bell Alley. In 1643–44 he was sent as an evangelist to East Anglia, working in Bedfordshire and Cambridgeshire. The parliamentary committee of Cambridgeshire disliked Denne and he was imprisoned briefly, but eventually became minister of the parish church at Eltisley. He joined Lambe on an evangelistic tour of Kent in 1645–66, preaching in Rochester and Canterbury. He was preaching in Spalding, Lincolnshire, the following June, where he was arrested for baptizing people during the night.

Between June 1646 and May 1649 Denne joined the Army, not as a chaplain, but as a soldier. He appears as one of the four Leveller leaders to be shot at Burford after the Army mutiny in May 1649. He alone was pardoned, and afterwards wrote a pamphlet *The Levellers' Design Discovered*.

Denne's preaching activity led by 1647 to the formation of the churches at Warboys and Fenstanton. He remained linked with the Fenstanton church – though never called its pastor – until November 1653, when they reluctantly accepted a request from Canterbury to let Denne become the minister. In the Fenstanton church there was an ongoing dispute about 'laying on of hands' and whether it was essential for all members. There were many members who began to set aside Scripture, and the ordinances of the Lord's Supper and Baptism, as being unnecessary because they had direct access to God through the Holy Spirit. Fenstanton did, however, practise footwashing, and also had the Lord's Supper at the end of a church meal. The church regularly helped 'poor' members of their own and other churches.

> ### TO THINK ABOUT . . .
> If you had been a member of the Fenstanton church what might have been your response to those claiming 'direct access to God through the Holy Spirit'?
>
> What would be the value of reintroducing the 'practice of foot washing' (John 13) today?

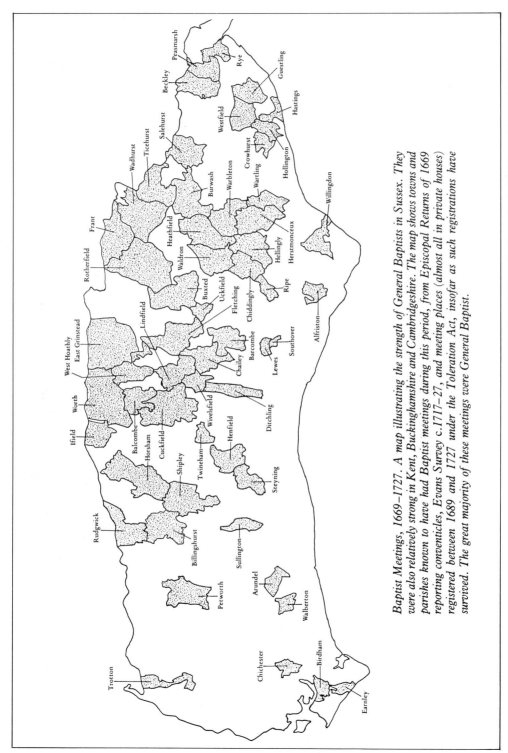

Baptist Meetings, 1669–1727. A map illustrating the strength of General Baptists in Sussex. They were also relatively strong in Kent, Buckinghamshire and Cambridgeshire. The map shows towns and parishes known to have had Baptist meetings during this period, from Episcopal Returns of 1669 reporting conventicles, Evans Survey c.1717–27, and meeting places (almost all in private houses) registered between 1689 and 1727 under the Toleration Act, insofar as such registrations have survived. The great majority of these meetings were General Baptist.

From Sussex believers: Baptist marriage in the 17th and 18th centuries by John Caffyn, by permission of Churchman Publishing.

THE IMPACT OF MATTHEW CAFFYN

Matthew Caffyn (1628–1715) was born of farming stock at Horsham, Sussex. While at Oxford during the first Civil War he adopted Baptist views. He returned to farm in Horsham, became pastor of the General Baptist church there and a Messenger of the General Baptist Assembly with, responsibility for evangelism in Sussex and Kent.

His geographical base is not without import-ance. The General Baptists in this part of the world were the successors of those influenced by earlier Anabaptist exiles. The General Baptists of the Midlands and Buckinghamshire had roots in the much older Lollard tradition, and this underlies continuing General Baptist divisions between 1670 and 1730.

Caffyn was strongly attracted to the Chris-tological views of Melchior Hoffman. These views were strongly repudiated by the Midland General Baptists and in 1673 Thomas Monck, a General Baptist Messenger from Berkhampstead in Hertfordshire, published *A Cure for the Cankering Errors of the New Eutychians* in which he repudiated the Melchiorite heresy 'that our blessed mediator did not take his flesh of the Virgin Mary, neither was he made the seed of David according to the flesh'. This view was confirmed by the General Baptist Messengers who gathered in Assembly in 1679. In that year the General Baptist Assembly also published an *Orthodox Confession of Faith* which sought to minimize differences with Calvinists, and it specifically repudiated the Hoffmanite teaching. Christ, they stated, is both 'coequal, coessential and coeternal with the Father' and was 'formed of the only seed, or substance of the Virgin Mary'. The 'denying of baptism is a lesser evil than to deny the divinity of Christ' they affirmed.

The Horsham Meeting House. The General Baptist meeting house, that became known as the Free Christian Church in 1879 and now the Unitarian Church, was erected in 1721. The land was transferred from John Dendy, 'chirurgeon', and John Geere, mercer, to nine trustees; the price paid for it was five shillings, with a rent of one penny per annum for a thousand years, 'if lawfully demanded'. In 1827 Ann Billingshurst, who had emigrated to America towards the end of the 18th century, wrote: 'I often wish I could be at Horsham Meeting, and hear such preaching as I used to hear . . .'.

Photograph from John Caffyn's Sussex believers.
By permission of Churchman Publishing.

Caffyn retained his unconventional ideas, despite the division it created in the General Baptist community. After the 1689 Toleration Act the General Baptists had two parties in direct conflict. The 1693 Assembly tried to compromise by condemning the heresy while at the same time affirming that Caffyn did not hold the view. At the 1696 Assembly the Western Association of General Baptist churches put the matter on the agenda, but it was suppressed. The result was a division which meant that there were two General Baptist gatherings each year, usually held in London at the same time. The Kent and Sussex churches, supporters of Caffyn, were known as the General Baptist Assembly, the others which came from London, the Midlands and the West, were known as the General Association.

The two groups re-united in 1731, on the basis of the so-called 'six principles' of Hebrews 6: 2, seventeen years after the death of Caffyn. But he was always in the background of the arguments which existed within General Baptist life.

Matthew Caffyn's window. Horsham Unitarian and Free Christian Church.

By permission of Horsham Unitarian Church.

TO THINK ABOUT . . .

To what extent can and should differences about Christology be accepted within a covenanted fellowship?

GENERAL BAPTISTS AFTER 1689

ORGANISED FOR ADVANCE

When the General Baptist Assembly met in the new era of toleration in 1689, the opportunity was open for the practical application of their doctrine of universal redemption. One of their most gifted leaders, Messenger Thomas Grantham (1634–1693), put it thus:

> The most glorious and worthy work to be done by God's people is to advance his truth, and to seek the salvation of the world by all possible means . . . all is but trifles in comparison.

However, that is not what happened. The General Baptists were connexionalists rather than independents. They had a three-fold ministry – Messengers, elders and deacons. The Messengers, although the last office to be developed by the General Baptists, were officers of the church at large, the elders and deacons were pastors and administrators in only the local congregation. Messengers were patterned on the New Testament work of Timothy or Titus. Grantham explained it:

> As God hath given to His Church a fixed ministry of Bishops, Elders, Pastors, etc., to take care of particular churches, so He hath given to her a travelling ministry, unfixed in respect of particular societies, to whom it pertains . . . to take all occasions to cause the light of the glorious gospel to shine unto such as sit in darkness, to plant churches, to confirm or settle them in the faith, to comfort and visit those who have believed through grace. (Underwood, *op. cit.*, p121.)

At a Church Meeting held at Horsham —
July 23: 1729 it was agreed:

1 That ye Widow Rowland Sen at Farnham
be allowed 6d ꝑ Week by the Church.

2 That Bro: Geere be paid out of the Con=
tribution Money 40 Shillings wch has been paid
by him on the Widow Rowlands Account at
Horsham, & that She be allow'd so ꝑ Year for
Mr Haylors Interest (wch he has been hitherto pleasd
to lay out upon her) so long as ye Church may think
She has Occasion for it.

3 That Old Sister Caffyn for ye future be allowd
Six Shillings ꝑ Month.

4 Agreed that a Letter be wrote to our Friends about
Thackham advising them to defer the Choice of
Bro: John Buckman to ye Office of an Elder for the
present till our Friends generally be satisfied for his
fitness for ye Work. Which was done accordingly.

Mathew Caffyn senr
Tho: Southon   Richard Deud Junr
Jno Geere   Jacob Caffyn   John Moss
Rich. Dowdy   John Snatt   John Tasker
Will: Agate   John Dowdy
                        / In Behalf of ye Whole

*The minutes of a meeting of the Baptist church at Horsham in 1729,
recording payments to be made to poor members of the meeting.*

The main task of Messengers was to 'preach the Gospel where it is not known and to plant churches where there is none' together with ordaining elders and administering the sacraments in remote churches.

FRUSTRATED HOPES

Sadly, Grantham's vision was not to be realised. The work of the General Baptists declined, it became harder and harder to persuade churches to offer elders and deacons for service in the wider work of Messenger. The predominant General Baptist view of a minister as someone who ministered only within one congregation for the whole of his life also frustrated the calling of Messengers.

The local Baptist churches were linked together in district Associations. The Associations joined in the General Assembly which functioned nationally, dealing with such matters as were referred to it by the local churches. Messengers, pastors and representatives from the churches comprised the Assembly. The Assembly easily became a court of appeal to which an aggrieved individual could apply for redress against a local church decision. In this way local disputes became generalised.

Time and time again the issue of marriage was discussed at the Assembly. The Assembly took the view that the Pauline restrictions on marriage in 2 Corinthians 6: 14–18 meant that an unbeliever is anyone who 'is not a member of the visible church of Christ'. This meant that those who married outside baptised churches were excommunicated, although leniency was used so that justice might be mixed with mercy. This not only drove many Baptist Christians out of their churches, it also turned Association gatherings into match-making occasions!

Should Christians allow their voices to mingle with those of unbelievers in singing the Psalms?

believers in singing the Psalms. They preferred that one believer sang representatively, just as one member might lead in prayer.

The General Baptists were the smaller of the two Baptist groups. It was reckoned that in 1718 about 19,000 'hearers' were regularly in attendance at 120 churches. Relatively strong in Kent, Sussex, Buckinghamshire and Cambridgeshire, with outposts in Lincolnshire and the West of England, they had little work elsewhere and were weak in London and Bristol. They were fundamentally a rural people, who preferred not to build chapels but rather to meet in barns, farmhouses and private dwellings. This was possible until owners died, and then a church might just disappear overnight, literally having nowhere to meet.

Long ministries in one church, an untrained ministry, a Biblicism which did not encourage thought and action, and the objective of marriage only within the community, all spelt out a recipe for decline rather than growth. Add to this the passing away of elderly, but strong, leaders at the turn of the century without their replacement, and the decline was almost inevitable.

> ### TO THINK ABOUT . . .
> You may or may not agree with the General Baptist stance on marriage in this period. But what policy do we or should we as Baptists have today concerning marriage?

The other matter which greatly vexed General Baptists was hymn singing. There were long discussions as to whether Christians should allow their voices to mingle with those of un-

> ### TO THINK ABOUT . . .
> It is perhaps easy with hindsight to be critical of the General Baptists in this period. What issues and circumstances today do you think could deflect churches from their priorities and aims?

Summarise below what you consider were the main features of General Baptist thought and practice. What do you believe has value for now?

The Origin and Development of English Particular Baptists: 1630–1690

ROOTS OF EARLY CHURCHES

The roots of the English Particular Baptists were in the same soil from which the General Baptists had already grown: the Puritan Calvinism of the early English Separatists. The first known Particular Baptist church grew out of an Independent (Congregational) church, and their 1644 Particular Baptist *Confession of Faith* drew extensively from the Separatist *Confession* of 1596.

Henry Jacob gathered an Independent Calvinist church in 1616. It was formed as a semi-Separatist community, its members occupying a middle position between Puritans who conformed to the Church of England and those Separatists who totally repudiated the state church as false. Organised as a covenanted fellowship of believers they refused to deny the Anglican Church completely.

By 1630 however, when John Lathrop was pastor, many in the congregation were urging a complete repudiation of the state church. On September 12, 1633, ten members of the congregation, after very lengthy debate, were given a formal release from fellowship. They established a fully Separatist group because they were no longer able to accept that parish churches could in any way be reckoned as 'true' churches. In this group Samuel Eaton, at that date certainly baptised as a believer by affusion, became a member and leading figure, and by 1638 was probably the pastor.

On June 8, 1638, the original congregation, which apparently retained fellowship links with the Eaton group, dismissed a further six from its number to join John Spilsbury. They were 'of the same judgment with Samuel Eaton', that is, convinced that 'baptism was not for infants but professed believers'.

In May 1640 the original Spilsbury congregation was divided for administrative reasons into two groups. One was led by Praisegod Barbone, and the other by Henry Jessey, converted in the early 1620s while at Cambridge University. Ordained a clergyman of the Church of England in 1624, Jessey became a family chaplain in Suffolk, where his Puritan sympathies were strengthened through contacts with the Winthrop family, who left England for the American Colonies to share in the establishment of the state of Massachusetts.

A discussion took place within the congregation, on the motion of Richard Blunt, a member of Eaton's group, about the correct mode of baptism: should it be by affusion or total immersion? Hearing that the Collegiants (a splinter group of the Mennonites) in Holland could advise on the matter, Blunt, who spoke Dutch, was sent over for consultations. One issue was over the proper agent of baptism; was baptism invalid if the wrong person performed it? This was not a new question since Helwys' group had raised it in Amsterdam thirty years earlier. They reached the same answer as then – the correctness of baptism did not depend on a succession of baptisers.

Blunt returned from Holland unbaptised, but reported his discussions to the London church. In January 1642 Blunt and a Mr Blacklock apparently baptised each other by immersion and then each baptised a number of others. There were fifty-three baptisms all together.

Praisegod Barbone resisted this move. He disliked self-baptising and claimed that some had now been baptised three times: once as an infant, once by sprinkling when a believer, and now by immersion as a believer. Thomas Kill-cop, another member of the baptised congregations, replied to Barbone in print, claiming that every Scripture which gave Barbone the right 'to erect a Church-State, gives us the same warrant to erect baptism'. John Spilsbury, in another publication, argued that the church had power under Christ to appoint people to a task, including the administration of ordinances such as baptism.

> **TO THINK ABOUT . . .**
> In a Baptist church in the 1970s a man, worthy in every respect, was barred from being elected to the diaconate because, although he had been baptised as a believer by affusion, he had not been immersed. What would your views be on the issue?

BELIEVER'S BAPTISM

Believer's baptism by total immersion, in the name of the Triune God, upon a personal confession of repentance for sin and avowed trust in Christ as Saviour and Lord, dates from this period. It is specifically commended in the 1644 *Confession of Faith*, and is the only valid form of believer's baptism thereafter for all Baptist congregations.

William Kiffin, who joined Eaton's congregation about 1637–38, began to preach among them and eventually became pastor. Kiffin wrote a sympathetic introduction to John Lilburne's *The Christian Man's Trial* (1641) in which he claimed that Christ gave his kingly power 'not to a Hierarchy, neither to a National Presbytery, but to a Company of Saints in a Congregational way.' By October 1642 Kiffin had become a Baptist.

In that year, at Southwark, on October 17, Kiffin debated for about five hours with Dr Daniel Featley on the issue of baptism. Kiffin argued in defence of believer's baptism, whilst Featley's reply was afterwards published in *The Dipper Dipt*, (1643).

Discussion about baptism continued in Jessey's church in 1643 and some joined Kiffin's congregation. A Quaker source claims that the

William Kiffin.

first baptised believer in Kent was Anne Stevens of Canterbury, who was 'Dipped into the Belief and Church of William Kiffin' in 1643–44. The Bristol *Broadmead Records* state that when the congregation moved to London after Bristol fell to Prince Rupert on July 26, 1643, 'those professors that were Baptized before they went up, they did sit downe with Mr Kiffen and his Church in London, being likewise Baptized'.

WHO PAYS?

Under Cromwell, when the traditional relationships between church and state were being widely debated, Baptists were faced with a number of awkward questions. For example, when the state offered to finance godly ministers who would preach the Word faithfully, should Baptist ministers take such money from the state? Particular Baptists generally answered negatively. Or, if a citizen accepted the role of the magistracy as just, should Baptists pay the tithe which provided the state with money to

The satirical title-page of Daniel Featley's The Dipper Dipt.   *By permission of the British Library.*

pay those godly ministers? It was a difficult issue, and many Particular Baptists thought the answer should be 'Yes', since they did not wish to be involved in civil disobedience. Once the Commonwealth period was over, however, the conviction that the Lord's people should support the Lord's work took hold and became the norm for Baptist churches.

TO THINK ABOUT . . .

Can you think of areas today where Free Church Christians are exercised over to what extent they should accept help from the state?

MILLENARIAN THOUGHT

Another area for discussion was the challenge of contemporary apocalyptic and millenarian thought, a debate intensified by the Republican political sympathies of some Particular Baptists in this period. The issue centred on the Fifth Monarchy movement. Fifth Monarchists were convinced of Christ's imminent return and that it would be to England that he came. Discussion raged around the prophecies of Daniel 2. The execution of Charles I in 1649 was seen as the end of the fourth monarchy spoken of in the book of Daniel. It was only, some believed, a matter of months, a year or two at most, before Christ came to reign.

The summoning of the Parliament of the Saints in 1653 augured well for the future. The nation was to be governed by the godly alone. The reaction when Cromwell dismissed the 1653 Parliament and eventually agreed to receive the title Lord Protector was intense. It was flying in the face of Christ's return. Was it not the act of Anti-Christ? Until this point Cromwell had seemed to be on the side of King Jesus. No wonder that Vavasor Powell sent his congregation home to pray over whether they would have the Protector or Jesus to reign over them.

Many people called for intervention and the overthrow of Cromwell to help bring in the Millennium. A small number of those urging this policy were Particular Baptists. They were concerned to secure freedom for worship, which Cromwell had promised, and freedom from the obligation to contribute to the financial support of the state ministers, because they had conscientiously withdrawn from that church in which 'new presbyter was but old priest writ large'.

There was a felt continuing link between the Fifth Monarchists of the 1650s and the underground, Independent congregations of the 1630s. They shared the same cause. When the matter of republicanism was posed by the Levellers under the leadership of John Lilburne, it was Kiffin, who had once supported Lilburne, who encouraged leading Baptists to withdraw their support.

TO THINK ABOUT . . .

How would you respond to this letter to the Baptist Times in 1950:

'I doubt the propriety of Christians taking any part either in voting or taking office in government, local or national . . . Christians should regard themselves as citizens of a kingdom of a far higher order . . . to be revealed . . . in the personal return of Jesus . . .'

TO THINK ABOUT . . .

In what circumstances could you envisage civil disobedience being appropriate in the cause of Christian social justice?

CONFESSING BAPTIST BELIEFS

The publication by seven London Particular Baptist churches of their 1644 *Confession of Faith* clearly brings the community into focus. It provides the basic framework for their understanding of the church and mission in this period. It was the theological equipment which enabled them to withstand all kinds of pressures, and not least those presented by the Society of Friends (the Quakers) which were to take over whole General Baptist communities in the 1660s and 1670s. Among the Particular Baptists at this time were men of strong intellectual ability, some of whom had received theological education at university. These men were also prepared to travel widely, exercising a personal ministry which developed links between all closed-communion Baptist churches.

IMPORTANCE OF THE 1644 CONFESSION

The 1644 *Confession*, as Dr B.R. White has shown, was widely acknowledged and used by the churches, being revised and reprinted on several occasions. Its phraseology shows dependence on the English Separatists' 1596 *Confession*. The 1644 *Confession* makes two modifications of the 1596 material. First, it adopts the distinctive five point plan of Calvinism accepted at the Synod of Dort in 1619.

The Five Points of Calvinism
- Total Depravity
- Unconditional Election
- Limited Atonement
- Irresistible Grace
- Final Perseverance of the Saints

Second, it gives full credence to the growing belief that the New Testament taught the baptism of believers only, by immersion.

The 1644 *Confession* deals with the doctrine of God, reviews the life of believers, and in the final section describes the church. The church is comprised only of professed believers; the ministry of the local church is placed firmly in the control of the independent local congregation. The separation of church and state is total, although obedience to the magistrate is commended without ambiguity.

TO THINK ABOUT . . .

In what ways is or could Baptist Association life today be modelled on the vision of the 1644 Confession of Faith?

RELATIONSHIPS BETWEEN CONGREGATIONS

The relationship between independent local churches is similar to the interdependence which characterises fellowship between Christians in a local church. The Confession says:

> And although the particular Congregations be distinct and several Bodies, every one is a compact and knit Citie in it selfe; yet are they all to walk by one and the same Rule, and by all meanes convenient to have counsell and help one of another in all needful affaires of the Church, as members of one body in the common faith under Christ their only head.

W.T. Whitley believed that, as Baptist churches began a life of associating together, Particular Baptist Associations developed by a conscious copying of the organisation of the New Model Army, in which many Baptists had served during the Civil Wars. But the word 'association', though widely used by Parliament and its army, was a late arrival among the Particular Baptists. They preferred the term 'General Meeting' for the periodic gatherings of their 'Messengers', which were not summoned on a county basis but drew on fairly large regions that included several counties.

The people who composed the Jacob–Lathrop–Jessey congregations had strong fraternal relationships. In 1638, for example, Samuel Eaton was arrested while worshipping in Jessey's congregation. In 1640 Richard Blunt, from Eaton's group, discussed the mode of baptism with both halves of the Jessey congregation. In 1642–43 William Kiffin, who was probably never a member of Jessey's church as such, was deeply involved in lengthy discussions with them on baptism.

It would appear that the publication by John Cotton, an Independent minister, of *The Keyes of the Kingdom of Heaven* was significant for the Particular Baptist understanding of relationships. He deals with Christ's power in an individual congregation, and also in neighbouring congregations 'in association with it'. Cotton considered 'an association or communion of churches, sending their Elders and Messengers into a Synod' an ordinance of Christ, on the basis of Acts 15.

Typical of the General Meeting held among Particular Baptists was that at Tetsworth, Oxfordshire, which brought together independent churches from a wide geographical area. In March 1653 the Messengers and ministers signed an 'Agreement' which was ratified later in the year by each church, so that its proper independency was affirmed. This Agreement outlined the doctrinal basis of the union between the independent churches, pledged loyalty to the common programme in mission of the churches, and affirmed contact with similar London Baptist churches. As each new independent church was admitted to the Tetsworth gathering it was asked to confirm acceptance of the Agreement.

> ### TO THINK ABOUT . . .
> Would such an Agreement help or hinder the work and 'common programme in mission' of the Baptist Association of which your church is a part?

SPREADING BAPTIST BELIEFS

The monument in the form of a pulpit at Ilston. Part of the inscription reads:
TO COMMEMORATE THE FOUNDATION IN THIS VALLEY OF THE FIRST BAPTIST CHURCH IN WALES 1649–60 AND TO HONOUR THE MEMORY OF ITS FOUNDER JOHN MYLES.

JOHN MYLES IN WALES

John Myles was baptised at Glaziers Hall, London, in 1649. He was commissioned to go to Wales and, by preaching the Gospel, to gather baptised churches which were to practise closed communion. He went in the name of the seven London churches who signed the 1644 *Confession*. He founded the church at Ilston, just outside Swansea, on October 1, 1649.

Early in 1650 a number from an Independent congregation in Llanigon, Breconshire, were won to the Baptist position. By July 1650 a third congregation had been formed at Llanharan, East Glamorganshire. The fourth church was formed on January 22, 1651 at Carmarthen, and a fifth church had been established at Abergavenny by August 1652. By late 1650 the elders and messengers of these churches were gathering at a General Meeting. From 1654 the General Meetings were held every half year, and in that year it was agreed that 'the appointed fast days should be continued: for that is the agreement of the churches of England, Scotland, Ireland and Wales, and our promise to God to them to observe it'.

Myles visited London at least once during this period and correspondence passed regularly between London and Wales. London advised on two specific matters: that the closed communion practice of the churches was to be maintained, and that a fellowship meeting in several different locations should not divide into independent congregations unless each group had someone able to provide pastoral oversight.

THOMAS TILLAM IN THE NORTH OF ENGLAND

Thomas Tillam, who describes himself as 'minister and messenger of one of the seven churches in London', was a member of Hanserd Knollys' church, in Swan Alley, Coleman Street. He went up to Northumberland and by July 21, 1652 he had formed a church at Hexham comprising five women and eleven men. He engaged in an evangelistic preaching tour of Cheshire in April 1653. In July he was involved in the formation of the church at Stokesley, Yorkshire.

Hanserd Knollys.

FURTHER EXPANSION

Expansion in Ireland

In Ireland, John Vernon and Thomas Patient maintained links both between the churches and with London. Patient, who had been one of the

signatories to the 1644 *Confession*, worked for the practice of closed communion in the Irish Baptist churches.

Expansion in the Midlands and West Country

The Midlands and the West Country also had similar gatherings. The Western Association, with Thomas Collier as one of its leading evangelists, stood off a little from the London group, perhaps for reasons of trade, but there was practical concern for those in financial need.

WILLIAM KIFFIN'S INFLUENCE

William Kiffin typifies the kind of personal involvement which was exhibited by the Particular Baptist leadership in this period. When the Tetsworth General Meeting was founded in June 1653, it was to Kiffin in London that they wrote. A month later Kiffin received a letter from ten Irish Baptist churches giving information concerning their arrangements for caring for each other. On July 24, 1653, Kiffin wrote to the Welsh Baptist churches, on behalf of the London seven, commending to them the Irish pattern of care. When Daniel King, in 1655, wanted to pass on information about the Midland Association, he corresponded with Kiffin in London. In 1657 Kiffin was a delegate to Devizes and gave advice from London on the matter of Baptist ministers receiving money from state funds. A year later in May 1658 he attended a meeting of the Western Association at Dorchester, where he used his considerable moral authority to argue against the adoption of Fifth Monarchist policies.

The organisation of the Particular Baptists in this period reveals that their leaders were concerned for the unity of the churches, cooperation between congregations, and the spread of closed-communion Baptist churches across the country.

> *TO THINK ABOUT . . .*
> **Would the personal involvement of Association or Union leaders in your church's life today be viewed as a welcome encouragement or an unwelcome interference?**

THE CHURCH UNDER PERSECUTION

With the restoration of Charles II to the throne of England there began a period of persecution for those who conscientiously refused to submit to the 'Clarendon Code', a set of new laws against those who would not conform to the re-established Church of England. It became virtually impossible to imprison a Dissenter illegally! The policy, however, was not applied uniformly over the country and in many areas there were times of peace, followed by periods of acute suffering.

FOCUS ON BRISTOL

By concentrating on one church, 'the church of Christ in Bristol' (now Broadmead Baptist Church), whose life was carefully chronicled during the period 1660–89, we can see how a particular congregation faced up to the persecutions of the Clarendon Code. Other churches suffered similarly.

Broadmead started about 1658 as an Independent, Separatist congregation, adopting Baptist views, but having a 'mixed' membership. That is, it allowed all to be members who confessed Jesus as Lord, and welcomed to the Lord's Table 'saints as saints' (as Bunyan would have expressed it). Baptism was a matter of personal conviction. As the period progressed, and under the pressure of persecution, Broadmead became a Particular Baptist church, and by 1689 it was in fellowship with the Western Association of Particular Baptist Churches. It is typical of the period as a Christian community which moved to a firm Baptist position.

The Broadmead congregation originated in the remarkable work of the wife of the vicar of St Ewen's, Bristol, **Dorothy Hazzard**. She was fearless in her Separatism. The group which she gathered round her declined to enter worship until her husband had completed worship according to the Book of Common Prayer, then they entered to hear the sermon. When Bristol was under threat from Prince Rupert, Dorothy Hazzard led 200 women and girls in the defence of the Frome Gate of the city against repeated Royalist assaults, losing everything when the castle was surrendered. A contemporary report described Matthew Hazzard's own involvement as that of a 'main Incendiary in this Rebellion violently egged on by his wife, whose disciple the silly man is'.

ATTEMPTS AT COMPREHENSION FAIL

At first Charles II offered a compromise on the religious issue. But he was under pressure from the restored Anglican Church to enforce religious conformity. He was also keen to provide a measure of toleration for Roman Catholics, under the guise of relief for Dissenters. Edward Hyde, Charles' Lord Chancellor (created Earl of Clarendon in 1661), skilfully presented legislation which would have allowed for comprehension and toleration. However, neither Anglicans nor Presbyterians were prepared to allow this and when Parliament met in May 1661 it ignored both toleration and comprehension and instead passed a series of acts of which, in fact, Clarendon was not the originator!

The rising of Fifth Monarchy men, led by Venner, in January 1661, had spread alarm about the political intentions of religious dissenters prior to the May 1661 Parliament. The Savoy Conference, at which Presbyterians and Anglicans met to discuss the religious future, was so manipulated that Presbyterians were compelled to petition the Anglican Bishops, now re-instated, regarding any future religious settlement.

THE ACTS OF THE CLARENDON CODE

1. THE CORPORATION ACT

This act passed in May 1661, was a measure political as much as religious in its intention. It required all persons holding municipal office to renounce the Solemn League and Covenant of 1643, made between Scotland and the English Parliament which had sought to maintain

בְּרֵאשִׁית הַקְּהַל אֱלֹהִים
Deus   Ecclesia   principio   in

J Chron: 4. 10 part from oh, to y word. Evil
nth of last word here LEACHARIM nded signifying TEAOΣ, Finis

אִם בָּרֵךְ תְּבָרֲכֵנִי לֵאלֹהַי וְהִרְבִּיתָ אֶת־
נְּבוּלִי וְהָיְתָה יָדְךָ עִמִּי וְעָשִׂיתָ מֵּרָעָה
לְאַחֲרִיתִי

Ἐγὼ περὶ αὐτῶν ἐρωτῶ, οὐ περὶ τῦ κόσμε ἐρωτῶ, ἀλλὰ περὶ ὧν
δέδωκάς μοι, ὅτι σοί εἰσι. Ἁγίασον αυτὸ ἐν τῆ ἀληθεία σε
ὁ λόγ῀ ὁ σὸς, ἀλήθειά ἐςι. (Κεφ 17 ΙΩΑΝ. 9. 17.)

Hebr: 10. 23 th part of
mathon 28. 20 from And lo. –
Κατέχωμεν τ ὁμολογίαν τ ἐλπίδ῀ ἀκλινῆ (πιςὸς δὲ ὁ ἐπαγγειλάμενο῀)
ἰδῦ, ἐγὼ μεθ᾽ ὑμῶν εἰμι πάσας τὰς ἡμέρας ἕως τ συντελείας τῦ αἰῶνο῀ Ἀμήν

Sicut igitur accepistis Christum Jesum Dominum ita in eo am-
bulare: qui dilexit nos et lavit nos a peccatis nostris
Per sanguinem suum: Et qui fecit nos Reges et,
Sacerdotes Deo et Patri suo: ei fit gloria
et robur in secula seculorum.

Amen

od who at sundry times and divers manners, spake
in time past unto the fathers By the Prophets hash in
these last dayes spoken unto us: by his Spirit by his Word
and Providences even by his Sonn whom he hath appointed
heir of all things. By whom also he made the World. This
God (we say) who worketh all things after the Councell of
his owne will. Havoing according to his determinate
purpose suffered his Church to be carryed into y wildernesse
of Antichristian darknesse; as he signified and foretold
by his servant y Apostle John, Revl: 12: 6 and that shee
should be there and Prophesy in Sack cloth 1260 yeares
Forwards

The opening page of the Broadmead Records.

TO THINK ABOUT . . .

We owe a great deal to churches such as Broadmead Bristol which carefully recorded and preserved accounts of their life and work. Do Baptist churches today care enough about recording for the future their life, worship and witness?

Presbyterianism as the state religion. All holding municipal office were to swear an oath of non-resistance to the established government of church and state. People with republican sympathies were thereby excluded from office. Those who took municipal office had first to receive the Sacrament according to the rites of the Church of England. This provision was intended to exclude all Roman Catholics, but it also effectively prevented Dissenters from holding such offices.

When Thomas Ewins, the pastor of Broadmead at this time and a city lecturer (preacher), was turned out of his lectureship by this Act, he still ministered to the Broadmead church. He was imprisoned for a month during the summer of 1661 for preaching in Bristol. The extended extract below indicates the effects of persecution on the Broadmead congregation.

> When King Charles II was brought from his Exile again into the Nation and to the Crown, Then Sathan stirred up adversaryes against us, and our Trouble or Persecution began. And then our friends of the Presbyterian party were turned out of their Publique Places as well as we. Then those who had preached against us for meeting in Private houses, they were faine to meet in Private houses as we had, and did doe. For then, when our Pastor, or Teacher, Mr Ewins, was turned out of those Publique places called Nicolas and Christ-church, (then) we first met every Lord's day at our Pastour's house in the Castle, and there we continued a long time; but being straitened for room, we took a large Place or Hall, towards the end of Broadmead, called the Fryars, which formerly had been some Chapel; and there we Continued, holding forth the Gospel of God's Free grace by our Lord Jesus Christ.

And in the 10 month 1660, Orders come that all above 16 years of age must take the Oaths of Allegiance and Supremacy; which many scrupled to doe, because of the Extensiveness of some words in the Oath of Allegiance; as the words Whatsoever and otherwise. Whereupon the Brethren only of our and Brother Hynam's congregation met together, and discoursed our Judgments, and searched the Scriptures, concerning our dutie and subjection to Magistrates; in which we all agreed, Concerning Civil matters they ought to be reverenced and obeyed. And to give them some assurance of it we drew up in Writing our sense,

Mr Thomas Ewins preaching from Prison, 1664.

and in what terms we could engage ourselves; which was Consonant to the Scripture, and we did judge it as full as the Oath of Allegiance; which we sent by two messengers to the Mayor of the City, who then was Sr Henry Creswick. He sent the same writeing up to the King and Council, and ordered us to be left alone for some time, until he had answer from above; which within a month came, and was that we must take the Oath according to the letter of the Law, and not in other words. But Sir Henry telling us they did not require us to oblige ourselves no further than the Scripture did require of us, whereupon divers members of both congregations took it. But some others, though they held an Oath for the end of Controversie to be lawful, yet were not then satisfied to take a Promissary Oath. And so in Peace we bare one with another, them that did, and them that did not. So that trouble passed over. (R. Hayden, (ed.) *Broadmead Records, 1640–1687, p*115.)

TO THINK ABOUT . . .
What are the differing attitudes today to the state and cooperation with state authorities when the church is suffering persecution?

---

2. THE ACT OF UNIFORMITY

Charles II delayed signing *The Act of Uniformity* for three months in 1662. As soon as it was passed, he issued an indulgence which dispensed with laws enforcing religious conformity and requiring oaths of office holders. But in 1663 Parliament made it clear this would not be tolerated, and the indulgence measures were dropped.

The 1662 Act had the effect of identifying those who would not conform or who dissented from these measures. *The Book of Common Prayer* issued in that year was ordered to be read by each minister on a given Sunday in August. The minister was then to give publicly his own unfeigned assent and consent to all and everything contained within it. Failure to do this entailed being deprived of the living. All future ordinands would be required to make such an affirmation.

The ejected ministers, who became known as Nonconformists or Dissenters, claimed that the authority of the church over matters of faith and order was distinct from, and not subordinate to, the state. They required all questions of faith and order to be brought to the touchstone of Scripture. They believed that the historic episcopate was neither an essential mark of the church nor a necessity for effective ministry; and that the orderly public worship of God did not have to be contained within the liturgy of a specific book. The effect in Bristol was to throw Presbyterians and Quakers together with Baptists and Independents, as all experienced some measure of persecution.

At Broadmead Thomas Ewins felt the sting of the now Anglican and Royalist City Council as it implemented the Act. One member of the Council in particular, Sir John Knight, made repeated and often violent attacks on several dissenting communities.

3. THE CONVENTICLE ACT

This Act introduced a persecuting measure. It began by reiterating the provisions of the act passed under Elizabeth I which enjoined attendance at the parish church. It then went on to outline legislation against 'the growing and dangerous practice of seditious sectaries . . . who under the pretence of tender consciences, do at their meetings contrive insurrections.'

TO THINK ABOUT . . .
In what respects do you think many people in our country have false ideas about what happens in our churches, their services and other gatherings?

Any person aged sixteen or over present at a meeting of five or more persons, other than those of the household, which had a service in any other form than that allowed by the Church of England Prayer Book, could be convicted on proper evidence and sent to prison for at least three months. Payment of a £5 fine could also be imposed. A second conviction would mean six months in prison and a £10 fine. A third conviction led to being sent for trial at the Quarter Sessions, where conviction could mean transportation for seven years, probably to the West Indies. A fine of £100 would secure release from transportation. Penalties were imposed on law enforcement officers who refused to apply the law.

Until now the Broadmead congregation had been required to support pastors who might be imprisoned, but now it could happen to any worshippers. Transportation was no empty threat. An existing letter from Ewins underlines this point. He said that all the members have a duty to bear witness at least once, though then the prospect of banishment should make them careful, remembering their family responsibilities.

But when may we say, Our testimony is finished? I answer, when you have witnessed against this late unrighteous act, or law of man, which is directly and so highly against the prerogative of Jesus Christ; or, when you have suffered the first penalty either by fine or imprisonment, then, I conceive, you have borne your testimony, and then you might come to family meetings, as Paul did at Corinth, Acts XVIII, 4; XIX, 8,9. Why should any fear or draw back, upon the account of the first penalty of this Act? It is not worth mentioning. You may redeem yourselves out for a shilling; if not they will turn you out in a week or two.

But some will say, They will do that but in policy, that they make take us again and hasten our banishment. I answer, let their ends be what they will, if you be out, you may then confine yourselves to private family meetings, and so escape banishment; having borne your testimony so fully, you may comfortably rest, and leave the work to those that have not yet been taken. (*Broadmead Records 1640–1687*, p62.)

TO THINK ABOUT . . .

For those of us who have never known persecution for our faith, these statements may come over as very poignant. How would you advise someone whose job depended in some measure on compromising their Christian stand?

4. THE FIVE MILE ACT

This 1665 Act was aimed at former ministers, who might be ministering to congregations which were now numbered among the Dissenters. It forbade them to come within five miles of any place where they had formerly carried out religious duties, or where they had been convicted of taking illegal dissenting worship.

The *Broadmead Records*, written by the church elder, Edward Terrill, take a regular account of what happened to the members during this extended period of persecution. He began writing the account about 1672, but it covers the period from 1640 onwards. In 1665 Terrill lists the disturbances which took place and those who were imprisoned, including himself. In November that year he reports a 'troop of horse came to the city, as reported on purpose to suppress the meetings, and they were very abusive to those they found'.

Clarendon fell from power in 1667. There was an attempt to pass another Bill of Comprehension which would have brought many Dissenters back into the established church. The measure failed.

5. THE SECOND CONVENTICLE ACT

Passed in 1670, this Act replaced the proposed Bill of Comprehension. It dispensed with transportation and introduced instead the possibility of limitless fines. The penalty for a first offence was a fine of five shillings and all subsequent offences meant a ten shilling fine. The fines could be obtained by 'distress and sale of the offenders goods and chattels'. If this did not produce enough funds, then the belongings of another person convicted at the same meeting could be sold to make up the deficit! The fines were divided three ways: one third to the Crown, another to parish poor relief, and a third to the informer.

A preacher or teacher at such a conventicle could be fined twenty pounds and the congregations' goods sold to meet the bill. Appeal to the Quarter Sessions against such a conviction was permitted but if lost, all the fines were trebled. A parish constable could break down the doors of a meeting on the receipt of information, and if he refused to act he could be fined £5. Justices who refused to act on information would be fined £100, and half of this would go to the informer. The Act was, in its own words, to be 'construed most largely and beneficially for the suppressing of conventicles, and for the justification and encouragement of all persons to be employed in the execution thereof.'

> **TO THINK ABOUT . . .**
> **Many of our fellow believers, in some parts of the world, suffer similar opposition. How would you advise them in the matter of their relationship with the state authorities?**

It is at this point that Terrill begins to talk of 'our persecutions'. The Bishop of Bristol urged the Act on his clergy pointing out its great advantages for Anglicans, and he himself appointed informers to visit most of the nonconformist gatherings over four consecutive weeks beginning May 10, 1670.

> The first Lord's day . . . the Informers from the Bishop, (that was then one Ironsides) came upon us; and because we did not know which way they would begin upon us, we shut our Publique Meeting-house door when we understood they

were coming. Then they fetcht Constables and brake open the door, came in and took our names, for which some of us were brought before the Magistrates and Convicted. Then, against the next Lord's day, we brake a wall up on high for a window, and put the speaker in the next house to stand and preach, whereby we heard him as well as if in the room with us. The Bishop's Informers come in again, take our names; for which we were again brought before the Mayor, and Convicted. So they did the 3d Lord's day. And the fourth Lord's day, the Mayor himself, with his officers and some Aldm came upon us, and turned us out; but seeing they could not make us refrain our Meeting they Raised the Trained Bands every last day of the week in the Evening, one band to keep us out of our places, and Nailed up our doors, and putt locks upon them; so they kept us out by force and power, That we were faine to meet in the Lanes and highways for several months. (*Broadmead Records 1640–1687*, p128.)

The Bristol harassments eased in 1671 when a mayor, sympathetic to Nonconformity, was in control of the city. At this time the congregation took over the rooms vacated by the Quaker meeting at the lower end of Broadmead, on which site the church has met ever since. In 1672 Charles II issued another Indulgence, inviting all Dissenters to register their meeting places. Many did so, including Broadmead, but some did not comply. The peace was short-lived. Charles II again found that Parliament was in no mood for measures which might allow Roman Catholics freedom under the guise of accepting Dissenters.

6. THE TEST ACT

The Test Act of 1673 was specifically designed to exclude Roman Catholics from all national and local offices, and from commissions in the army and navy. The holders of such posts had to take the oath of allegiance and receive the Lord's Supper according to Anglican rites. Evidence had to be presented from the parish minister who gave communion, his warden, and two other witnesses on oath. Failure to produce such evidence was a bar to these offices. The Act was passed to prevent Catholics from obtaining office and to curb the activities of the Catholic Duke of York.

TO THINK ABOUT . . .

What reactions do you have to the fact that often in the history of Christianity in this country, Roman Catholics have been subjected to the same deprivations and restrictions as Protestant Dissenters.

COURAGE UNDER TRIALS

'OUR PERSECUTIONS'

Terrill's *Broadmead Records* are very full from 1672 onwards. They reveal a picture of continuing persecution for the next fifteen years. John Hellier, a constable for the parish in which Broadmead met, Ralph Ollive the Mayor, and the landlord of a public house in the Broadmead area, together with every encouragement from the new Bishop of Bristol, Guy Carleton, launched a determined attack on Dissenters in Bristol from 1674, and Broadmead suffered as much as any. The attack, which lasted over ten years, was encouraged by the fact, mentioned above, that a third of the fines went to the local parish poor relief and a third to the informers themselves.

Thomas Hardcastle, the Broadmead pastor at this time, was imprisoned for a considerable period. Some of the most wonderful expressions of faith in a time of persecution are contained in the twenty-two letters he wrote to the congregation from prison. They were read, instead of the sermon, each Sunday afternoon.

> Hardcastle understood the situation demanded a close look at the congregation's attitude to worship, and the inner drives which motivated the congregation. He believed it was good that persecutions should come because they would not only deepen faith and patience, but they would eventually bring about the conversion of many. Hardcastle did not see a quick end to the persecutions and said that greater trials and troubles would come: 'these are but the footmen you have been running with; these are but the little figures of Anti-Christ'.

> This brought Hardcastle to a lengthy discussion of the nature of Christian faith at its deepest point. He talks of the precious gift of faith in God as a veritable shield in danger. This is the kind of faith by which the just shall be able to live: a faith which brings a deep and lasting joy. Such faith takes the warnings which God's judgments provide, looks upon life as a pilgrimage to God, and is capable of overcoming the world. When Christians are obedient to Christ, then despite all outward factors, they will enter into the very presence of God. (*Broadmead Records 1640–1687, p66.*)

Thomas Hardcastle.

> **TO THINK ABOUT . . .**
> 'He believed it was good that persecutions should come . . .' Do you think Christian history vindicates Terrill's remark. Can you think of examples from more recent history which confirm his belief?

It was teaching of this nature and calibre which sustained the church in these dark days of persecution and in the years after 1680.

In 1680 the most severe persecutions broke out.

On the 22nd, being Ld's day, we met at Br. Terrill's, at the upper end of Redcross Lane, about 6 and 7 in the morning. But while Mr. Enoch Prosser, a Gifted Br. belonging to Mr. Keech of London, who came to our Fair, was preaching, about ten, Hellier, Sheriff Knight, Bp's Register, and Constables came, to the number of about 20. The Sheriff and Hellier with others knock at the Street Door, but none answered. And they sent to Tilly's for an Iron Crown, wherewith they broke some Battens, but could not enter after much Labour. Others of them laboured hard with a Bar at the Back door, but could not get in. Then Edw.

Summers, a vile young man, a Butcher, with others, got into Capt. Vaughan's Orchard behind the House; but neither They, nor those at the Street Door, could get in. They behind broke a Window and its Shutter, driving the Bar into the Room where Several people were. Br. Terrill offered to open the Doors if they would stay till he had tyed up his mastiff dog, but they would not. So he let them alone, till, after much fruitless Labour, they were willing to accept his offer. He opened the Back door, and they that came in there let in their Gang at the Street door; and one of them threatened to shoot the Dog, which they saw tied, and strove to come at them. Then Jno. Hellier arrested Mr. Terrill in the King's Name. (*Broadmead Records 1640–1687, p236.*)

The Earl of Shaftesbury was at the centre of intrigue in 1680, when he advocated putting the illegitimate, but Protestant, Duke of Monmouth on the throne when Charles II should die, instead of the Catholic James, Duke of York. The discovery of the Rye House Plot in 1683 meant that Monmouth had to flee the country and in 1684 the Lords Lieutenant of the various counties were ordered to seize the arms of those disaffected to government. The list of arms

seized in Bristol has survived. It reveals massive dissenting support for Monmouth in all the congregations including Broadmead. After Monmouth's abortive rising in the West, the infamous Judge Jeffreys severely punished Dissenters. At his command seventy-four were hanged in Dorset, and two hundred and thirty-three in Somerset. Eight hundred and forty were transported to Barbados. Congregations assembled in the countryside in order to avoid arrest. Hardcastle's successor, George Fownes, was kept in prison for over two years, and died in Gloucester prison in 1685.

When James II came to the throne in 1685 as an avowed Papist, the country again experienced considerable unrest. The laws against Dissenters were ferociously applied. Courts were crowded with victims, worshippers pursued through the countryside, and many prisons overflowed with Nonconformists.

One interesting development which these years produced was a willingness among Dissenters to raise funds for the defence of those prosecuted under the Clarendon Code. On one occasion when Broadmead worshippers were being chased through the woods, a certain Mr Ford from Taunton, a dissenting minister, was drowned. The matter was taken through the courts and brought to a successful conclusion when the constables responsible were punished. Terrill and others enlisted the support of various attorneys, and were quick to point out defects in the warrants and other legal documents which technically made them invalid.

> ## TO THINK ABOUT . . .
> **What evidence can you gather from the world-wide Church today that hardship strengthens the bonds of mutual care and sacrificial support?**

Many suffered abuse at the hands of informers in these years. In court they were often ridiculed. In overcrowded prison cells they experienced extreme privation. Heat, cold, filth and disease made conditions intolerable, and a bribed or vindictive gaoler could make matters even worse. Several prisoners died, most were released with their health permanently impaired. For the majority the seizure of goods, added to imprisonment, spelt financial ruin. But out of it all, there was revealed a strength of character which brought a new lustre to the name Puritan.

THE GLORIOUS REVOLUTION

Eventually James recognised the futility of such ferocity and in 1687 issued a declaration allowing liberty of conscience which effectively nullified the Test Act. He appointed several Roman Catholics to office in government and the armed services. He also attempted to set up a commission to assess the damage caused to dissenting meeting houses and property during the last ten years, with a view to making reparations. Dissenters recognised that James' true objective was to advance Catholicism and refused co-operation.

Dissenters and Anglicans, united for a brief time in opposition to a Catholic King, now worked for the enthronement of James II's daughter, Mary, who was married to the Protestant William, Prince of Orange. In May 1688 James tried to enforce the reading of his Indulgence in all the London parish churches, but the bishops refused to allow it, petitioning the King not to make alterations in religion without the sanction of Parliament. The bishops, who were for a time imprisoned in the Tower, were eventually tried and acquitted, to be received in London with great acclaim. Eventually, without further bloodshed, James II fled the country and William and Mary were established on the throne by act of Parliament.

A **Toleration Act** was passed in 1689 allowing freedom of worship to Dissenters, but the Test Act remained unrepealed. Dissenters were effectively still barred from public office. It should not be assumed, however, that they took no interest in public affairs.

CHURCH ORGANISATION

THE BEGINNINGS OF THE BROADMEAD CHURCH

Broadmead originated in that Puritan Separatism which characterised the Cromwellian period. As early as 1613 a Puritan minister at Bristol had gathered a group of interested lay people around him. In 1639 this group centred its activities on a newly arrived minister at St Ewen's, Bristol, Matthew Hazzard. He married a widow in the group, Dorothy Kelly. Broadmead was first formed in the Hazzard's home.

The disturbances of the times brought a Welsh influence to bear on the Broadmead congregation. The congregation at Llanvaches, near Chepstow, under the leadership of William Wroth and then Walter Craddock, came to Bristol in 1642, and the two groups met for worship under Craddock's leadership at the Dolphin Inn, James' Back. When Bristol fell to Prince Rupert in 1643, this whole group migrated to London, where some joined Kiffin's congregation, while others went to Jessey's church.

With the return of Bristol to Parliamentary control in 1645, some of the Bristol folk returned and met under the leadership of an Anglican Puritan, Nathaniel Ingello. They were a 'church within a church'. Eventually this group fell out with Ingello who was a little too wordly for them. They called Thomas Ewins, then pastor at Llanvaches, formerly a member at Jessey's London church, to be minister. He was appointed the City Lecturer in Bristol and remained at Broadmead till his death in 1670.

Baptism first became an issue at Broadmead in the early 1650s when one or two members left to join 'the other baptised congregation' in Bristol, that is Henry Hynam's Particular Baptist congregation at the Pithay. Eventually it was decided that baptism was a matter of individual conscience, and that both baptised believers and paedo-baptists would be admitted to full membership of the church and to the Lord's Table. Thomas Ewins was baptised by Jessey in London in 1654, and he afterwards baptised others who requested it.

KEY LEADERS IN BROADMEAD'S EARLY HISTORY

One of the Broadmead leaders was Robert Purnell, a carpet weaver who lived on James' Back, Bristol. He had an irenical Christian spirit, as can be understood by this short quotation from one of his several books, *Good Tydings for Sinners, Great Joy for Saints* (1649), in which he describes the 'true Church state' which he would like to see, presumably, at Broadmead:

> The ground of this communion shall be spiritual union: and when the day is dawned, and the day-star risen in our hearts, Ephraim shall not envy Judah, nor Judah vex Ephraim; Presbyterians shall not bitterly cry out against Independents, nor Independents have such hard thoughts of Presbyterians. Yea, they shall be ashamed to own one another by their fleshly titles, but look upon and love one another as Christians, members of the same body, heires of the same promise, children of the same father: having all the same spirit, all clothed with the same robe, inclined to the same work; ruled by the same Word and Spirit. And so their love of each other shall arise from union in the same Spirit. And against this church–state the gates of hell shall not prevail.

TO THINK ABOUT . . .
To what extent can the spirit of this statement be formative for Christians today in facing the ecumenical challenge to unity?

The congregation in these years was led by gifted ministers and, with the exception of Ewins, all had had a university education at either Oxford or Cambridge. Though their training had been in Calvinist theology, all of them were marked by a catholicity of spirit which was a little unusual in this era. Ewins and Hardcastle both held the 'open communion' position, treating 'saints as saints', which was rare in those days. There was co-operation in several matters with other Baptists and Dissenters. They shared a burial ground with the Particular Baptists at the Pithay from 1679 onwards. They raised a common fund for keeping the city gate keeper 'sweet', and for securing legal aid for members who were taken to court.

BROADMEAD WORSHIP AND CONGREGATIONAL LIFE

The worship was public, with lengthy prayers by the elders, the reading and exposition of the Scriptures, and Psalm-singing. In the seventeenth century, on account of illiteracy, a person would usually give out the first line of a Psalm and then the congregation would join in singing it. But at Broadmead books were in evidence and the congregation sang in unison, especially when magistrates came in to arrest them!

A Pitch Pipe used to give the note for unaccompanied singing in church services.

There was a regular mid-week meeting called a Conference, at which there were sessions for guidance in which the interpretation of the Scriptures played a vital part. All members could participate by free discussion. Usually held on Tuesdays, the meeting was maintained, even at the height of the persecutions, from 1672 onwards.

The church meeting was held after public worship. Applications for membership were received and members would be subjected to discipline. Only the members could remain for this purpose. Admission to the church was usually by profession of faith in Christ, made before all the church members, who would then vote either for or against admitting the applicant. The church withdrew its fellowship from those who 'walked disorderly'. Charges could range from the very serious, such as fornication or drunkenness, to such matters as going to hear the Quakers and speaking evil of the Bishop of Bristol.

> ### TO THINK ABOUT . . .
> **What reasons can you give for discipline, in the sense described here, being little practised today? In what situations could you envisage discipline being applied by a contemporary Baptist church meeting.**

The church observed the two ordinances: baptism and the Lord's Supper. Baptisms were usually taken by the pastor, though Thomas Jennings, a member of the church for some years, was officially appointed the baptismal administrator during the pastor's absence, usually because he was in prison, but sometimes because he was ill. Not all who asked for baptism were accepted, and not everyone who was baptised came into membership. Ewins had to face the matter of how to acknowledge the children of believing parents, and instituted a kind of seventeenth-century infant dedication service. Some of his opponents derisively called it 'dry baptism'.

The Lord's Supper was a monthly service, and there was usually a day of preparation in the week preceding it. Only the pastor could preside at the Lord's Table. During a vacancy of the pastorate or when the minister was in prison, the Lord's Supper was not administered. At the height of the persecution the church discussed at some length whether it was legitimate to have the Lord's Supper on any day other than a Sunday. They decided that it was.

WORSHIP AND STEWARDSHIP

THE PASTOR'S ROLE IN WORSHIP

Robert Robinson.

A century later, in very different circumstances for Dissenters, there is an interesting note in the Cambridge Baptist Church book for 1769 in which **Robert Robinson**, the pastor, argues that the worship is something which is specifically in his control. On November 18 that year the church book records:

> The pastor this day complained that, whereas the manner of conducting the public worship of the assembly was a branch of the duty which belonged to his office, he had been interrupted in this part of his work by certain heady people. They had not only found fault with certain tunes, which the best judges of music in the assembly had approved as proper church-music; but had done this at a lecture on a Lord's-day evening, a service which the church did not require, and over which they claimed no authority. A service which the pastor

began and continued by desire of the gown and town. That his aim in diversifying the manner of worship in lectures was the good of his hearers in general, and the growth of the church in particular. That for these purposes he sometimes indulged even the prejudices of his hearers, by introducing a sprightly tune, and by preaching in another language and in another manner than he did in the CHURCH'S WORSHIP. That he devoted the Thursday evening lecture to the church, the Lord's-day evening lecture to the gown and town, and the monthly lectures in the country villages to the country-people, and thought it his duty to vary them all as well as he was able. He begged the church to believe the goodness of his intentions, to claim no jurisdiction over his lectures, but to leave him an entire liberty of conducting them as he judges most conducive to the public edification. All this was allowed. And indeed, what sort of discipline has that church, which, having no confidence in its pastor, submits his office to the control of every disaffected brother, however destitute of pastoral abilities he may be?

It is interesting to note that Robinson is quite clear as to his role in worship and how that worship must be varied to meet the needs of various groups not only within the church but also the community.

> ### TO THINK ABOUT . . .
> **What views do you have on this debate, as lively now as in Robinson's time, about the extent to which the minister or designated leader of worship should have complete say in the ingredients of a service and the manner of preaching?**
>
> **How can we preserve the balance between form and order and freedom and spontaneity?**

FINANCIAL STEWARDSHIP

The same church book also records the four types of monetary collections which were made each year in the church. It illustrates the pastoral care and concern of all through the pastor. Money taken at the Lord's Supper was for their own members. They took a second collection at Christmas to help their own members and those of the congregation. A third collection was taken at Mid-summer to help with the expenses relating to the upkeep of the premises. Fourthly, there were occasional collections for other ministers in need, or for churches which had building repair programmes, although the latter were usually confined to one a year.

The collection each Lord's Supper, Robinson recorded, was approximately a guinea each time. He then outlines how the money for the church's poor was spent.

> I find by the Poor's Book that from Jan 1st to June 24th 1774 there has been distributed among the poor of the church and auditory, in money, clothing, firing, etc., twentyfive pounds one shilling . . . Last Christmas the deacons purchased 40 ells of hemping at 1s.4d. per ell, which they distributed in shirting, shifting, etc., 45 yds of baize at 1s.1d. per yard for petticoats, beside stockings, handkerchiefs, and flannel waistcoats . . . Two children of the widow Nottage and one of Will Johnson's have been taught to read and write by the deacons' allowance. Two old men and two widows have weekly payments . . . The whole of the last six months is about £25.

This was all part of the work of the church which flowed out of its regular commitments in worship, and this was not uncommon among churches of the period. There was great variety in worship in the period, and undoubtedly much depended on the pastor's leadership, but there was a wholesome, caring concern in many Baptist congregations which is not always evident from the records.

> **TO THINK ABOUT . . .**
> In our age of state provision and welfare, unknown in Robinson's day, what opportunities still remain to congregations for 'wholesome, caring concern'?

HYMN SINGING

Hymn singing amongst Baptists caused great controversy for a good number of years. Eventually the impetus given by Isaac Watts encouraged Particular Baptists to pursue this with enthusiasm, and the thrilling songs of the evangelical revival under the Wesleys secured the tradition in the churches.

An example of the church's 'wholesome, caring concern'.

The growing practice of hymn writing encouraged John Ash, minister of Pershore, and Caleb Evans, principal of the Bristol Academy, to publish in 1769 *A Collection of Hymns adapted to Public Worship*. It was the first compilation of hymns by different authors, with Watts and Doddrige predominating. Also in this collection were the first published hymns of Anne Steele (1717–78), from Broughton in Hampshire, whose hymns have been widely used in Britain and America.

John Rippon, trained at Bristol by Caleb Evans, published his own Selection (1787) which became the ground work of the Psalms and Hymns collection and what is now today *The Baptist Hymn Book*.

A nineteenth-century contributor to Baptist hymnody, under her pen name of Marianne Farningham, was Marianne Hearn, of College Street, Northampton. Author, lecturer, and known to thousands through the length and breadth of the country as editor of the Sunday School Times, her Easter hymns and poetry were widely appreciated.

> ### *TO THINK ABOUT . . .*
> **What distinctive contributions to enriching Christians' worship and strengthening Christians' faith have come from hymns and spiritual songs written in the eighteenth, nineteenth and twentieth centuries?**

Summarise below what you consider were the main features of early Particular Baptist thought and practice. What do you believe has value for now?

UNIT 5

Scripture, Church and Ministry

Having established the historical roots of Baptist churches prior to 1700, it is important to recognise that the churches arose from distinctive principles which shaped Baptist identity profoundly. The principles grew out of an understanding of the nature and authority of Scripture and a deep desire to re-create the apostolic understanding of the Church. Baptist identity springs, not from a desire to establish the validity of believer's baptism, but out of a clear conviction that putting God's Word at the centre provides an adequate answer to the question: What is the Church?

This present unit reviews the diversity of early Baptist thought in respect of Scripture, the Church and its ministry. Later chapters will continue an historical discussion of these themes, together with those concerning the two sacraments of baptism and the Lord's Supper, mission, religious liberty and unity.

> **TO THINK ABOUT . . .**
> 'Baptist identity springs, not from a desire to establish the validity of believer's baptism, but out of a clear conviction that putting God's Word at the centre provides an adequate answer to the question: What is the Church?' Is this true for you?

SCRIPTURE

THE CENTRALITY OF SCRIPTURE

Baptists in the seventeenth century regularly issued statements about their beliefs; these were called Confessions of Faith. The roots of such works are found in sixteenth-century Anabaptist writings and much more clearly in the Puritan and Separatist tradition of the English churches. The Confessions were issued both by Associations and Assemblies of the Particular and General Baptists.

These Confessions used Scripture to illustrate the doctrinal statements made. The references were not cosmetic but essential to the understanding of the document and made it clear that Scripture is the controlling factor in the establishment of doctrine. We can illustrate from the Particular Baptist 1644 *Confession*:

> The Rule of this Knowledge, Faith and Obedience, concerning the worship and service of God, and all other Christian duties, is not mans inventions, opinions, devices, lawes, constitutions or traditions unwritten whatsoever, but only the word of God contained in the Canonical Scriptures.

In this written Word God hath plainly revealed whatsoever he hath thought needful for us to know, believe, and acknowledge, touching the Nature and Office of Christ, in whom all the promises are Yea and Amen to the praise of God. (Articles 7 & 8, 1644 *Confession*.)

The central place of Scripture is again evident in Article 22:

> . . . Faith is the gift of God wrought in the hearts of the elect by the Spirit of God, whereby they come to see, know, and believe the truth of the Scriptures, and not only so, but the excellence of them above all other writings and things in the world, as they hold forth the glory of God in his attributes, the excellency of Christ in his nature and offices, and the power of the fullness of the Spirit in its workings and operations; and thereupon are inabled to cast the weight of their souls upon this truth thus believed.

The General Baptist equivalent to the Particular Baptist 1644 *Confession* was the *Faith and Practise of Thirty Congregations* 1651, drawn up at an Association meeting in Leicester by delegates from a wide geographical area. There is a profusion of Scripture references throughout the document, and the attitude to Scripture is best summed up in Article 46:

> That whosoever shall preach, teach, or practise any doctrine in the worship of God, pretending it in the name of Jesus Christ, which is not to be heard or read in the record of God, which was given by inspiration of the Holy Ghost; such teachers are liable to the curse of God, howsoever countenanced by men.

TO THINK ABOUT . . .
'The Bible says . . .' Is this as much an adequate statement of ultimate authority for Baptists now as in the seventeenth century?

SCRIPTURE IN THE ASSEMBLY

In the seventeenth century both the Particular and General Baptists met in national Assembly and issued Confessions of Faith. The Particular Baptist Assembly issued in 1677 the *Second London Confession*. It was an era of persecution when it was important to affirm Particular Baptist unity with Presbyterians and Congregationalists in the Westminster Confession. It was re-drafted in 1688 by William Collins of Petty France, London, and agreed in 1689 by representatives of many 'London and country' Particular Baptist churches.

The role of Scripture was much more fully developed in the 1677 *Confession*, the first article of which read:

> The Holy Scripture is the only sufficient, certain and infallible rule of all saving Knowledge, Faith and Obedience; Although the light of Nature and the works of Creation and Providence do so far manifest the goodness, wisdom and power of God, as to leave men inexcusable; yet they are not sufficient to give that knowledge of God and His will, which is necessary unto Salvation. Therefore it pleased the Lord at sundry times, and in divers

manners to reveal himself, and to declare His will unto His church; and afterward for the better preserving and propagating of the Truth, and for the more sure Establishment and Comfort of the Church against the corruption of the flesh, and the malice of Satan, and of the World, to commit the same wholly unto writing; which make the Holy Scriptures to be most necessary, those former ways of Gods revealing His will unto His people being now ceased.

The authority of Scripture, it continues, does not depend 'upon the testimony of any man or Church; but wholly upon God (who is truth itself) the Author thereof; therefore it is to be received, because it is the Word of God'. Even though we have all the testimony of the Church, and the nature of the revelation, 'our full persuasion, and assurance of the infallible truth and divine authority thereof, is from the inward work of the Holy Spirit, bearing witness by and with the Word in our hearts'.

Everything necessary for man's salvation is contained in the Scripture and nothing is to be added to it, 'whether by new Revelation of the Spirit, or traditions of men'. The first phrase excluded Quaker claims, and the second, Anglican or Roman Catholic.

TO THINK ABOUT . . .
These very two issues, 'new Revelations of the Spirit' and 'traditions of men' are matters of debate today. How would you relate them to your own understanding of the authority of Scripture? Do these seventeenth-century statements help?

'The infallible rule of interpretation of Scripture,' declared the confession, 'is the Scripture itself: And therefore when there is a question about the true and full sense of Scripture (which is not manifold but one) it must be searched by other places that speak more clearly.'

The General Baptists' 1679 *Orthodox Creed* was written with the intention of uniting and confirming 'all true protestants in the fundamental articles of the Christian religion'. In the General Baptist churches the Hoffmanite theology (see page 17) of a leading General Baptist Messenger,

Matthew Caffyn, who was preaching widely in Kent and Sussex, was an added inducement to expound the orthodox position.

The *Orthodox Creed* centres on Christology, because as the Preface remarks, 'we are sure that the denying of baptism is a less evil than to deny the Divinity or Humanity of Christ.' Article 19 is concerned with the relationship between the Old and the New Testament concluding: 'the Old and New Testaments, like the faces of the Cherubins look one toward another, and hold forth the self-same Gospel salvation to them and us.'

> The authority of the holy scripture dependeth not upon the authority of any man, but only upon the authority of God, who hath delivered and revealed his mind therein unto us, and containeth all things necessary for salvation. (Article 37.)

In less thorough terms than the Particular Baptists, the Article excludes:

> pretended immediate inspirations, dreams, or prophetical predictions . . . We do believe, that all people ought to have them in their mother tongue, and diligently and constantly to read them in their particular places and families for their edification and comfort; and endeavour to frame their lives,

according to the direction of God's word, both in faith and practice, the holy Scriptures being of no private interpretation, but ought to be interpreted according to the analogy of faith, and is the best interpreter of itself, and is sole judge in controversy.

For a proper understanding of Baptist faith and order it is essential to recognise the controlling influence of the Scriptures. Whether Baptists are in church meeting, Association gathering or national Assembly, the final court of appeal is the Scriptures. It provides the frame-work for understanding the covenanted nature of the church local and universal. It is the magnetic north to which all discussions of belief and practice for individuals or churches constantly turn. It provides the authority and pattern for the ministry of Word and sacrament and is the motivation for Christian mission.

TO THINK ABOUT . . .
What might later historians detect were the things which challenged the authority of Scripture in Baptist churches today?

THE CHURCH

THE DISTINCTIVENESS OF DISSENT

The Anglican understanding of the Church of England as the church by law established was an inclusive idea. The baptism of infants signified not only their acceptance within the church community of divine grace, but also their initiation into the temporal community of the nation. The Reformation in England had resulted in the severance of all links with the ecclestiastical and temporal powers of the see of Rome. Control in the Church of England, as in the nation, was directly under the Sovereign, who worked through bishops in the House of Lords in the appointment of all ministers of the Church of England, and through both Lords and Commons in controlling the laws and liturgical practice of the established church.

The concept of an independent gathering of adult believers, who pledged personal loyalty first to Christ and then to each other as in the body of Christ, was completely foreign to the Church of England as established by Queen Elizabeth and her successors. But for Dissenters the independency of the local congregation, where Christ was King, was paramount. The members themselves provided from their own physical and spiritual resources for the chapels and their own ministers. Christian commitment was worked out in the holy living of members of the congregation and in a Christian life-style in the local community. It is almost impossible to overstate the importance for such congregations of the independence of the local church. But this is not to deny that they also shared in a wider association of interdependence between churches of the same denomination. Such interdependence was worked out with Christians of a like mind on the basis of common doctrinal beliefs, ecclesiastical polity and in mission to an unbelieving world. Each congregation understood itself to share in God's covenanted love made known through Christ.

> **TO THINK ABOUT . . .**
> **In your own understanding of the Christian doctrine of the Church, how important and central would be any or all of these features?**

A COVENANTED PEOPLE

Long before John Smyth adopted a General Baptist position, the concept of the divine covenant dominated his thought about the Church. He defined a 'visible community of saints' as 'two or more joined together by covenant with God and themselves . . . for their mutual edification and God's glory'. God covenanted to be their God, 'to give Christ' and 'with Christ, all things else'. Christians entering this covenant agreed to obey all God's commandments. Christians also had a duty to each other as believers, which he termed 'the duties of love'. Smyth maintained this covenant grace became contemporary when people accepted it within the context of a local congregation.

The final seat of church authority, for Smyth, was in the covenant community. 'Unto whom the covenant is given, unto them the power of binding and loosing is given. The covenant is given to the body of the Church . . . therefore the power of binding and loosing is given to them.'

For Smyth, believer's baptism 'doth visibly declare' a promise which had been inwardly received, a covenant which had already been entered. It was a covenant involving the 'mutual consent of both persons contracting together'.

Covenant theology was central also to the Particular Baptists. Dr B.R. White has shown that the ancestry of the 1644 *Confession* is a Confession of 1596, which influenced not only John Smyth but all the Separatists in the Robert Browne tradition.

Articles 33 and 34 of the 1644 *Confession* state that:

> Christ hath here on earth a spiritual Kingdom, which is the Church, which he hath purchased and redeemed to himself, as a peculiar inheritance: which Church, as it is visible to us, is a company of visible saints . . . To this Church he hath made his promises, and given the signs of his Covenant, presence, love, blessing and protection . . .

Dr G.F. Nuttall, in *Visible Saints: The Congregational Way, 1640–60* (1957) p. 77, describes the use of the covenant in a local church. 'Along with its binding and voluntary aspects, both of which were regarded as vital, in church circles the covenant did express, almost before all else, the entering into fellowship, the giving of themselves up to God and to one another intended by those who took part in it'. Baptist churches used the covenant in a distinctive way. At the Western Association gathering at Taunton in 1654 it was asked: 'whether any are to be received into the Church of Christ only upon a bare confession of Christ being come in the flesh and assenting to the doctrine and order laid down by him?' The answer was unequivocal: 'They may not be admitted on such terms without the declaration of the experimental work of the Spirit upon the heart, through the Gospel and suitable to it, being attended with tokens of conversion to the satisfaction of the administrator and brethren or church concerned in it.'

The use of the word 'experimental' indicated the experiential and personal nature of conversion and it was a distinction of consequence for Baptists. Presbyterians, for example, using the same covenant theology, only required a simple subscription to the doctrines for admission to membership.

Within the local independent congregation the commitment to the covenant was often linked to the Confession of Faith affirmed by the local church. At Frome, Somerset, for example, the church book begins with a Calvinistic statement of Faith. This is followed by a three point covenant to which members are to subscribe at the same time.

These are (i) to be regular in worship; (ii) to care

and be cared for in the Lord; and (iii) to accept financial responsibility for the ministry. Then it continues:

> Now upon these conditions:
> *Qu.1.* Do you solemnly give yourself up to the Lord and to the Church to watch over and be watched over, to perform all the duties, and enjoy all the privileges of the House of God?
> *Qu.2.* Do you solemnly agree to receive this person as a member of the Society, to watch over . . . in the Lord and to be watched over, according to the Gospel Rule?

TO THINK ABOUT . . .
What evidence of a personal experience of God and an understanding of Christian truth do you think should be requested today from applicants for church membership?

Towards the end of his life Benjamin Keach produced, alongside a reprint of the 1689 *Confession*, a church covenant which was the combined basis of membership in his Horsly Down church. The local independent congregation was not narrowly conceived in its churchmanship. The document reveals that the church believed itself to be affirming the theology and life-style of the mainstream Protestant, Reformed, churches.

> We believe a true church of Christ is not National nor Parochial but doth consist of a number of godly persons who upon the Profession of their Faith and Repentance have been baptized and in solemn manner have in a Holy Covenant given themselves up to the Lord and one another, to live in love and to endeavour to keep the unity of the Spirit in the bond of peace; Among whom the Word of God is duly preached; Holy Baptism and the Lord's Supper and all other ordinances are duly administered according to the Word of God and the institution of Christ in the primitive Church; watching over one another and communicating to each other necessities, as becometh saints; living Holy Lives, as becomes their sacred profession and not to forsake the assembling of themselves together as the manner of some is; not to take leave to hear where they please in other places when the Church is assembled, but to

worship God and feed in that pasture or with that Church, with whom they have covenanted and given themselves up as particular members thereof.

Benjamin Keach.

A PRIESTLY PEOPLE

Separatism provided for both General and Particular Baptists an understanding of the independence of each gathered fellowship of believers, which was fundamental to the concept of interdependence which these churches also held.

The clearest statement of this was made by the General Baptist founder, John Smyth, who wrote about it in *The Differences of the Churches of the Separation* (see, *The Works of John Smyth*, 2 vols, edited W.T. Whitley, Cambridge, 1915, pp. 274 ff). Smyth developed the idea of the visible church as a 'kingly priesthood . . . and the Saints are Kings and Priests unto God'.

Smyth argued that it is the congregation, 'saints as kings', who rule the visible church. They are children of the Kingdom who accept the government of Christ the King in each congregation. As part of this congregational kingship the 'saints as priests' have the responsibility of offering up spiritual sacrifices acceptable to God. Smyth deals at length with how such worship is to be conducted, and elaborates on the responsibilities of presbyters or elders. The eldership 'is to lead and moderate the Church actions and speeches' but Smyth made it clear that the ultimate authority rests with the 'saints' who are 'kings and priests unto God'. The saints are 'all interested in all parts of administration though the elders lead and moderate them'. It is the saints 'jointly who have all power both of the kingdom and the priesthood immediately from Christ'. Therefore, if there is no elder in a congregation, it does not lack power 'to preach, pray, sing psalms and . . . administer the seals of the covenant' and can properly 'admonish, convince, excommunicate, absolve, and all other actions either of the kingdom or the priesthood'.

> **TO THINK ABOUT . . .**
> Do you believe John Smyth offers any help at this point in discovering appropriate styles of leadership for Baptist churches today?

Even when the church has chosen elders it 'loses none of her former power, but still retains it entire unto herself to use' when occasion demands. 'The presbytery has no power but what the Church has and gives to it, which the church upon just cause can take away.' In fact the church has some power which the eldership on its own does not possess, that is the power to elect elders to office and also to excommunicate.

> **TO THINK ABOUT . . .**
> Do these statements fit with your own understanding of the power of the church in relation to the minister/elder.

This ultimate congregational control of the life of the church has been distinctive for Baptists from the beginning. Indeed, Smyth went so far as to say that though the deacons 'are the hands of the church' and servants of the congregation, nonetheless, 'the church is the owner and primary possessor of the treasury, and the chief lord of it under Christ: and unto the church must account be made finally.'

A DISCIPLINED PEOPLE

Seventeenth-century church books reveal at least seven issues which often occupied the members' attention. The meetings, which were frequently held following Sunday worship, dealt with:

(1) the appointment and care of church officers, including the minister;
(2) admissions to membership;
(3) the support of those in physical need and distress;
(4) discipline cases;
(5) the calling out of people to exercise a preaching gift;
(6) the upkeep of the building; and
(7) matters theological and practical, involving relationships with other local Baptist churches or the Association.

> **TO THINK ABOUT . . .**
> How do these seven points compare with the agenda of a current Baptist church meeting agenda?

The gathered fellowship of believers demanded a godly life-style. The Particular Baptist 1644 *Confession* makes it clear that every member of each church is subject to the 'censure and judgment of Christ', a power which 'is given to every particular Congregation and not one particular person, either member or officer, but the whole'. Therefore 'the Church ought with great care and tenderness, with due advice to proceed against her members'. To this end Christ has 'given authority, and laid duty upon all, to watch over one another'.

The General Baptist *Orthodox Creed* of 1678 established a discipline procedure, based on Matthew 18:15 ff., but urged that an offender be tendered 'an admonition of repentance . . . with gravity, love and authority, and all this without hypocrisy or partiality, praying for the sinner . . .'

Church discipline among Baptists was corrective but rarely vindictive. Discipline was motivated by love. It was first of all necessary to determine whether the conduct alleged was contrary to Scripture. Hearsay evidence was never enough – the church meeting required incontrovertible evidence of the offence in question, and would send its leaders to establish facts with the people concerned.

The church dealt differently with those who succumbed to sudden temptations and those who were persistent transgressors. The Soham Baptist Church's 'Principles of Church Order and Discipline' maintained that there was a great difference between 'being overtaken by temptation and running into it'.

TO THINK ABOUT . . .

Do you consider that the exercise of discipline is or is not adequate in contemporary Baptist churches? Does the practice of seventeenth-century Baptists offer any helpful guidance in these matters?

The covenant which members had taken 'to watch over one another in love and tenderness, remembering that we are in the body and liable to sin', meant the members owed it to each other to give thought to an action, provide Biblical evidence for its prohibition, explain its detrimental effects, and pronounce judgement on it.

Effective discipline required dealing with people personally. When that failed certain procedures were adopted. The truth of the accusations had to be verified by witnesses. Visitors were then appointed from the church, who personally informed the offender of the church's concern, privately. If the offender did not respond positively, it could end with public censure, but this was a last resort. There was an avoidance of severity, a leaning towards mercy, and prayers for the offender. The hope was always that repentance would bring restoration to fellowship.

Throughout the churches discipline was an essential expression of genuine Christian compassion. To ignore the faults of a fellow believer was to fail him or her in love. A healthy concern for the moral and spiritual welfare of one's fellow members was considered the true compassion.

AN ASSOCIATING PEOPLE

The preamble to the 1644 *Confession* underlined the conviction that the churches which so covenanted together shared a common life:

> . . . though we be distinct in respect of our particular bodies, for conveniency sake, being as many as can well meet together in one place, yet all are one in Communion, holding Jesus Christ to be our head and Lord; under whose government we desire alone to walk.

The mutual relationship between Particular Baptist churches is illustrated in a programme of evangelism which began in the London churches, but which reached to the Midlands, Northumberland, Kent, the West Country, Ireland, Wales and Scotland.

At a meeting of church representatives at Tetsworth, Oxfordshire, in 1653, the churches signed an 'agreement' acknowledging mutual interdependence and agreed to confer on three matters. These were:

(1) advice on controversial matters which could not be resolved by one church on its own;
(2) the provision of financial support for any of the congregation in need; and
(3) the common planning, for the greater glory of God, of anything which required 'the joint carrying on of the work of the Lord that is common to the churches'.

TO THINK ABOUT . . .

How would Baptist churches today be affected if these three principles from the 1653 agreement were consistently and widely implemented?

The principle of association was on the analogy that what happened in the local gathered fellowship of believers should also appertain between churches with a shared faith and order.

> There is a like relation betwixt the particular churches each towards other, as there is betwixt particular members of one church. For the

Churches of Christ do make up but one body or church in general under Christ their head . . . we conclude that every church ought to manifest its care over other churches as fellow members of the same body of Christ in general.

The *Second London Confession* of 1677 described the mutual care of churches for each other in the following terms:

As each Church, and all the Members of it, are bound to pray continually, for the good and prosperity of all the Churches of Christ, in all places, and upon all occasions to further it . . . so the Churches . . . ought to hold communion amongst themselves for their peace, increase of love, and mutual edification.

Any problems can be resolved when many Churches holding communion together, do by their messengers meet to consider, and give their advice in or about that matter in difference, to be reported to all the Churches concerned; howbeit these messengers assembled, are not entrusted with any Church-power properly so-called . . . to impose their determination on the Churches, or Officers.

The General Baptist *Orthodox Creed* of 1678 stated that the covenant idea held a central position in their thinking. The new covenant is the basis for man's acceptance before God, since the old covenant has failed. The new covenant in Christ is the basis of a new relationship between God and humanity, and on it the Church is built. This new covenant is of God's 'free grace and love to fallen man' and is freely and fully offered to all men on the terms of the Gospel, viz. repentance and faith.

For General Baptists the relationship between churches was deliberately connexional.

There is only one invisible catholic Church of Christ. Nevertheless, we believe the visible Church of Christ on earth, is made up of several distinct congregations, which make up that one catholic church, or mystical body of Christ. And the marks by which she is known to be the true spouse of Christ, are these, viz.

- Where the word of God is rightly preached,
- and the sacraments truly administered, according to Christ's institution and the practice of the primitive church;
- having discipline and government duly executed

by ministers or pastors of God's appointing and the Church's election,
- that is a true constituted church.

The General Baptist understanding of the power of the Assembly is expressed in Article 39:

General Councils or Assemblies, consisting of Bishops, Elders and Brethren, of the several churches of Christ . . . and the churches appearing there by their representatives, make but one church and have lawful right, and suffrage in this general meeting, or assembly, to act in the name of Christ; it being of divine authority and is the best means under heaven to prevent heresy, to preserve unity and superintendency among, or in any congregation whatsoever within its own limits, or jurisdiction.

Appeals concerning any injustice, schism or heresy in a particular congregation were dealt with by a majority vote in the Assembly.

TO THINK ABOUT . . .
Should Association gatherings still be concerned with matters of 'injustice, schism or heresy in a particular congregation'?

A MISSIONARY PEOPLE

New thinking about the nature of the Church came from the Particular Baptists at the end of the eighteenth century through the writings of **Andrew Fuller**, minister at Soham, Cambridgeshire, and a significant theological thinker.

Fuller's expression of evangelical Calvinism challenged the high, or extreme, form of Calvinism that prevailed among Baptists in his day. *The Gospel Worthy of All Acceptation* (1784) was theological dynamite which exploded into a new understanding of the Church among Baptists.

Andrew Fuller.

microcosm of the universal Church. When churches associate Fuller claimed that such unity was a matter of mutual consent and fellowship in the service of the Gospel, and not the result of an authority imposed on the churches from without.

William Carey, using this as a foundation, enquired at length into the 'obligations of Christians to use means for the conversion of the heathen'. This new understanding of God's mission through the Church led to the founding of the Baptist Missionary Society in 1792 and five years later the organisation of the Baptist Home Mission Society.

DANIEL TURNER – THE CHURCH

Another eighteenth-century Baptist writer who gave some thought to the nature of the Church was Daniel Turner, minister at Abingdon. His *Compendium of Social Religion* (1758) begins with a summary of the New Testament meaning of the word Church. He claimed first that the word described:

> the whole number of truly pious or peculiar people of God . . . the mystical body of Christ [who are the] invisible catholic or universal church, part of which is triumphant in heaven and part militant on earth. [But the word also described] the whole body of those that make any visible profession of a religious regard to the revealed will of God . . . which may be called the apparent or visible catholic church. [By visible, Turner meant] what falls under human cognisance and judgment. [Third, the word Church denoted] one particular society of Christians.

He argued the missionary nature of the Church on two premises. First, it is the obligation of all 'to whom the Gospel is published to repent and believe the Gospel'. Second, that being so, every member of the Church must do their utmost to 'further the discipling of all nations'. The charge of the Risen Christ to go and make disciples is still binding on the Church.

Andrew Fuller's doctrine of salvation caused him to describe the Church as 'the whole Assembly of the saved' which embraced in 'one community all ranks and degrees of men as brethren'. Fuller used many other Scriptural images to define the Church. It was:

> a vessel living in a tempestuous sea; a bush on fire, yet not consumed. In the very worst times God has had a remnant, and since the Church is built on a rock, the gates of hell shall not prevail against it.

Using the image of a human body (I Corinthians 12:24), he explained the Church was composed of many members, one in grace (charis) but differing in gifts (charismata). The local church is a

A local church comprises those who meet for fellowship and worship at the same time in one convenient place. It is distinguished from the 'civil societies of the world by the spiritual nature and design of its constitution and government'. The members of the church 'devote themselves to God through Christ, in obedience to the call of the Gospel'. The church owns Christ 'as their only Saviour and the Sovereign of their consciences, and his word as the only perfect and infallible rule of their faith and practice in matters of religion'. Such a church is a 'voluntary society, formed by mutual consent and confederation' which submits to Christ by the same sign of devotion, baptism with water in the name of the Trinity.

The chief ends of church fellowship are the preservation of the faith, worship and blessings of the Gospel in their power and purity; the support and encouragement of the public ministry of the Word, for the conversion of sinners and the edification of the saints; and the continual manifestation of the wisdom, power, grace and glory of God by Christ in the world.

Though churches are independent of each other, it is necessary and prudent for them to be in touch about 'their own mutual comfort, purity and edification', to share in the 'communion of saints', and 'unite their counsels by social meeting of their respective elders and messengers by agreement, provided they assume no arbitrary jurisdiction or decisive power and authority over any particular churches or persons . . .'

The issue of authority in the eighteenth century made both Daniel Turner and Andrew Fuller cautious about the 'churchly power' of an Association. One way through this difficulty was

the adoption of the so-called 'society' method. Of this the Baptist Missionary Society was a typical example, since it allowed a new understanding of the church by the establishment of a voluntary society. It gave shape to a new understanding of the interdependency of Baptist churches as they worked out God's mission together. The method gave autonomy to the local church, but it also provided for Baptists a Society model for doing together what no one local congregation could do on its own. In the next century the same 'society method' would make possible the formation of the Baptist Union as an agency for united Baptist work in Britain.

> **TO THINK ABOUT . . .**
> Have we anything to learn from Daniel Turner's model of the 'society'? How would you justify the tension in our thought between the independency and the interdependency of the local church to someone alien to a Baptist understanding of the church?

THE MINISTRY

Among English Baptists there has never been complete clarity and agreement on the fundamental point of the relationship between ministry and church. Both the General and Particular Baptists were agreed about the need for ministry in the church, and both would have subscribed to the 1644 *Confession* of the Particular Baptists that: 'every church has power given them from Christ for their better well being, to choose to themselves meet persons into the office of Pastors, Teachers, Elders, deacons . . .'. How ministry related to the church was a matter for divergence between the Particular and General Baptists.

MINISTRY AND THE CHURCH

Early **General Baptists** concentrated attention on the local, independent, covenanted fellowship. Helwys said: '. . . the officers of every church or congregation are tied by office only to that particular congregation whereof they are chosen'. The covenant theology of the

Separatists was in part responsible for this view since it emphasised the independence of each congregation, and as a consequence the minister was limited strictly to the church which called him. The minister had first to be a covenanted member of the local church before he could be called to ministry within it. Another corollary was that ministry was not an absolute necessity for the existence of the church. Smyth wrote: 'The brethren jointly have all the power both of the kingdom and priesthood immediately from Christ . . . and that by virtue of the covenant God maketh with them.'

Particular Baptists in the seventeenth century,
who also shared covenant theology, did not draw
the General Baptist conclusion. Individual
churches were indeed 'a compact and knit city in
itself . . . yet are they all to walk by one and the
same rule', having counsel and help from all the
churches 'as members of one body in the
common faith under Christ their only head'.

The growing awareness of a wider relationship
between the ministry and the churches
developed, surprisingly, among the General
Baptists through the office of Messenger. A
Messenger was someone commissioned by a
church to preach the Gospel and form new
churches, or who was sent by one church to
another to discuss matters of common concern
or settle a dispute. However, a reluctance to let a
good local minister become a Messenger resulted
in a steady decline of this office in the eighteenth
century.

ASSOCIATION GATHERINGS

Another factor in developing the recognition of a
broader relationship between the ministry and
the churches was the regular coming together of
Baptist churches in Association gatherings.
Associations were a vital part of early Baptist
life, and after the persecutions ceased it was not
surprising that both General and Particular
Baptists took the opportunity to meet nationally
to restore effective Association life. It was the
breadth and depth of relationship discovered in
Association life which strengthened the conviction that extreme isolationism was a denial of

fellowship among churches, and that unity
would better advance Christ's cause.

Daniel Turner's *Compendium of Social Religion*
presents a broad Particular Baptist view of the
ministry and church. The fundamental unity of
the whole Church was demonstrated by the way
in which churches 'unite their counsels by the
social meetings of respective elders and
messengers'. He understood the ministry to be
to 'the church in general' and encouraged
ministers to preach, administer the sacraments
and share in ordinations in churches other than
their own, as opportunities arose. He had a
strong sense of the wider fellowship of the
churches which ministers must serve.

John Gill, another Particular Baptist with high
Calvinist sympathies, whose influence at this
time was immensely greater than Turner's,
urged quite the opposite opinions. A minister
must be a member of the church to which he
ministers. When he is a pastor he may not act
ministerially in any other congregation. His task
is within that one local fellowship. However, the
growth of Association life indicated the future
was with men like Turner and Andrew Fuller.
At Fuller's ordination, for example, were
ministers from several other churches representing the wider fellowship. When he considered
moving from Soham to Kettering, he discussed
the decision privately with local ministers and
churches.

MINISTERIAL AUTHORITY AND STATUS

The status and authority of the ministry within
both General and Particular Baptist *Confessions*
provides a point of unity. 'The visible Church of
Christ, being completely organised according to
the mind of Christ, consists of officers and
members: and the officers appointed by Christ
to be chosen by His Church . . .' is the view of

the *Orthodox Confession*. The Particular Baptist *Somersets Confession* of 1656 states: 'That the authority of Christ in an orderly ministry in His Church is to be submitted to'.

The church has power to act against the minister if doctrinal error or immorality is evident in the minister's life. Equally, 'the work of preaching the Word is not so peculiarly confined to them but that others also who are gifted, and fitted by the Holy Spirit for it, and approved, and called by the Church, may and ought to perform it'.

> ### TO THINK ABOUT . . .
> Do you believe that that principle holds true for today? If so, do you see any signs of the preaching function within Baptist churches extending beyond ordained ministers to 'others also who are gifted, and fitted by the Holy Spirit for it, and approved, and called by the Church . . .'?

The appointment of ministers among early Baptists was in three stages.

• There was first an election by the church when the minister was 'chosen by common suffrage of the Church'. The election was by the 'most voices of the members of the church in full communion'.

• The second factor was the approbation of the church. Approbation was the 'examining and finding the officer elect to be according to the rule of his office', with the members making their objections known, particularly if they were unwilling to give the minister support.

• Finally there was ordination by the elders together with other ministers of the churches. The ordination had three facets: 'the power which the church commits to the minister; prayer made by the whole church for the minister that he may faithfully serve; and a charge given to the minister to look to his office in all parts of it'.

At Hitchin in 1785, Robert Robinson was invited to share in an ordination and induction service for Mr Geard, and recorded the following note for the Cambridge Baptist Church book:

> The order of the ordination was this. The Revd Mr Simmons, pastor of the Baptist Church at Bedford began in singing. The Revd Mr Ryland senior, pastor of the Baptist Church at Northampton, prayed and opened the nature of the work. Mr Simmons prayed. Mr Ryland sang. Robinson took the church's account, the pastor's confession of faith, and prayed the ordination prayer, laying hands on Mr Geard, who was kneeling, and the other pastors laying their hands also. The Revd Mr Rippon, pastor of a part of the people of the late Dr Gill, sang. The Revd Hugh Evans, pastor of the Baptist church, and divinity tutor of the Baptist Academy at Bristol, preached to the pastor. The Revd Mr Cole, pastor of the Baptist Church at Whitchurch, Hants, prayed. Mr Rippon sang. The Revd Mr Jones, pastor of the Baptist Church at Hempstead, preached to the people. And the Revd Mr Gill, pastor of the Baptist Church at St. Alban's, prayed and dismissed the assembly.

FIT PERSONS FOR MINISTRY

Early Baptists used passages from the Pastoral Epistles to define the type of person fit for the ministry. The relationship between education and ministry is best described in the addition made to the General Baptist 1691 *Confession*.

> We believe that learning the languages, to whit, Hebrew, Greek, Latin, etc. is no qualification so absolutely necessary to the being of a minister, or Elder, but that a person may very possibly be sufficiently qualified without it; though we readily grant that the learning of languages may be useful in its place, and as a servant to help, etc., but to make it a qualification, absolutely necessary to the being of a minister, we dare not.

The Broadmead elder, Edward Terrill, whose will of 1679 resulted in the establishment of Bristol Baptist Academy, encouraged a spiritual and educated ministry among Particular Baptists. The early years of Bristol Academy were not easy but were formative, and the support it gathered during the next century put an educated ministry firmly in place among Baptists of future generations.

The front entrance of the present Bristol Baptist College, with a reminder that, founded in 1679, it can claim to be the oldest Baptist college in the world.

In the eighteenth century a man was called to the ministry by his own church. If he showed ability in prayer and speaking he would be invited to preach at a church meeting. Having passed that hurdle, and after further preaching at subsequent church meetings, he would be called to a preaching ministry, and a day of exhortation would be held. After this the person would enter on a preaching ministry until he was called to be pastor of a specific congregation. When that happened he was ordained, even though there was sometimes a gap of several years between being called to preach and settlement as a pastor.

TO THINK ABOUT . . .

Does this pattern for the calling and final settlement of a minister in a church have any advantages over the pattern which operates today in most Baptist churches?

The path of one such candidate for the ministry, James Bicheno, is related in detail in the Cambridge Baptist Church book. The matter was first raised by Robinson, the pastor, on May 14, 1775.

> The church was called to meet after the Lord's Supper, and, the house being cleared of all but members, the pastor desired Mr James Bicheno to withdraw, and then informed the church that Mr Bicheno had informed him that he had a great desire to devote himself to the ministry, that the Revd Mr Wells of Royston had very generously offered to recommend him to an academy for the sake of literary attainments, that he [the pastor] had examined him, and thought him a person of promising abilities, which under proper tuition might serve the church of Christ . . . advised him to proceed on the Bristol plan. That the school at Bristol was a noble institution, well calculated to prevent the evils that had been complained of in other schools, particularly that of sending learned, but irreligious, men into the ministry, that they received none but such as were members of Baptist churches . . . whose gifts the church had tried, and who were recommended by that church. That the Baptist cause suffered much for want of a pious, but far more for want of a learned ministry, that the church had in the present case, two extremes to avoid, on the one hand, the quenching of the spirit, and on the other, the encouraging of ignorant, conceited, and unqualified spirits to go into the ministry, who would disgrace the church that sent them, and injure the best cause in the world.

TO THINK ABOUT . . .

What models/patterns of ministerial training do you consider are best suited to avoiding the extremes of, on the one hand, 'the quenching of the Spirit', and on the other, 'the encouraging of ignorant, conceited, and unqualified spirits to go into the ministry . . .'?

The church meeting agreed to try the young Bicheno's gifts and appointed a small group to hear him preach, which included the pastor and deacons. On July 6 the report was brought to the church meeting. They reported he had natural abilities for the work, that morally he was unblameable, but they doubted if he had that 'modest diffidence which, in their opinion, is essential to the ministry.' The church members therefore decided to put the decision off for three months. At a church meeting six months later, the pastor told the church they·should finish the affair. In the meantime someone had made objections to Bicheno on the grounds of his moral failure. The charges were examined by the church which decided they were unfounded and more than a year after the first discussion in church meeting he proceeded to Bristol Academy.

FUNCTIONS OF MINISTERS AND DEACONS

The functions of ministers were described by early Baptists in terms of their tasks, for example, messenger, elder, pastor, and deacon. In 1611 General Baptists had two types of officers, elders and deacons. Deacons could be either men or women. The *Orthodox Creed* 1678 lists three types of officers:

> The visible church of Christ, being completely gathered and organized, according to the mind of Christ, consists of officers and members; and the officers, appointed by Christ, to be chosen by his church, for the peculiar administration of ordinances, and execution of the power and duty Christ hath enjoined them to the end of the world, are these three, viz., Bishops (overseer or shepherd), or Messengers; and Elders, or Pastors; and Deacons, or Overseers of the poor.

Among Particular Baptists the 1644 *Confession* listed four types of officers, in line with the general Calvinistic practice.

> Every Church has power given them from Christ for their better well-being to choose to themselves meet persons into the office of Pastors, Teachers, Elders, Deacons, being qualified according to the Word, as those which Christ has appointed in his Testament for the feeding, governing, serving and building up of his church, and that none other hath power to impose them, either these or any other.

It is doubtful if such a fourfold ministry was put into practice in Baptist churches, since later editions of the *Confession* omit pastors and teachers, and the 1677 *Confession* has only two types of officers, bishops or elders, and deacons.

The minister was supported financially in Baptist churches, though in the beginning it was recognised that ministers should not be averse to 'labour with their hands that they may not be overchargeable'. The practical result was that while some congregations could support a full-time ministry, the majority were served by men who had a trade.

The General Baptist Messenger was essentially an evangelist, planting new churches, advising them in their early development and also offering advice to the churches who had appointed him. But the term was also used by both General and Particular Baptists of a representative of a congregation at an Association gathering, or of one who carried greetings to another church.

The General Baptist elder or pastor, and the bishop or elder of the Particular Baptists, fulfilled the functions normally associated with a minister today. Their task was to 'feed the flock'. In more detail this meant to 'attend the service of Christ in his Church, in the Ministry of the Word and Prayer, with watching of their souls as they that must give account to him'.

Among General and Particular Baptists the functions of deacons, who were ordained, were based on Acts 6, namely, 'to relieve the necessity of the poor and impotent brethren concerning their bodies'.

> **TO THINK ABOUT . . .**
> In what ways do Scripture, tradition and contemporary circumstances shape your own convictions about the leadership and ministerial needs of Baptist churches?

Daniel Turner in the eighteenth century echoed the early Confessions, though by this time the administration of the sacraments was explicitly stated to be the duty of a bishop, elder or pastor. Deacons 'are to take the care and management of the secular affairs of the church, that the bishop or pastor may be more at leisure to attend to the spiritual'. Turner also emphasised the leadership role of bishop or pastor, and called for an 'orderly and right execution' not of any new laws but 'of those already made by Christ himself'.

Baptists in the Eighteenth Century: Defending and Spreading the Faith

SETTING THE SCENE

SOCIAL CONDITIONS

Eighteenth-century Baptist churches were parochial. But that is only to describe the age in which they witnessed. The rural world was marked by tradition. The vast majority farmed as their fathers had before them. Enclosure was only slowly making ground. The landed gentry added to their estates by shrewd purchase and selective marriages. In times of low grain prices, tenant farmers might find it difficult to pay rent to their landlords, with eviction a real threat. The lot of the agricultural labourers, among whom were a number of Baptists, was even more precarious. Rural poverty and increasing population meant a slowly accelerating drift to the towns and industrial villages as the century progressed. In towns, the poor crowded ten to a room, alongside their poultry, cattle and even horses, in weatherboard, back-to-back houses.

'Trade is the wealth of the world', claimed Daniel Defoe in 1728, and his contemporaries in England agreed. Trade was the source of England's growing prosperity. Between 1750 and 1780 England experienced the birth of an industrialised society and the revolution in agriculture which changed the face of the countryside. Industrial middlemen pressed for the production of more goods. Coal was required, for example, and the invention of the steam pump by Thomas Newcomen, for many years pastor at the Dartmouth Baptist Church, enabled deep seam mining to replace open-cast works, because the pump could effectively remove the flood water from the pits.

The Steam Pumping Engine invented by Thomas Newcommen, as early as 1705.

TO THINK ABOUT . . .

How, in a few sentences, would you attempt to summarise the social conditions and values of late twentieth-century Britain?

The textile industry brought a golden age to weavers, particularly in the cotton trade. Baptist life in Lancashire and Yorkshire was transformed by the planting of industries in places like the Rossendale Valley or the Yorkshire Dales. It was also the time when the English countryside we know came into being. There were 642 Enclosure Acts in this period.

INTELLECTUAL CURRENTS

The arts and sciences flourished under the watchful eye of Dr Johnson, who dominated the scene in his own peculiar, truculent way. Thomas Gray's *Elegy* caught the feeling of the times and was a bestseller. Goldsmith and Sheridan brought wit and humour to the English stage. Artists captured the glories of rural England in these years. Gainsborough pictured the elegance of the fashionable world. Hogarth, in his biting, satirical cartoons, depicted the manner of life of the vast majority who lived in the middle of violence, vice and poverty.

Henry Cavendish at Cambridge University explored the separation and identification of gases and experimented with electricity. Joseph Priestley, a political as well as a theological radical, was a scientist who isolated oxygen and discovered the law of inverse squares in physics. Adam Smith's *Enquiry into the Wealth of Nations* (1776) established political economy as a social science. Gibbon's *Decline and Fall of the Roman Empire* (1776) was a breakthrough in historical writing, careful in its scholarship and confident in its judgement.

Monarchy in Britain was constitutional. The King depended on Parliament for his income and for the pay of the armed services. Ministers of the Crown were appointed by him at his personal will and pleasure, but the Ministers so appointed were answerable to Parliament.

In this century religion was commonly approached through reason. The religious certainties of previous generations became a confusing complex of probabilities arising out of human thought. The Deists' God was the divine watchmaker who had put the world together, wound it up, and now left it running without further interference. Matthew Tindal, a leading Deist, claimed in 1730 in *Christianity as old as Creation* that 'the religion of nature is absolutely perfect'.

John Tillotson, Archbishop of Canterbury under William III, believed that 'with charity and mutual forbearance the Church may be peaceful and happy without absolute unity of opinion'. The Latitudinarians saw themselves as champions of orthodoxy against the encroachments of Deism. They engaged in an elaborate rational defence of Christian revelation but often seemed lax about precise Christian formulations of dogma, leaving as much room as possible for individual judgement.

> *TO THINK ABOUT . . .*
> **What features of eighteenth-century thought and culture still seem to have influence in shaping contemporary attitudes to religion and world views?**

SPIRITUAL AWAKENING

Into this complex situation John Wesley's Methodism was born. Rationalism had dealt a blow to personal religion. John Wesley offered a way to life, now, which would transcend the ever-present reality of death, and the miseries of present poverty. He reaped a rich harvest.

Wesley did untold good, but he was a man of his age. Politically he was a Tory: 'The greater share the people have in government', he wrote, 'the less liberty civil or religious does a nation enjoy.' He welcomed the suppression of John Wilkes and his liberal views, had no sympathy with the rebels in the American Colonies, and thought the French Revolution was Satan's work.

Methodism was the lost soul of Anglicanism. Wesley never wished to break with the established church, and did his best to hold his movement within it. He had little sympathy with Calvinistic theology or the republican leanings of Dissent.

> *TO THINK ABOUT . . .*
> **Is history doomed to throw up movements which represent 'the lost soul' of more established, comfortable forms of religion? If so, what contemporary examples can you cite?**

'Wesley reaped a rich harvest'.

THE SALTERS' HALL DEBATE

THE TRINITY QUESTIONED

At the opening of the eighteenth century there emerged in England two forms of anti-Trinitarian thought: Arianism and Socinianism. Both taught a subordinationist view of Christ in relation to the Father.

Arians acknowledged the pre-existence of Christ, thought him in some sense divine and retained the idea of the atonement in respect of Christ's death. However, they regarded Christ as different in essence from God. These views were first propounded by the Alexandrian priest, Arius, and then rejected by the Council of Nicaea in 325 AD.

Socinians completely rejected the Trinitarian formulations of the fourth-century Councils of the Church. They believed Christ was a man whom God made worthy of adoration. Modern day Unitarians often hold this view of the person of Christ.

In 1687 Stephen Nye, an Anglican priest, published *A Brief History of the Unitarians, called also Socinians,* which disseminated anti-Trinitarian views. Certain measures were adopted to curb the spread of these views, such as the Blasphemy Act 1698, which made those propagating them liable to three years imprisonment. But the heresy gained ground.

William Whiston, a Cambridge Professor of Mathematics, published in 1710 a book called *Primitive Christianity Revived* which set out an Arian interpretation of Christianity. For this he was deprived of his post at Cambridge.

TO THINK ABOUT . . .
Should Christians have spent so much time and energy over the years debating the issue of Christ's deity? Why do you answer as you do?

THE SALTERS' HALL MEETING

In the dissenting world the matter came to a head when all London dissenting ministers were asked to give advice about views which were then being propagated by two Exeter Presbyterian ministers. The meeting was convened in 1719 at Salters' Hall, London, an important centre of Dissent. The question at issue was whether the matter could be resolved by an appeal to Scripture only, or was it right also to appeal to the creeds of Christendom? The creeds drew the Trinitarian understanding as an inference from the Scriptures.

The majority of Presbyterian and General Baptist churches took their stand on the sufficiency of Scripture alone. Most Congregational and Particular Baptist churches insisted further on subscription to a Trinitarian creed. Within a century many Presbyterian, and General Baptist churches connected with the original General Baptist Assembly, became Unitarian. The Congregational and Particular Baptist churches not only remained Trinitarian but also continued to honour the theology of John Calvin.

The attitude of the General Baptists to this issue was established when, in dealing with the Caffyn

> **TO THINK ABOUT . . .**
> This issue is still alive and still opinion is divided. It is focused for Baptists in the question: Should we have a fuller credal statement than we have already? What do you think?

dispute, the Assembly claimed in 1697 that if members debated the Trinity they 'must do so in Scripture words and terms' and 'in no other'. The Bible, however, nowhere mentioned the Trinity. Trinitarian thought is implicit, not explicit, in Scripture. Alongside this, the philosopher John Locke was encouraging Dissenters at large to test revelation by reason, not by the theological schemes of Athanasius or Calvin – and when they used that method they frequently ended up with unorthodox answers! The General Baptist literalism in regard to Scripture, which led them into the practice of foot washing and anointing with oil, also led them to suspect doctrine not based on explicit Scripture references. Their predilection for Arianism, inherent in their origins, made them grow liberal in theology and the final outcome was the denomination's demise.

THE NEW CONNEXION OF GENERAL BAPTISTS

As the General Baptist churches declined in the eighteenth century, many becoming Unitarian in doctrine (a legacy of Caffyn), the effect of the Evangelical Revival was to remind some of these churches of their origins in a lively evangelistic community.

> **TO THINK ABOUT . . .**
> Why do you think homes have sometimes been important centres for the gathering of believers at times of spiritual ferment?

THE REVIVAL'S IMPACT ON BAPTIST GROWTH IN THE MIDLANDS

One aspect of the Revival was the meeting of new Christians in people's homes for mutual support and further evangelistic outreach.

In Leicestershire one of the Revival's preachers was a certain David Taylor. He was a servant in the household of Selina, Countess of Huntingdon. Among the converts he gathered in the

villages around was **Samuel Deacon**, a Leicestershire farm hand, who later became a leader among the General Baptists of the New Connexion. In 1745 a meeting house was built for Deacon's congregation at Barton Fabis, despite much local opposition. By 1755 this congregation had adopted the rite of believer's baptism without any direct contact with regular Baptist churches. As the work expanded into the adjacent counties of Nottinghamshire, Derbyshire and Staffordshire, new meeting houses were built to accommodate the emerging congregations. Within twenty-five years the combined membership of these churches exceeded nine hundred people.

FORMATION OF THE NEW CONNEXION

At the same time, but completely unrelated to Deacon's work, a young Yorkshireman, **Dan Taylor**, began preaching among the Wesleyan Methodists around Halifax. Taylor became unhappy with some of the pastoral care aspects of Methodism and left the local Methodists. He formed an independent congregation at Wadsworth, near Heptonstall. He used the newly built chapel as a day school during the week. By a study of the New Testament he enabled the congregation to discover the nature of church order and persuaded them to adopt believer's baptism. Local Particular Baptist ministers refused to baptise Taylor and his members because of their Arminian theology. They advised him to go to Leicestershire to seek baptism from a General Baptist minister.

Dan Taylor.

Taylor undertook the journey with a friend and on the way called at Gamston, in Nottinghamshire, where there was a General Baptist church. The minister, Joseph Jeffries, baptised Taylor in the local river and introduced him to the General Baptist churches of the Midlands.

In May 1763 Taylor attended the Lincolnshire General Baptist Association meetings and soon after was ordained a minister by Gilbert Boyce. In 1764 Dan Taylor met Samuel Deacon, the convert of David Taylor, whose churches had now adopted believer's baptism but were unwilling to join the Lincolnshire General Baptist Association because of its tendency to Unitarian theology. The relationship between Taylor and Deacon developed quickly and as a result Dan Taylor realised that the old General Baptists were not evangelical as he understood that word. He concluded that it required a completely new beginning. Therefore, in 1770 Dan Taylor called together a number of colleagues who shared his evangelical Baptist sympathies and they formed the New Connexion of General Baptist Churches.

DECLINE OF THE GENERAL BAPTISTS

The original General Assembly of Baptist Churches heard each succeeding year a story of churches in decline, pastorless, and moving towards Unitarian views. This was encouraged by John Evans, a relative of the Bristol Academy's Principal, Caleb Evans, and who had also trained at Bristol. Over the next thirty years John Evans taught his Socinian sentiments to prospective Old General Baptist ministers and led them to adopt rationalist ideas and unorthodox patterns of theology.

In 1801 the Old General Baptist Assembly criticised the New Connexion for taking as its name the Free Grace General Baptists. A year later the Assembly revealed its further decline into Unitarianism by admitting as a personal member William Vidler, an avowed Baptist–Universalist minister. His preaching caused the final break for many free-thinkers, or Unitarians, from the Old General Baptist Assembly. Many former General Baptists became Unitarian and new chapels were opened across the country.

There was a travelling Baptist–Unitarian missioner, Richard Wright, ably supported by Robert Aspland, minister of the now General Baptist–Unitarian chapel at Newport, Isle of Wight. In due time a a number of General Baptist churches joined existing Presbyterian–Unitarian congregations, as at Boston, Portsmouth, Lewes, Taunton and Hull. However, it was not until 1916 that the Old General Baptists officially joined the Unitarians and in 1929 became part of the newly-founded General Assembly of Unitarian and Free Christian Churches.

TO THINK ABOUT . . .

In what ways is a church's understanding of who Jesus is – that is a church's Christology – related to its spiritual vigour, its attitude to mission and to worship?

GROWTH OF THE NEW CONNEXION

Meanwhile the story of the New Connexion was closely entwined with the personal story of Dan Taylor as the eighteeenth century turned into the nineteenth. Self-educated but widely read, Taylor was thirty-two years old when the New Connexion came into being. He engaged in a considerable pastoral work among the churches of the New Connexion and, when size prevented that, he developed a wide-ranging ministry through the printed word. In 1790 his *Essay on*

the Truth and Inspiration of the Holy Scriptures warned of the dangers inherent in drifting from evangelical truth. The *General Baptist Magazine*, which became the *General Baptist Repository*, was a constant source of information and news for the expanding new denomination. To counter the views of John Evans, in 1798 Taylor founded the Mile End Academy for the training of New Connexion ministers. The success of the New Connexion was in the emerging industrial towns of the Midlands and the North. Frequent ministerial conferences were encouraged and Association life was vigorous, giving vision to the ordinary members of the churches.

TO THINK ABOUT . . .

Do you think that today a vigorous Association life depends on the initial vigour of the member churches? Or, as is maintained here of the churches of the New Connexion, does a vigorous Association lead to ordinary church members being inspired?

The New Connexion formed its own Missionary Society in 1816. After 1832, when the Calvinistic Confession of Faith was dropped by the Baptist Union in favour of a unity based on those whose faith was 'usually denominated evangelical', the Baptists of the New Connexion moved closer to Particular Baptist churches and eventually, under the leadership of John Clifford, became integrated in the Baptist Union in 1891.

PARTICULAR BAPTISTS AND THE EVANGELICAL REVIVAL

To preach the Gospel to the world was very much part of the practice of the early Calvinistic Baptists in England. They would have concurred with the 1656 *Somersets Confession* which stated that:

> as it is an ordinance of Christ, so it is the duty of his church in his authority, to send forth such brethren as are fitly gifted through the Spirit of Christ to preach the Gospel to the world.

Richard Davis, an Independent minister at Rothwell, Northamptonshire, was thought to be the father of high Calvinism (sometimes referred to as hyper-Calvinism). Nevertheless, he regarded a vigorous policy of evangelism as essential for a church and was himself a successful exponent of this in the early eighteenth century. From among those churches he founded, some eventually became Baptist churches.

THE LINGERING INFLUENCE OF HIGH CALVINISM

London Baptists in this century were dominated by a devotion to an ever more rigid form of hyper-Calvinism. The three primary exponents of it were Baptist ministers who came originally from Northamptonshire. **John Skepp**, Baptist minister at Curriers' Hall, London, expounded his views in a posthumously published series of sermons in 1722. In these he established, at least to his own satisfaction, that it was wrong to use moral persuasion in presenting the Gospel. In this he echoed the teaching of his mentor, an Independent minister, Joseph Hussey. Hussey's own book of 1707 summed up the position in its title, *God's operations of Grace; but no offers of Grace*.

John Gill from Kettering settled as pastor in the Baptist church at Southwark following the ministry of Benjamin Stinton. Gill had been a close friend of Skepp, and working closely with another Baptist minister, **John Brine**, he developed Skepp's views in some depth. Brine, minister at Cripplegate, London, entered the debate in 1743 with a book which refuted the principles of Davis' successor at Rothwell,

John Fawcett.

Matthias Maurice. Maurice's book, *A Modern Question Modestly Answered* (1737), asked whether it was not the duty of the unconverted to believe in the Gospel of Christ? He answered his own question in the affirmative and claimed it would be a failure in any preacher not to offer the Gospel. A supportive Baptist view was published in 1752 by Alvery Jackson. Called *The Question Answered*, it argued that a balanced evangelical theology demanded that preachers offer the Gospel to all who will receive it.

Gill and Brine disagreed and they were ministers with great influence in the middle years of the eighteenth century. They published much and their books were on the shelves of all orthodox Particular Baptist ministers. They often preached at ministerial ordinations and inductions. For almost fifty years this type of teaching, concentrating almost exclusively on the quality of life within the church, robbed many Particular Baptists of evangelical preaching.

> ### TO THINK ABOUT . . .
> Are there other examples from Christian history of concern for the purity of the church robbing Christians of a zeal for mission?

THE EMERGING INFLUENCE OF EVANGELICAL CALVINISM

It was George Whitefield's Calvinistic strand of the Evangelical Revival rather than the Arminian preaching of the Wesleys which influenced Particular Baptist churches. In the north, **John Fawcett**, converted through the preaching of Whitefield, went on to become a significant Baptist minister in the founding of both the Baptist Missionary Society and Northern Baptist Education Society, the precursor of the Rawdon Baptist College. His evangelical influence in the Yorkshire and Lancashire Associations was considerable.

One of Fawcett's members at Wainsgate, Hebden Bridge, was **John Sutcliffe**. In 1772 he entered Bristol Baptist Academy for ministerial training. He settled at Olney, Northamptonshire, in 1775 and for four years was a close friend of the Olney Rector, one-time slave-ship captain, John Newton. Newton's diaries testify to their close relationship and in 1776 Newton provided hospitality at his rectory for the Baptist ministers met in Association.

By 1780 Sutcliffe was in trouble with some among his hyper-Calvinist congregation who felt that he did not properly or sufficiently teach true Calvinism. At an Association gathering in 1783 Sutcliffe affirmed that any person who did not know Christ as Saviour was the neighbour with whom Christians needed to share the Gospel. In 1784 Sutcliffe issued, through the Northamptonshire Baptist Association, a *Call to Prayer* which arose from his reading of the works of Jonathan Edwards, a Congregational minister in Massachusetts, America.

The Call was for concerted prayer for the general revival and spread of religion, centring in regular meetings on the first Monday of every month. The call was set out in these terms:

> The grand object in prayer is to be that the Holy Spirit may be poured down on our ministers and churches, that sinners may be converted, the saints edified, the interest of religion revived, and the name of God glorified. At the same time remember, we trust you will not confine your requests to your own societies; or to your own immediate connection; let the whole interest of the Redeemer be affectionately remembered and the spread of the Gospel to the most distant parts of the habitable globe be the object of your most fervent requests.

Another work that moved Sutcliffe deeply was the journal of David Brainerd, Edwards' son-in-law, who had died of the privations experienced while preaching the Gospel to the American Red Indians. In 1785 William Carey was for a while a member of Sutcliffe's church and from that time both became deeply committed to the missionary task facing the church. Sutcliffe's challenge to pray each month for the revival of religion around the world was taken up across Britain by Baptist churches and was a significant factor in the founding of the Baptist Missionary Society.

TO THINK ABOUT . . .

Is there a case for arguing that activism is such a mark of our age, that as Baptists we have failed to heed the challenge of Sutcliffe's 'Call to Prayer'?

Another Northamptonshire Association minister of this period was **Robert Hall, Snr**, of Arnesby, Leicestershire. In 1779 Hall preached an Association sermon on Isaiah 65:14, which was later published as the book *Help to Zion's Travellers* (1781). It set aside the hyper-Calvinism of the day and urged a new involvement in mission. 'I do not remember to have read any book with such raptures', wrote William Carey to the friend who had given him a copy. Thereafter Carey would walk twenty miles to hear Hall preach. When Carey died in India many years later, among his few possessions was a well-thumbed, worm-eaten, copy of Hall's book, with Carey's own notes made over the years, on almost every page.

TO THINK ABOUT . . .

What may we learn from noting that evangelistic endeavour in this period arose partly out of vigorous theological wrestling and reflection?

Robert Hall's communion table, kept still at Arnesby Baptist Church, and showing the section removed from the back of the table to accommodate Hall's portly figure.   *By permission of Arnesby Baptist Church*

THE BRISTOL ACADEMY AND EVANGELICAL CALVINISM

Evidence of the evangelistic concern among Particular Baptists is found within the churches and ministers of the Western Association. From the days of Edward Terrill, the Broadmead Elder who, by his will of 1679, endowed a programme for the theological education of potential ministers, there had been a concern for an educated and evangelical ministry in the West Country.

Andrew Gifford Jnr.   *By permission of the British Library.*

In Bristol, three generations of the Gifford family, who were based on the Pithay church, played a significant role. Andrew Gifford, Snr, was known as the 'Apostle of the West' because of his evangelistic preaching and church planting ministry. William Bagley, the co-pastor of Andrew's son, Emmanuel Gifford, recalled how at the close of a sermon Emmanuel would offer Christ to sinners in a most affectionate manner. Andrew's grandson, also Andrew, was minister at Eagle Street, in London, and often went to hear George Whitefield preach, claiming that he

would light his 'farthing rushlight' at the evangelist's 'flaming torch'. When Whitefield died it was Gifford who edited a volume of the evangelist's sermons.

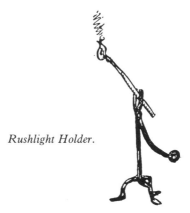

Rushlight Holder.

The Bristol Baptist Fund was founded in 1717 and was used, under the provisions of Terrill's will, to support ministers in training with the Broadmead pastors. The scheme for ministerial training was put on a sound footing by Bernard Foskett, while minister at Broadmead from 1726 to 1758. During those years he trained over

Bernard Foskett.

Hugh Evans.

Caleb Evans.

eighty ministers in equal number from Wales and England. John Rippon said of Foskett: 'some good scholars and several of our greatest ministers were educated by him'.

He was followed as pastor and teacher at Broadmead by Hugh Evans, a Welsh minister whom he had trained some years earlier. Hugh was followed by his son Caleb Evans, who had also trained under Foskett. Caleb recalled hearing his father preach at Broadmead: 'Hearing the awful terrors of the law and the astonishing grace of the Gospel I was brought in very dust before the throne of a Holy God, and enabled to magnify the riches of free grace.' This was Calvinism with an evangelical heart that gripped the soul of a man. Caleb's own personal Confession of Faith began by affirming the right of private judgement in religious matters as the undoubted and inalienable privilege of every rational, intelligent creature. 'I am accountable to God' he claimed, 'I cannot deny the doctrine of election . . . this is the deepest lesson I learn from it . . . with the deepest humility every believer ought to say "by the grace of God I am what I am".'

The Bristol Baptist Academy in this period was the only effective Baptist training institution for ministers, most of whom served the West Country. The libraries of Andrew Gifford, Jnr, together with that of Dr Llewellyn, both evangelical Calvinists, came to Bristol in the 1780s. Some books and support for ministerial training in the American Colonies went via a former Foskett student, Morgan Edwards, who was closely involved in the establishment of Brown University.

> **TO THINK ABOUT . . .**
> **Which contemporary books of theology/biblical study, etc., would you like to see passed on to future generations?**

Caleb Evans had wide interests. He was involved in day schools at Downend and Broadmead. His Association sermon in 1775 attacked the Test and Corporation Acts and appealed for 'constitutional liberty'. In 1778 he attacked John Wesley's defence of Government action over the revolt in the American Colonies, even though he did not personally espouse republicanism. A decade later he was vigorous and ardent in his support of Bristol's Anti-Slavery Group.

ROBERT ROBINSON AND RATIONAL DISSENT

Robert Robinson was another convert of Whitefield. He became the minister of St Andrew's Street Baptist Church in Cambridge. He was a fine example of those Baptists who sought to promote 'rational religion', fostered free enquiry and sought to establish liberal sentiments. The Rational Dissenters were ministers of outstanding ability who stood for reform and toleration, with equal liberty and justice for all.

Robert Robinson.

Robinson had a passionate concern to remove the social and political disabilities which shackled Dissent in his day. In 1778 he published a series of lectures which had been given at the Eastern Baptist Association, under the title *The Principles of Nonconformity*. They were approved by the Marquis of Lansdowne in the House of Lords, attacked by Edmund Burke in the Commons, and defended by Charles James Fox. The result was that the book went through many editions. Robinson's book was admired by Dissenters and reviled by their enemies, since it argued that *people* are the origin of power in Government. Benjamin Flower, Robinson's friend and editor of the *Cambridge Intelligencer*, reviewed the book thus: 'Few ministers of religion have been so well acquainted with foundation principles of good government, or have inculcated such sentiments of civil and religious liberty as Mr Robinson.' A later publication by Robinson, *Political Catechism*, revealed his pre-occupation with political matters. In its preface he hoped for 'the everlasting death of toryism and the joyful resurrection of honest men'.

Robinson was a founder member of the Cambridge Constitutional Society which was concerned with electoral reform. Among fellow-Baptist ministers who shared this concern were Mark Wilks and Joseph Kinghorn, both in pastorate at Norwich. Robinson had deep sympathy with French Revolutionary thought and translated into English the *Paris Revolutionary Magazine*. He was more deeply attached to the cause of the Republicans in the American Colonies and openly campaigned for them in their struggle for independence.

Like all Rational Dissenters, Robinson held firmly to the view that God revealed himself in history and that God's will and purpose for mankind were best understood in this context. His two major historical works, *Ecclesiastical Remains* and *A History of Baptism* were the fruit of years of historical research in which he used the past to illustrate the themes of God's action in the present.

Robinson's book *A Plea for the Divinity of our Lord Jesus Christ* went through four editions in the year of its publication. It was a response to the convictions of Theophilus Lindsey, an Anglican priest, who in 1773 became a Unitarian and opened the first Unitarian chapel in 1774. Lindsey's decision called forth a lot of literary attacks, but Lindsey reckoned that Robinson's book was one of the very few that required an answer.

> **TO THINK ABOUT . . .**
> Is Robinson's brand of Rational Dissent an inevitable, desirable, or undesirable consequence of Baptist convictions about freedom of conscience and toleration?

House at Kettering in which the Baptist Missionary Society was formed.

THE FOUNDING OF THE BAPTIST MISSIONARY SOCIETY

In the seventeenth and eighteenth centuries Protestantism in general showed a lack of concern for the vast non-Christian world. It was engrossed with theological and ecclesiastical affairs, to the exclusion of concern for a world without Christ, except for the slaves of the New World and the North American Indians. Many of the Reformers would have argued that the Apostolic mandate was addressed to the apostolic age and was fulfilled then. The promises in the New Testament concerning the 'Gentiles' belonged to those nations who received and held fast the Gospel and were now part of the Christian community. Islam and other pagan religions were such as had, under one dispensation or another, rejected the light of revealed truth and sinned away their day of grace. Also many believed that the world would shortly perish. Calvin's doctrine of election and predestination, whilst not incompatible with evangelism at home and abroad, did not seem to encourage it.

Particular Baptists in their *Somersets Confession* and the 1660 General Baptist *Standard Confession* both claimed, in the words of the latter:

> Christ hath commanded that the Gospel (to wit, the glad tydings of remission of sins) should be preached to every creature (Mark 16: 15) . . . [and that ministers] ought to exercise their gifts not only in the Church but also (as occasion serves) to preach to the world, they being approved of by the Church to do so.

The Baptist Missionary Society was founded on the prayer-call of John Sutcliffe and the

Northamptonshire Association; the theology of Andrew Fuller expressed in his book *The Gospel Worthy of all Acceptation* (1785); and in the burden on Carey's heart for the unevangelised millions of his day, which found expression in *An Enquiry into the Obligations of Christians to use means for the Conversion of the Heathens* (1792).

Andrew Fuller.

TO THINK ABOUT . . .

Sutcliffe's prayer-call urged the following seven points:

" I. Consider Christ's readiness to hear and answer prayer, especially on these subjects. . . .
II. Consider what the Lord has done in times past, and that in answer to prayer. . . .
III. Let the present religious state of the world be considered to this end. . . .
IV. Consider what God has promised to do for his church in times to come. . . .
V. If we have any regard to the welfare of our countrymen, connection and friends, let this stimulate us in this work. . . .
VI. Consider what is suggested is so very small. . . .
VII. And lastly. It will not be in vain, whatever be the immediate and apparent issue of it. . . . "

What relevance do these points have for today?

The prayer-call was taken up by the Particular Baptist churches, and the expectation of revival was uppermost in the minds of the ordinary church members, as month by month they sought it from God in prayer. The high Calvinism of John Gill, which resulted in arid, dry, 'non-invitation' preaching, was superseded by the neo-Calvinism of Fuller, which clearly laid the responsibility for taking the Gospel to spiritually destitute men and women on Christ's disciples.

ANDREW FULLER'S GOSPEL UNDERSTANDING

The root of the matter was this: Have the unconverted a duty to believe the Gospel? Abraham Taylor's tract, *The Modern Question*, demonstrated that 'the eternal God does by his word make it the duty of poor unconverted sinners, who hear the Gospel preached or published, to believe in Jesus Christ'. The book had a catena of texts demonstrating that John the Baptist, Christ and the Apostles all *did* offer grace and salvation to the unconverted. It was a study of this book which led Andrew Fuller to attempt a modification of the hyper-Calvinism of his day,

and this in its turn provided the theological impetus to world mission among Baptists. Fuller wrote thus of this early reading:

The principal writings with which I was first acquainted were those of Bunyan, Brine and Gill. I had read pretty much Dr. Gill's *Body of Divinity*, and from many parts of it had received considerable instruction. I perceived, however, that the system of Bunyan was not the same as his; for that while he [i.e. Bunyan] maintained the doctrines of election and predestination he nevertheless held with the free offer of salvation to sinners without distinction. These were things which I could not then reconcile, and therefore supposed that Bunyan, though a great and good man, was not so clear in his views of the doctrines of the Gospel as the writers who succeeded him. I found indeed, the same things in all the old writers of the sixteenth and seventeenth centuries that came my way. They all dealt as Bunyan did, in free invitations to sinners to come to Christ and be saved; the consistency of which with personal election I could not understand.

The Gospel Worthy of all Acceptation, or the Duty of Sinners to Believe in Jesus Christ (1785),

AN

ENQUIRY

INTO THE

OBLIGATIONS OF CHRISTIANS,

TO USE MEANS FOR THE

CONVERSION

OF THE

HEATHENS.

IN WHICH THE

RELIGIOUS STATE OF THE DIFFERENT NATIONS
OF THE WORLD, THE SUCCESS OF FORMER
UNDERTAKINGS, AND THE PRACTICABILITY OF
FURTHER UNDERTAKINGS, ARE CONSIDERED,

BY WILLIAM CAREY.

For there is no Difference between the Jew and the Greek;
for the fame Lord over all, is rich unto all that call upon him.
For whofoever fhall call on the name of the Lord fhall be faved.
How then fhall they call on him, in whom they have not
believed? and how fhall they believe in him of whom they
have not heard? and how fhall they hear without a Preacher?
and how fhall they preach except they be fent?

PAUL.

LEICESTER:

Printed and fold by ANN IRELAND, and the other Book-
fellers in *Leicester*; J. JOHNSON, St. Paul's Church yard;
T. KNOTT, Lombard Street; R. DILLY, in the Poultry,
London; and SMITH, at *Sheffield*.

[Price One Shilling and Six-pence.]

MDCCXCII.

The title page of Carey's 'Enquiry'.

presented Fuller's resolving of the issue, which was based entirely on Jonathan Edwards' particular distinction between natural and moral liability. Its publication launched him into a sea of controversy for the rest of his life, but 'Fullerism', as it came to be known, or 'moderate Calvinism', proved to be the significant factor in establishing the principle of world mission among Baptists.

Fuller stated his thesis in the first part of his book. His proposition was that it is the duty of all who hear the Gospel to believe in Christ with such a faith as issues in salvation. What is this saving faith? It is a real belief of God's report or record concerning his Son (Mark 6:15–16; John 20:31), which includes personal trust in Christ's promises.

The second part comprised arguments to prove that faith in Christ is the duty of all who hear the Gospel. Unconverted sinners are commanded, exhorted and invited to believe in Christ for salvation. The Gospel requires obedience and such obedience includes saving faith. Scripture ascribes the want of faith in Christ to men's depravity, and God has threatened and inflicted the most awful punishments on sinners for their not believing on the Lord Jesus Christ.

The next section answered specific queries relating to election, particular redemption, and human inability to do what God commands. Concerning the duty of preachers, Fuller said:

'I believe it is the duty of every minister of Christ plainly and faithfully to preach the Gospel to all who will hear it . . . I therefore believe free and solemn addresses, invitations, calls and warnings to be not only consistent, but directly adapted, as means, in the hand of the Spirit of God to bring them to Christ. I consider it as part of my duty which I could not omit without being guilty of the blood of souls.'

WILLIAM CAREY'S 'ENQUIRY'

William Carey also believed that it was the duty of sinners to believe in Jesus. Therefore, he claimed, it meant that all mankind must be presented with the Gospel. Carey's *Enquiry*, begun while he was minister at Moulton, Northampton, was published in 1792 at

The scene of Carey's baptism in the River Nene. Behind are the walls of Northampton Castle. The scene today is quite different.

Leicester. He wrote in the Introduction:

As our blessed Lord has required us to pray that his kingdom may come, and his will be done on earth as it is in heaven, it becomes us not only to express our desire of that event by words, but to use every lawful method to spread the knowledge of his name.

Carey recognised that individual efforts were being made:

but they are inconsiderable in comparison of what might be done if the whole body of Christians entered heartily into the spirit of the divine command on this subject. Some think little about it, others are unacquainted with the state of the world, and others love their wealth better than the souls of their fellow-creatures.

The first section of the *Enquiry* argued that Christ's commission to his disciples was still binding on the Church, a position now so generally accepted that it is difficult to appreciate how revolutionary a view it appeared in 1792.

It seems as if many thought the commission was sufficiently put in execution by what the apostles and others have done; that we have to attend to the salvation of our own countrymen; and that if God intends the salvation of the heathen, he will some way or other bring them to the gospel or the gospel to them.

Carey's cottage at Moulton. The internal picture looks through the door to the back kitchen where he did his work.

TO THINK ABOUT . . .

Was it helpful for them that the missionary mandate came as a fresh insight? What fresh insights have come to the church today and issued in vigorous action?

The next section presented a wide-ranging view of missionary endeavours from the New Testament period to his own day. It contained a survey of the countries of the world, with their religious allegiance shown as either Christian, Jewish, Islamic or pagan. He estimated the world population at 731 millions, of whom about 420 millions were pagan. The challenge is obvious 'to Christians, and especially to ministers, to exert themselves to the utmost.'

A number of impediments prevented more being done for 'the conversion of the heathen'. Carey listed these as:

> their distance from us, their barbarous and savage manner of living, the danger of being killed by them, the difficulty of procuring the necessities of life, or the unintelligibleness of their languages.

Carey was impressed by the efforts of traders and comments:

> It is no objection to commercial men. It only required that we should have as much love to the souls of our fellow-creatures and fellow-sinners, as they have for the profits arising from a few otter-skins, and all these difficulties would be easily surmounted.

Carey then suggested a way forward: 'The first, and most important of these duties which are incumbent upon us, is fervent and united prayer.' He mentioned the Association prayer-call of Sutcliffe, and recognised that 'our monthly prayer meetings for the success of the Gospel have not been in vain'. However, 'we must not be contented . . . with praying, without exerting ourselves in the use of the means for obtaining those things we pray for.'

He put forward a 'society' idea, with a competent committee to administer its affairs.

> I do not mean to confine it to one denomination of

Christians, I wish with all my heart that every one who loves our Lord Jesus Christ with sincerity, would in some way or other engage in it. But in the present divided state of Christendom, it would be more likely for good to be done by each denomination engaging separately in the work, than if they were to embark in it conjointly.

> ### TO THINK ABOUT . . .
> In the light of this statement, how do you think Carey would regard the many para-church missionary agencies currently at work?
>
> Does Carey's conviction need to be modified, bearing in mind that ecumenical co-operation together with partnership with national churches are believed by many to be the right ways forward in missionary strategy?

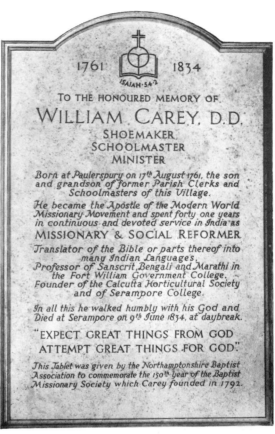

Memorial Tablet to William Carey in Paulerspury Parish Church.

William Carey.

'Surely', Carey concluded, 'it is worth while to lay ourselves out with all our might, in promoting the cause and kingdom of Christ.'

Within thirty years the theology of Fuller, linked with the 'society' method of Carey, transformed the face of Baptist church life in England. Responses to social and organisational factors undoubtedly contributed to the transformation, but as Dr Champion has suggested, there was at this time a 'renewed theology' which led to a 'rediscovery of mission and the creation of organisations for the fulfilment of mission'.

The willingness of Carey to translate his vision into reality by sailing with Dr John Thomas in 1793 assured the successful launching of the Baptist Missionary Society. The whole venture centred in a Biblical and theological understanding of the church's task. Only one thing needed attention – the financing of the object in view.

TO THINK ABOUT . . .

Why would you argue that the title of Carey's book: 'An Enquiry into the Obligations of Christians to use means for the Conversion of the Heathens' is or is not relevant today as a summary of the missionary mandate?

FINANCING THE MISSIONARY SOCIETY

The *Periodical Accounts* of the Society made the position quite clear.

> As such an undertaking must needs be attended with expense, we agree immediately to open a subscription list for the above purpose, and to recommend it to others. Every person who shall subscribe ten pounds at once, or ten shillings and sixpence annually, shall be considered a member of the society.

The reason for this method was that it was impossible to raise support from the whole Church of Christ, or even from the churches of the Baptist denomination, so finance had to be raised on the voluntary principle. It was a matter of expediency. The second resolution passed at the foundation meeting of the Society in October 1792 reads:

> As in the present divided state of Christendom it seems likely that each denomination, by exerting itself separately, is most likely to accomplish the great end of a mission, it is agreed that this society be called, The Particular Baptist Society for Propagating the Gospel among the Heathen.

It was now for the individual churches, and their members, to decide whether they would support the mission or not. Many supported the work generously, and it succeeded. But the fund raising was on the 'voluntary' principle, which was then widely used by most philanthropic organisations. The 'voluntary' principle was not a vital theological, nor even an historical Baptist, principle. It was simply the most convenient expedient for the financial support of the venture.

TO THINK ABOUT . . .

What theological principles do you think have a bearing on the matter of support for ministry in this country and overseas? Should expediency have a place in determining methods of raising financial support?

The Society's current logo points clearly to the authority for and theme of its continuing mission to the world.

UNIT 7

Baptism and the Lord's Supper: Ordinance or Sacrament?

BAPTISM

BAPTISM AND CHRISTIAN INITIATION

There were many lively debates about baptism in seventeenth-century England. It produced its own literature from the public disputations held, and one of the most important of these took place in 1642 at Southwark, London, between William Kiffin, the Particular Baptist leader, and an Anglican priest, Daniel Featley. Featley published *The Dipper Dipt* (1642) in which he argued the validity of infant baptism by equating baptism and circumcision. On the basis of 1 Corinthians 7:14 and Acts 2:39 Featley claimed that children are comprehended in Christ's covenant and therefore fit subjects for baptism. Featley's book called forth several other pamphlets which opted for one side of the argument or the other.

The main replies were given through the *Confessions of Faith* where emphasis was put first on the mode of baptism. The 1644 *Confession* stated:

> The way and manner of dispensing this ordinance the Scripture holds out to be dipping or plunging the whole body under water. It states that the meaning of baptism is: First the washing of the whole soule in the blood of Christ: Secondly, that interest the Saints have in the death, burial, and resurrection: Thirdly, together with a confirmation of our faith, that as certainly as the body is buried under the water, and risen again, so certainly shall the bodies of the Saints be raised by the power of Christ, in the day of resurrection, to reigne with Christ.

The General Baptist *Orthodox Creed* (1678) and the Particular Baptist *Second London Confession* (1677) both speak of baptism as an ordinance of Christ which is in force until he comes again. They agree it is a sign of the believer's identity with his Lord in life, death and resurrection, which signifies a known remission of sins and new life in Christ. Baptism is always in the name of the Trinity, and the mode required is the immersion of the person in water. Both understand baptism as the seal of the covenant between a believer and God. Particular Baptists describe baptism as an 'ordinance' but General Baptists prefer to speak of 'this holy sacrament'.

The relationship between baptism and the Lord's Supper was spelt out in an appendix to the 1644 *Confession* published in 1646. It stated:

> Though a believer's right to use the Lord's Supper do immediately flow from Jesus Christ, apprehended and received by faith, yet inasmuch as all things ought to be done not only decently but also in order . . . accordingly the Apostles first baptized disciples and then admitted them to the use of the Lord's Supper . . . We therefore do not admit any to the use of the Supper, nor communicate with any in the use of this ordinance, but disciples baptised, lest we should have fellowship with them in their doing contrary to order.

An untypical Baptist, John Bunyan, vigorously opposed such a view. He repudiated the view that baptism was the 'initiating and entering ordinance' of the church. People were admitted because of faith in Christ and a subsequent holy life. Bunyan affirmed that Christ, not baptism, was the door of the sheepfold. Baptism was therefore not a pre-requisite for communion in the Gospel of which the Lord's Supper was a sign. Baptism's role was to strengthen faith.

MEMBERSHIP: THE PROCESS AND THE REASONING

The process of admission to membership, baptism and attendance at the Lord's Supper became, by the eighteenth century, a process in which one part soon followed upon the other. Robert Robinson, minister of the Cambridge Baptist Church in this period, described the three parts of this one process in the pages of the church book.

In 1761 he recorded on December 10:

This day Robert Silk, Miss Gifford and others were admitted members. The manner of the admission follows. R. Silk, having given notice of his design to the pastor, who had conversed with them in private, attended. The pastor stood at the head of the [communion] table; the deacons next him on each side, and the members in the table and adjoining pews: sitting. The pastor began by a short discourse on the nature of Christ's kingdom, qualifications of his subjects, etc, and closed by proposing R. Silk to them for a fellow-citizen. Then he spent a few minutes in prayer. Silk, who stood at the bottom of the table-seat . . . was asked to speak as in the presence of God the truth only. He was told that faith and repentance were the two prerequisites to church-fellowship. The first he was desired to speak: the last, he was told, would be inquired in his life. The man then gave an account of his former profane life, and of his late change, declaring his faith in the Gospel of Christ. When he was ended he was desired to withdraw.

In Silk's absence the pastor recapitulated what had been said by R. Silk, and observed, that though a profession of faith in Christ was necessary to church fellowship: though the practice was clearly apostolical: though the custom of this church, and others of the same discipline, was preferable to the customs of those churches, which either on the one hand required nothing but a decent conduct, and sometimes not that; or on the other, imposed creeds on their members to subscribe; not suffering people to express their own ideas in their own language: though this church, like the churches of the first 300 years after Christ, required those that were to be baptized to renounce the devil and all his works, and to declare their faith in Christian truths; yet after all, he said, we ought not to forget that this, with every other institution, is subject to gross abuses and fallacies. He said, that all men showed themselves to others by their bright sides; that the temptation to do it in this case was strong; that all a man said about his own experience was in reality no more than the man's opinion of himself; that if men were subject to partiality, it was when they judged their own cause: that all the man had said might be true, for it was not impossible: it might also be false, for some men are capable of anything. He said there were two things extremely important. One was whether his moral conduct was upright, for that proved the goodness of faith, and such a member would be an honour to any society in the world; the other was whether his temper was captious and litigious: free from that he would be a son of peace in the church. He added, the man is withdrawn to give room for free debate. The members all approved what he had said; and his neighbours spoke well of his life. He was then recalled. The pastor inquired what he thought of baptism. He desired it by immersion. The Covenant was read, and he was asked whether he would make that his rule of conduct to us. He agreed. He was then told that the pastor would inquire his character, and if that were good, would fix a day to baptize him. The pastor prayed and dismissed the assembly. This was last church meeting. In the interim, his character had been inquired, he had been baptized, and was now presented to the church again. The pastor asked whether the church was willing to receive him. They voted by holding up their hands. The pastor then took him by the hand and said, 'I give you the right hand of fellowship; a token of full communion with this church of Christ.

> *TO THINK ABOUT . . .*
> **In receiving members, what aspects of the practice at Cambridge is echoed in the practice of your church? Are there any valid aspects of the Cambridge practice you feel are missing today?**

BAPTISMS AT WHITTLESFORD

A few years later, in 1767, there was an unusual day of baptisms at Whittlesford, near Cambridge. Robinson recorded the meeting of the Cambridge and Saffron Walden Baptist churches for a joint open-air baptismal service in the local mill pond.

> This day the two churches of Walden and Cambridge met by mutual consent at Whittlesford to administer the ordinance of baptism in public (as now) in the presence of many hundred spectators; so John the Baptist administered it; sometimes in private; so S. Paul administered it to the jailor, though never in the night, because we are not only not persecuted, but we are protected by law. Circumstances must determine when a private, or when a public baptism is proper. Previous to this, twenty-five had professed their faith and repentance to the church at Walden; and twenty-one had done the same at Cambridge; and all had desired baptism by immersion. Dr Gifford at ten o'clock, mounted a moveable pulpit near the river in Mr Hollick's yard, and, after singing and prayer, preached a suitable sermon on the occasion from Psalm cxix.57. After sermon, then men retired to one room, the women to two others, and the baptizer, Mr Gwennap, to another to prepare for the administration. After about half an hour, Mr Gwennap, dressed as usual (except a coat, which was supplied by a black gown made like a batchelor's) came down to the waterside. He was followed by the men, two and two, dressed as usual, only, instead of a coat, each had on a long white blaize gown, tied round the waist with a piece of worstead-binding, and leaded at the bottom that they might sink; they had on their heads white linen caps. The women followed, two and two, dressed as usual, only all had white gowns, holland or dimitty. Their upper-coats were tacked to their stockings, and their gown leaded, lest their clothes should float. Mr Gwennap sang an hymn at the waterside, spoke about ten minutes on the subject, and then taking the oldest man of the company by the hand, led him to a convenient depth in the river. Then pronouncing the words, I baptize thee in the name of the Father, of the Son, and of the Holy Ghost, he immersed the person once in the river. Robinson stood in a boat, and, with other assistants, led the rest in, and, having wiped their faces after their baptism, led them out. Mr Gwennap added a few words more after the administration at the water-side, and concluded with the usual blessing.

In the eighteenth century the baptismal discussion was calmly controversial and its content primarily academic. William Wall, not a Baptist, published *A History of Infant Baptism* in 1705, which all parties to the discussion agreed was basically correct in its historic statements. A leading Baptist minister, John Gale, published a refutation of Wall's main arguments for infant baptism in his book *Reflections* (1711). Gale's argument was that historically there was no evidence of infant baptism prior to 250 AD. He dealt with the mode of baptism, then the qualifications of those to be baptised, refuting

Baptisms at Whittlesford.

TO THINK ABOUT . . .

The picture records a baptism in 1965 at an old open baptistry at Old Southwick, Wilts.

Would it be feasible and fruitful for Baptists to revert more often to public open-air baptisms? Have we become too comfortable and sheltered in our practice?

any link between Jewish and Christian baptism. Wall and Gale were both re-published as the nineteenth century opened and secured far greater interest than when originally published.

It is almost impossible to exaggerate the impact of the Anglo-Catholic Tractarian Movement in Nonconformist churches. The word 'sacrament' now became totally unacceptable in Baptist circles. The Tractarian leader, John Keble, in his *Village Sermons* of 1850, spoke of infant baptism as a 'coronation in which the meanest child is made a priest and king to God the Father . . . Once a child is baptised he is a Christian forever unless by his own sin he cast away the grace granted him.' (Quoted in Himbury, D.M. *British Baptists – A Short History*.)

Baptists, in this period, tended to give a higher priority to what the individual believer did than to God's action in baptism. Baptists regarded this ordinance as primarily a testimony to personal faith in Christ and a disciplined following of the example of Jesus.

TO THINK ABOUT . . .

How can we ensure our doctrine of baptism stresses the Biblical emphasis on the gracious action of God as well as the testimony of the baptised?

C.H. Spurgeon, in a sermon published in the *Metropolitan Tabernacle Pulpit* of 1864, based on Matthew 16:15–16, expressed his deep conviction that baptism without saving faith availed nothing. He contrasted the baptismal teaching of Jesus with the doctrine of baptismal regeneration taught in the *Book of Common Prayer* and the *Thirty-nine Articles* of the Church of England. The sermon went through many editions and over 150 tracts came from other people who responded to Spurgeon's attack.

THE LORD'S SUPPER

EARLY BAPTISTS ON THE LORD'S SUPPER

Smyth held that 'only baptised persons must partake'. He went on to argue that the outward act itself:

> does not confer and convey grace and regeneration to the participants or communicants; but as the Word is preached, they serve only to support and stir up the repentance and faith of the communicants till Christ come . . . The preaching of the Word and the ministry of the sacraments, represented the ministry of Christ in the spirit; who teaches, baptises, and feeds the regenerate, by the Holy Spirit inwardly and visibly.' (Lumpkin, *op.cit.*, *p*137–138.)

The General Baptist 1651 *Confession*, quoting the 1 Corinthians 11:23–26 passage, stated:

> 'Jesus Christ took Bread, and juice of the Vine and brake, and gave to His Disciples, to eat and drink with thanksgiving; which practise is left upon record as a memorial of his suffering, to continue in the Church until he come again.' (*ibid*, *p*183.)

The General Baptist 1678 *Orthodox Creed* has a statement about the purpose of the Lord's Supper in Article 33. It is 'for perpetual remembrance, and showing forth of the sacrifice of himself in his death' which will confirm the faithful in Christ's atoning work, assure them of their place 'in the covenant of grace' and testify to their 'communion and union' with Christ and each other. (*ibid*, *p*321.)

The bread and wine of the Supper 'signify to the faithful, the body and blood of Christ, or holdeth forth Christ and him crucified.' The elements are received in both kinds from the minister, but no unbaptised or unbelieving person may communicate. The Roman Catholic view of transubstantiation and the Lutheran concept of consubstantiation were both specifically repudiated. Frequent communion was

recommended, with an insistence on personal examination by participants.

A typical administration of the Lord's Supper among General Baptists was recounted by Thomas Grantham, a leading minister and Messenger. It began with preaching and prayer as on other occasions and allowed time for the 'decent' preparation of the elements and the Table. There followed an exhortation to 'due humility and reverence' and the Scriptural authority for the Supper. The minister spoke of the 'mystical signification of the Cross', and stated the spiritual qualifications necessary for all who were to participate.

The bread and wine were blessed and distributed separately with the appropriate words of institution. The meal concluded with an exhortation to gratitude, a prayer of thanksgiving, and a fellowship offering. The offering was for the purchase of bread, wine and plate as necessary, and to express love in relieving 'the necessities of the saints'.

The final act was a 'hymn of praise'. In General Baptist parlance this was *not* a congregational hymn. It was a 'solo outburst of praise to God by the elder conducting the Supper'. Most General Baptists followed the Lord's Supper with an 'agape', which they claimed was according to the Scriptural pattern. It recognised the distances from which people often came. It was 'necessary that the congregation should be refreshed before it be dismissed'. The agape meal was defunct by the early eighteenth century, though the phrase 'Leg of Mutton Baptists' lingered on!

The Particular Baptists followed the Westminster Confession much more closely than the General Baptists. The 1644 *Confession* contained no reference to the Supper but the 1677 *Confession* remedied this deficiency.

The Supper was a 'perpetual remembrance' which confirmed the faith of all believers in its benefits and was a 'bond and pledge of their communion with him and each other'. The meal was not a 'real sacrifice . . . but only a memorial of that one offering up of himself, by himself, upon the cross, once for all'.

Both elements were given to all participants, and neither were to be 'reserved' for later use. Though in worship the elements are rightly called the 'body and blood of Christ', they remained 'only Bread and Wine as they were before'.

'Worthy receivers' of the ordinance had inward faith and 'spiritually receive and feed upon Christ crucified and all the benefits of his death'. Ignorant and ungodly people were not fit to receive communion and should they do so, 'eat and drink judgment to themselves'. (Lumpkin, *op. cit.*, *p291–293*.)

THE LORD'S SUPPER AT CAMBRIDGE

Robert Robinson at Cambridge recorded their usual procedure in the church book:

As soon as the afternoon public service was concluded, such as chose to go home went. Such as chose to be spectators, went up into the galleries. The outer gate was fastened for the avoiding interruption; always hurtful in public worship, particularly so in the Lord's-supper-time. Mary Morris, the servant of the church, covered the table with a clean linen cloth, and sat thereon bread in a basket, the crust being taken off; two borrowed silver cups: and three pints of red port

wine. The pastor took his seat at the upper end of the table. The deacons next him, two on each hand. The elder-men members at the table. The younger in the pews on the pastor's right hand. The women in pews on his left. The pastor began with a short discourse on the occasion, nature, benefits, etc, of the ordinance.

Then he read 1 Cor.xi.23, till he came to the words, 'took bread', then, taking the bread in his hand, he read, 'and when he had given thanks' and said, 'Let us do likewise', on which, the congregation rising, he gave thanks. This ended, and the church sitting down again, he added, 'When he had given thanks, he brake it;' and broke the bread. During which he spoke of the sufferings of Christ, etc. Then, delivering the plates of bread to the deacons, he said, 'Take eat: this is my body which is broken for you: do this in remembrance of me.' The deacons then carried the bread round to the members; during which the pastor and all the church sat silent. The deacons at their return took bread and ate; the pastor last of all because the servant of all. After he had eaten the bread he rose again and added, taking the cups into his hands, 'After the same manner also, the cup.' The congregation rising again he gave thanks again. Then he poured the wine from the bottles into the cups, discoursing as while he broke the bread. The deacons rising at the close, he gave them the cups, saying 'This cup' and so on to the end of the 26th verse. After the deacons returned, and were seated, they drank, and last the pastor; all sitting silent from the delivery of the cup to the deacon. The pastor rising subjoined, Our Saviour and the disciples 'sang an hymn and went out', let us do likewise. An hymn of praise was then sung, after which a collection for the poor was made; the blessing added; and the assembly dismissed. The whole time was about three-quarters of an hour.

> ## *TO THINK ABOUT . . .*
> **Little seems to have changed over the years in the basic form and practice of celebrating the Lord's Supper in Baptist churches. How important is continuity in tradition? How do you distinguish between living tradition, which is worth perpetuating, and dead tradition which is not?**

Pencil drawing of John Bunyan by Robert White.
From the Cracherode Collection in the British Museum and
reproduced by permission of the British Library.

JOHN BUNYAN AND TERMS OF COMMUNION

John Bunyan, not a typical Baptist, since his church practised open membership and open communion, acknowledged only two sacraments. Bunyan said both:

are of excellent use to the church in this world; they being representations of the death and resurrection of Christ, and are, as God shall make them, helps to our faith therein. But I count them not the fundamentals of our Christianity, nor grounds or rule to communion with saints; servants they are, and our mystical ministers, to teach and instruct us in the most weighty matters of the Kingdom of God; I therefore here declare my reverent esteem of them; yet dare not remove them, as some do, from the place and end where by God they are set and appointed; not ascribe unto them more than they were ordered to have in their first primitive institution. It is possible to commit idolatry even with God's own appointments. (Offor, *Works of Bunyan*, II, p604.)

TO THINK ABOUT . . .
To what extent do you agree with Bunyan's position? In what other matters is it possible for Baptists to 'commit idolatry even with God's own appointments'?

Bunyan's view found acceptance with Henry Jessey and some other Baptist congregations, but William Kiffin opposed it on behalf of Particular Baptists.

Bunyan's *Difference in judgment about water baptism no bar to communion* (1673), raised an important issue. May those who are not baptised as believers share communion with those who are baptised believers? 'The Church of Christ,' wrote Bunyan, 'hath no warrant to keep out of communion the Christian that is discovered to be a visible saint of the word, the Christian that walketh according to his own light with God.'

The matter of admission to, or exclusion from, the Lord's Supper was closely related to the issue of membership in a Baptist Church. General Baptists were largely strict communionists, holding fellowship at the Lord's Table only with those who were fellow Baptists. The Particular Baptists had a majority of their churches practising closed membership and closed communion. 'Terms of communion' dominated the eighteenth and nineteenth-century discussion among Baptists.

TO THINK ABOUT . . .
What 'terms of communion' do you believe ought to operate in a local church.

ABRAHAM BOOTH AND ROBERT ROBINSON

In the eighteenth century Abraham Booth and Robert Robinson argued the issue in two books. Robinson's book *The General Doctrine of Toleration applied to the Particular Case of Free Communion* (1791) dealt with the issue of whether only those baptised by immersion should be admitted to communion, or whether all Christian believers were to be welcomed. He argued against 'sacramental tests and in favour of "mixed" or "free" communion. He was all for the widest possible fellowship around the Lord's Table, viewing any attempt to impose restrictions as contrary to that spirit of freedom in which he so fervently believed.' (G.W. Hughes, *With Freedom Fired*, *p*52.) At the close of the book Robinson imagined a strict communion church where a revered member rises to propose the admission of ten members on profession of faith. They are known to favour infant baptism, but their known Christian faith makes them fit to be members of the church. The door opens, and in come John Calvin, William Tyndale, John Owen, Matthew Henry, Isaac Watts, and five ladies known for their Christian good works.

'Robinson then addresses the pastor of the church and asks what he will do. Will he not rise and "collect the votes of justice, gratitude and love", opening the doors of the church to those who are righteous and keep the truth?' (Hughes, *op. cit.*, *p*53.) Robinson went on to claim that Peter and Christ himself would welcome them as inheritors of the Kingdom of God.

Robert Hall the Younger.

Abraham Booth replied for the closed communion, closed membership position. Robert Hall summarised his arguments as follows:

(1) The priority of Christian Baptism to the Lord's Supper;
(2) the implicit priority of baptism to the Supper in the Apostolic Commission;
(3) the apostolic practice of baptising prior to allowing believers to partake of the Supper; and
(4) the united practice of all Christian Churches.'
(See, B.R. White, 'Open and Closed Membership', *Baptist Quarterly*, Vol. 24, *p*330–334.)

HALL AND KINGHORN IN THE NINETEENTH CENTURY

A generation later Robert Hall, who published *On Terms of Communion*, 1815, felt the necessity of replying to Booth's points before presenting his own arguments in favour of open communion.

He pointed out:

- that baptism 'as a Christian institution had no existence during the personal ministry of our Saviour';
- that it is unjustified to deduce an invariable rule from an implicit priority;
- that circumstances alter cases and the two ordinances 'do not so depend one upon the other that conscientious use of the first forfeits the privilege, or cancels the duty, of observing the second'; and
- this plea assumes the impossibility of the 'universal prevalence of error' and ill becomes 'the members of a sect, who upon a subject of much greater moment have presumed to relinquish the precedent and arraign the practice of the whole Christian world.' (White, *ibid.*, 333.)

Positively Hall stressed the obligation of Christian love and the toleration of disagreement on secondary matters, since paedo-baptists are part of Christ's Body.

No man or set of men, are entitled to prescribe as an indispensable condition of communion what the New Testament has not enjoined as a condition of salvation.

Those who allowed only baptised believers to sit at the Lord's Table were making a shibboleth of baptism, demanding more of Christians than Christ himself; 'investing every little Baptist teacher with the prerogative of repelling from his communion a Home, a Leighton, or a Brainerd, who the Lord of glory will welcome to his presence.

TO THINK ABOUT . . .
What is your own reaction to Baptist churches today which have an 'open table' yet a 'closed membership'?

Joseph Kinghorn.

Joseph Kinghorn, of St Mary's Church, Norwich, replied to Hall in *Baptism: a term of communion at the Lord's Supper* in which he defended the strict communion position. His conviction that infant baptism was no baptism meant that 'it was not according to the law of Christ that persons not baptised should come to the Lord's Table'. Those who favoured mixed communion yet declined to admit non-baptised persons into church membership virtually admitted that the strict communionists were right.

Andrew Fuller's modified Calvinism of the period became a primary factor in Baptist development in Britain. When 'Fullerism' was linked with Hall's plea for open communion and closed membership, some churches feared the demise of the doctrines of God's sovereign grace. William Gadsby and his followers in Lancashire and Yorkshire, with others in East Anglia, responded by the formation of Strict and Particular Baptist Associations. These were Calvinist in doctrine, practised closed membership and communion, and continue outside the structures of the Baptist Union to the present day.

THE NORWICH TEST CASE

Was it possible for churches to change their position without becoming embroiled in disputes about the original Trusts of the churches? There was a test case in the mid-nineteenth century. Some members of St Mary's, Norwich, wished the church to change from a 'closed' to an 'open' position. In 1833 William Brock became minister in succession to Kinghorn who, as already noted, was a closed communionist. Brock told the members he was an open communionist, and they informed him that he was welcome as pastor as long as he did not preach against strict communion. The church had many paedo-baptists in the congregation and some members were distressed that fellow-believers could not join them at the Lord's Table. In 1838 Brock was absolved from his pledge and administered communion to paedo-baptists, at first in his own home. But then in 1845 he instituted two monthly communion services, one for the strict communionists and the other for the paedo-baptists. This step proved divisive. He left Norwich in 1848 on medical advice and moved to Blooms-bury Chapel in London, whose congregation later sent financial help towards the costs of the Norwich chapel case as the matter developed.

The next pastor at Norwich, George Gould, was also an avowed open communionist. In 1857 the church decided to open its communion service to all believers and have a special service for those who conscientiously objected to the presence of the unbaptised at communion. The strict communionists, a vocal rather than a powerful minority, withdrew and formed a separate congregation. Through one of the Trustees the group issued a writ claiming the property as their own. The matter went before the Master of the Rolls who ruled that on the basis of historical precedent, 'Particular Baptists had had in each case, "from the earliest time" liberty to regulate their practice, "either to the Strict communion or to the Free or Mixed Communion, as it might seem best to Congregation".' (B.R. White, *ibid*, *p*333.) The Master of the Rolls concluded: 'I am of the opinion therefore, that this congregation is at full liberty to alter its practice in respect of Communion, if such should be the opinion of the majority of its members.'

> **TO THINK ABOUT . . .**
> Are Trust Deeds mill-stones round the necks of churches, impeding change and the work of the Spirit, or are they proper and necessary guarantees of good order and responsible stewardship?

C.H. Spurgeon, who was responsible for the planting of over a hundred congregations, formed churches which were closed in membership but open in respect of communion.

Dr Michael Walker, in a recent study on Baptist attitudes to the Lord's Supper, claimed that at the outset of the nineteenth century the Baptist approach was influenced by the Puritan Calvinist tradition from which the churches had sprung. This, he argued, was evidenced in the communion hymns of eighteenth-century Baptists. Faced with the Anglo-Catholic emphasis on sacramental grace, most Baptists adopted a Zwinglian view of the sacrament, regarding it as simply a memorial event.

In addition there were a further series of Baptist controversies surrounding the Lord's Supper. Robert Hall maintained a Calvinistic view of the Supper. There was a growing indifference among Baptists as to who should preside at the Lord's Table. As the century closed the temperance movement's campaign to replace fermented with unfermented wine at communion made for further controversy surrounding the Lord's Supper, with the result that attendance at it became even more irregular. This in turn made it an increasingly ineffective instrument of church discipline in Baptist churches.

As Baptists moved into the twentieth century, those who shared the anti-sacerdotalist views of Clifford were in the ascendancy when it came to the observance of baptism and the Lord's Supper. It would not be until the 1960s that the Calvinist tradition would begin again to challenge the Victorian Baptist understanding of baptism and the Lord's Supper.

Baptists and the Transformation of the World

SIGNS OF RENEWAL

The census of 1851 – the only official census of religion ever taken in Britain – revealed the considerable growth of Baptist churches. The census reported about 366,000 Baptists. The Particular Baptists had 1491 chapels in England and 456 in Wales. The New Connexion of General Baptists had 179 chapels in England and 3 in Wales. The Old General Baptists (mostly Unitarian) had 93 chapels.

What was it that had so transformed the situation? In part it was the difference in ethos between the dullness of Brine and Gill and the vigour of Fuller and the younger Robert Hall. Hall's description of Gill's eighteenth-century classic *Body of Divinity* as a 'continent of mud' typifies the changed mood. The theological shift was of Copernican proportions but there was much more than that involved. There was a renewed Association life across the country, itinerant preaching, Sunday Schools, overseas mission, and an expanding programme of ministerial education. Many 'Fullerites' believed themselves to be living in a new era for the denomination in which there was a conscious return to its roots in evangelical Calvinism.

There was an increasing range of literature which presented the new spirit of the times. The theme of missionary advance and endeavour, at home and overseas, was presented each year in the pages of John Rippon's *Baptist Annual Register*, published from 1790 to 1802, together with historical themes which reminded the Baptist family of its glorious past. The *Periodical Accounts* of the Baptist Missionary Society and its successor, the popular *Missionary Herald*, were telling the story of missionary advance across the world.

There was a new engagement with the problems which faced communities around the

John Rippon.

world as well as at home. Carey appalled by the custom of widow burning in India; Grigg and Rodway unable to accept the conditions for black people in Sierra Leone; Knibb prepared to walk barefoot through the land rather than withhold the story of the Jamaican Baptist slaves; all contributed to a growing concern in

The chains and whip illustrated in the panel were brought home by William Knibb and used to hang on the wall outside the General Secretary's office in the Baptist Union's London headquarters. The statement below is the text of the inscription beneath the panel.

THESE CHAINS WITH THE WHIPS WERE RECOVERED FROM BENEATH THE FOUNDATION STONES OF THE ALMS ROOMS IN CONNECTION WITH THIS CHURCH. THEY WERE PLACED THERE BY WILLIAM KNIBB THE EMANCIPATOR, ON THE ERECTION OF THE BUILDINGS, AS A MONUMENT OF GRATITUDE TO GOD FOR THE LIBERATION OF THE SLAVES IN BRITISH COLONIES UNDER THE MINISTRY OF REV JOSEPH IVIMEY.

THE CHAINS HAD BEEN STRUCK FROM THE LIMBS OF SLAVES ON EMANCIPATION DAY, 1835. "WHERE THE SPIRIT OF CHRIST IS THERE IS LIBERTY."

Baptists were among those instrumental in bringing an end to the slave trade. This fact was honoured and illustrated in a terracotta panel above the fireplace in the Shakespeare Room of the BU headquarters in London. The panel shows the liberation of slaves in Jamaica and includes a representation of William Knibb.

the Baptist consciousness for liberty, physical and spiritual, personal and political, at home and abroad.

The church was on the move. There was talk of the spread of 'Catholic Christianity', a phrase which had nothing to do with Roman Catholicism and everything to do with evangelical Christians from all denominations, whether Churchmen or Dissenters, Arminians or Calvinists, who gladly shared in proclaiming the Gospel and rejoiced at 'the funeral of bigotry' by which Christians had been kept apart.

There was a growth in the work of ministerial and lay itinerant evangelists who took up the challenge of preaching the Gospel in rural areas in a variety of ways. This development within the churches of the older Dissent was of special significance and has been carefully researched by D.W. Lovegrove, in *Established Church, Sectarian People: Itinerancy and the Transformation of English Dissent, 1780–1830*. (CUP, 1988.)

> ### TO THINK ABOUT . . .
> What factors within society or the Church contribute in certain periods of history to 'the funeral of bigotry'? Are those factors at work in our own age?

> ### TO THINK ABOUT . . .
> If it is true that at present there is renewed life and vigour among Baptists, what do you think future historians might identify as the marks of that renewal? Are there any parallels with the nineteenth-century signs of renewal?

ITINERANCY AND BAPTIST GROWTH

GROWTH IN RURAL COMMUNITIES

In the nineteenth century the Baptist community in Britain grew in size and significance, and this was especially true of the rural areas in the first part of the century.

It was dynamic village preaching by both ministers and lay people which was responsible for this remarkable growth. The breakthrough among Particular Baptists into a moderate Calvinism was important, and the influence of itinerancy among Methodists showed a way forward, but perhaps the greatest force was the breakthrough created by the formation of the Baptist Missionary Society.

Soon after the founding of the Baptist Missionary Society, at a general meeting in Birmingham in 1795, the challenge of 'the heathen at home' was countered by setting aside funds for the cause of home mission. There were two preaching tours organised in Cornwall in 1796 and 1797. These were led by William Steadman of Broughton, Hampshire, helped by a Bristol Academy student, Francis Franklin, who was eventually to become the pastor at Coventry.

William Steadman.

Help was also given by the fund to various ministers for expenses incurred in local village preaching. For several years Thomas Wastfield, a schoolmaster from Imber, Wiltshire, was enabled to itinerate in the Vale of Pewsey and the upper Avon Valley. By 1810 every English county had a dissenting itinerant society of some sort, many of them Baptist. This was a positive force in breaking down the isolation of independent churches and encouraging a deeper Association life.

TO THINK ABOUT . . .

To what extent is itinerancy still a method for Baptist churches and Associations to use in encouraging rural and urban congregations?

It also produced a shift in understanding of what it meant to be a Baptist minister. It was no longer sufficient to think of ministry in the static terms of the ministry of Word and Sacrament and the pastoral care of the people of God. It encouraged a new relationship between ministers and members who were engaged in this village preaching programme. It created an expectation of evangelistic pastors, like John Saffrey of Salisbury, who supported both home and overseas mission, and itinerated regularly in the villages round Salisbury. In the year 1796–1797 there were twenty-six members added to the Salisbury church and in the next twelve months nineteen more. Of these, nine were from surrounding villages into which the Salisbury Baptist itinerant preachers had recently gone. The adoption of itinerancy by Baptists marked the transition from their relative obscurity in the eighteenth century to their prominence in the next.

Itinerancy made striking progress in this period and one major contributory factor was that first the Bristol and later the Bradford Academies provided a number of ministers who were trained in village preaching and convinced of the need for aggressive evangelism.

TO THINK ABOUT . . .

In what ways ought Baptist colleges to be training men and women to minister specifically in rural and urban contexts?

The success of the initial phase of itinerancy meant the Gospel penetrated new communities, drawing a considerable accession of hearers and a lesser number of members to new Baptist churches. The place of adherents, as distinct from members, in these churches produced an increasing breakdown of Baptist churchmanship. Itinerancy concentrated on principal gospel themes but it lacked an emphasis on the obligation of church membership, encouraging the development of a rural chapel culture, conscious of its Nonconformity rather than specific denominational allegiance.

These results were not so evident at the time and Baptists were pleased to co-ordinate their efforts in the work of the Baptist Home Missionary Society, founded in 1797.

BAPTIST HOME MISSIONARY SOCIETY

By 1820 full-time evangelists were employed, with some success, to supplement local ministries. Typical was the missionary to East Kent, who each week travelled some seventy to eighty miles, preached in five villages, ran a Sunday School of fifty children and conducted two prayer meetings; every fortnight he exchanged loan tracts and sold copies of the Bible; in addition he preached frequently in the open air at various unevangelised villages. By 1825 the Baptist Home Missionary Society supported twenty-five such missionaries, and in 1835 there were a hundred working across the country.

After 1835 the Society increasingly turned its attention to the rapidly expanding population in the north of England. By 1850 one third of its three hundred stations were in urban situations, many of them in Lancashire. The Society also began to direct some evangelists to revive established churches through special 'protracted meetings', rather than planting new causes.

The word *revival* is a clue to much thinking about mission in the nineteenth century. **Charles Hill Roe**, the dominating secretary of the Baptist Home Missionary Society in 1835, spent five years reviving existing 'feeble' churches. The revival services he conducted were based very much on the American model of Charles G. Finney's *Lectures on Revivals of Religion*. Roe's health collapsed under the strain of work, and **Thomas Pulsford** took over the itinerating work in the north of England in 1839. Pulsford's 'flame of Pentecostal fire' was carried with vigour through the churches for a decade.

A growing tide of criticism, the deterioration of the Society's finances in the later 1840s, and the departure of two committee members to America were too much for the evangelist system. Criticism focused on the pressures that itinerant evangelists put on those unqualified and unprepared to accept baptism and church membership. New converts, inflated with a sense of their own importance, lost confidence in their pastors whom they compared unfavourably with dynamic evangelists. The emphasis on

revivals did damage to the Home Mission Society's task of 'extension'; and evangelists were increasingly asked to cultivate new areas, not to revive old ones. The result of such criticism was the termination of Pulsford's appointment. Baptists continued to benefit from the revivals but their commitment was cautious and often uncertain.

> *TO THINK ABOUT . . .*
> **To what extent are these criticisms of itinerant evangelists valid for today? How most fruitfully should itinerant evangelists relate to local churches?**

J.H. HINTON – A PLEA FOR PERSONAL EVANGELISM

John Howard Hinton, Secretary of the Union 1841–1866.

This cherished feeling of exemption on the part of Christians at large . . . is one of the greatest evils of the present age. [There was no hope for a] revival of religion, until this vast slumbering body is aroused to throw off the incubus, and to bend its energies to the effort. [The Church had become a refuge from the world's trials. It should be as a] fortress from which the soldiers of the cross are continually issuing, to assail the Kingdom of darkness, and rescue the captives of Satan. Hence, finally, it arises that even the ministry of the divine word has undergone a most injurious modification. The pastoral character in great part absorbs the ministerial. The edification of the Church takes precedence over the conversion of the world . . . its main address no longer to sinners but saints.

> *TO THINK ABOUT . . .*
> **What steps could be taken by the Union and Associations to ensure that Hinton's call to personal evangelism by *all* members has relevance for contemporary Baptist churches?**

J.H. Hinton was typical of many Baptist ministers who stirred his members to take up personal evangelism. *The Means of a Religious Revival* (1828) began as a sermon on Matthew 5:13, given to his Reading congregation. Hinton complained that far too many Christians left evangelism to the minister. He called for a new commitment to personal evangelism by all members.

Hinton followed the sermon, which was printed, with two series of lectures in 1830 and 1831. The first was titled *Individual Effort for the conversion of sinners enforced.* Hinton's 'moderate Calvinism' was evident as he argued that all Christians are responsible for the condition of fellow men and women and must exert themselves to convert sinners. He discussed direct and indirect means of conversion, and the close connection between prayer, labour and success. *The Active Christian* published a year later is a straightforward guide to personal evangelism. Subsequently the two series were published under a joint title *Individual Effort and the Active Christian.* Another popular work of

Hinton's provided a theological basis for such practical books on personal evangelism. It was called *The Holy Spirit's Work in Conversion.*

When Hinton wrote an introduction to his collected works in 1865 he said these books:

> are to me an affecting memorial of a period of general religious excitement – too transient, alas! and unproductive – to which they owed their origin; but the topics treated of are not temporary or of an evanescent interest.

ROBERT HALL – PREACHER AND REFORMER

There is no doubt that itinerancy was a powerful and formative influence within Baptist churches as the nineteenth century opened. But the century was also productive of great ministers who were primarily powerful as preachers. Even into the middle of the present century it was possible to find copies of an old print hanging in chapel vestries which was a composite etching of Baptist worthies at the opening of the Victorian period, gathered around a vestry table. One man, standing in front of the group which includes Carey, Fuller, Ryland, Knibb, Foster, Kinghorn, dominates the scene. He is Robert Hall, prince of preachers, social reformer and champion of liberty.

PRINCE OF PREACHERS

The nineteenth century was the age of preaching, and Hall possessed great pulpit power. He brought to it a devotional spirit, a brilliant intellect and a profound grasp of philosophy, theology and public affairs. Primarily a doctrinal preacher on faith's fundamentals, Hall's sermons were firmly rooted in events. *The New York Observer* once commented:

> The springs of political government have also felt the touch of his unobtrusive but mighty hand. There is not perhaps a man living . . . of whom the English politicians stand so much in awe. He explains to them the British Constitution, points them to the path of duty, arraigns them before the tribunal of the public, sifts all their proceedings, and dares even to speak against Mr Pitt!

> **TO THINK ABOUT . . .**
> **What do you think explains the comparative lack of influence on national life exerted by contemporary Christian preaching?**

One such sermon was delivered at short notice when he was called on unexpectedly to preach at Broadmead, Bristol. It was October 19, 1803. In the chapel a large congregation containing many servicemen in uniform waited for the 'public fast day' service to begin. The fast had been called as Napoleon stood poised to invade Britain. The oratory was superb as Hall concluded that 'the intoxication of his greatness is the omen of his fall'. *Sentiments Proper to the Present Crisis* became a best seller.

Another sermon, published in 1800, which attracted wide interest was *Modern Infidelity Considered.* It went through many editions, was quoted at length by Sir James Mackintosh during his law lectures at Lincoln's Inn, and brought many to hear Hall during his ministry at St Andrew's Street, Cambridge. The sermon attacked the irreligion which was rooted in the philosophy of the French Revolution. 'Atheism is an inhuman, bloody, ferocious system . . . its first object is to dethrone God, its next to destroy man.' Hall contrasted the moral results of irreligion and the ethical fruits of Christianity.

More typical of his preaching is this series of brief extracts from an evangelistic sermon which appealed direct to the person.

Baptist Leaders in Early Victorian Period. Left to right back row: Joshua Marshman, William Ward, William Knibb, Thomas Burchell, John Rippon, Dan Taylor, J.G. Pike, William Steadman, Samuel Pearce. From left to right front row: William Carey, Joseph Kinghorn, John Ryland, Robert Hall, Andrew Fuller, J. Foster.

To be a partaker of Christ is to be at peace with God; to have peace of conscience, to possess a beneficent interest in all things, and an assured hope of everlasting life. He came that you might have life, and more than life. He came to give rest to your souls, to afford you strong consolation under the sorrows of the world, support in the hour of death, and an entrance when your mortal course is ended into the glory to be revealed . . .

While the bare possession of Christianity will bestow neither profit nor delight, the possession of it in reality will be replete with both . . .

Is the Saviour, the Lord of his Church, wooing your souls? Is he asking leave to come in? . . . Open the door and let the King of Glory come in . . .

> ### TO THINK ABOUT . . .
> **From the cursory consideration above of Hall's preaching, what do you glean about his balance between personal salvation and social change?**

SOCIAL REFORMER

An appeal on the subject of the Framework Knitters' Fund appeared as an anonymous tract in 1819. War and industrialisation made the period after the Napoleonic wars one of the most desperate. The government pursued a repressive policy against all who tried to organise workers in defence of their basic pay. Flying in the face of the Combination Acts, the tract argued for a workers' 'Union' among the stocking-makers of the area to prevent starvation and raise basic wages. The workers would contribute to a central fund from which fellow unemployed workers would be paid. The problem was that the stocking-makers already lived on starvation wages. To be out of work was even worse, so many workers would accept lower wages, a position which manufacturers exploited to the full to reduce overheads. The *Appeal* sought capital for the proposed central fund. It would benefit workers by supporting the unemployed and thus remove a cause of low wages. It would help by relieving the already over-strained parish poor-relief. Local tradesmen would benefit because the purchasing power of the workers would be increased and debts reduced.

The pamphlet called down the wrath of William Cobbett, author of *Rural Rides*. At this point Robert Hall revealed that he was the author of the pamphlet and replied on behalf of the workers. Hall viewed Cobbett as 'shrewd, intemperate, presumptuous, careless of the truth of his representations and indifferent to their consequences.' Cobbett claimed employers could not afford to pay their workers more and the whole scheme would encourage idleness. Hall replied that already many employers in three counties had seen the wisdom of his suggestion and responded with gifts for the capital of the union.

CHAMPION OF LIBERTY

Hall opposed the slave trade, as had Caleb Evans and Robert Robinson before him, long before Knibb went to Jamaica with the Baptist Missionary Society. He said the slave trade 'degrades human beings from the denomination of persons to that of things . . . The sale of human flesh is the most atrocious of social crimes.' He opposed the trade as 'most iniquitous in its origins, most mischievous in its effects, and diametrically opposed to the genius of Christianity and the British Constitution.'

One of Hall's most enduring publications came early from his pen: *Apology for the Freedom of the Press* was first published in 1793 and re-issued, largely unchanged, in 1822. From the beginning of his ministry Hall believed that Christianity was consistent with a love of freedom. He reasoned that fellow ministers should be involved in civil affairs, to cherish freedom, to work for it and when it was secured to maintain it. The *Apology* demanded universal adult suffrage, annual parliaments, and the independence of the House of Commons from the paralysing control of the rich. He asserted the need of a free press, a free church and a free state in which people governed themselves.

> ### TO THINK ABOUT . . .
> **What freedoms do you think Christians should be campaigning for today?**

BAPTISTS AND RELIGIOUS LIBERTY

The concern for religious liberty and basic human rights was deep-rooted in Baptist life. Both Robert Hall and Robert Robinson inherited an abiding concern for religious liberty from their Baptist forebears. The Baptist concern for religious freedom and toleration stemmed from a fundamental conviction about human liberty which originated in the Gospel. Both General and Particular Baptists expressed this principle in their earliest thought and life.

The belief that each person is competent to enter on a personal relationship with God heightens the importance given to the validity of private judgement in religious matters. For such a freedom to be established in religious matters it was necessary to have a free church in a free state. Baptists believed that the state had no right to coerce religious opinions or practices, but it did have the duty of sustaining a religious pluralism in the community.

As John Smyth's personal Confession of Faith stated, the powers of magistracy were valid in temporal matters only. The King must 'leave Christian religion free to every man's conscience and . . . handle only civil transgressions . . . for Christ alone is King and Lawgiver of the Church and conscience.' Smyth viewed persecution as stupid, immoral and inimical to the advancement of true religion.

Thomas Helwys, in *A Short Declaration of the Mistery of Iniquity* (1610), gave religious toleration the first and finest defence it had received in England until that time. He, too, was firm in his belief that a ruler's power must be limited to temporal matters, since a confusion with spiritual issues had resulted in much suffering. To use the temporal power to destroy false churches was contrary to the Gospel. It was the task of spiritual forces to 'abolish the man of sin, the mystery of iniquity, which is this beast.' Nothing is more objectionable in spiritual affairs than forcing people to adopt certain religious attitudes. Since each person has competence before God in religious matters, it is a fundamental requirement that everyone shall have liberty to seek this truth in his or her own way. Helwys looked for complete religious freedom as well as total toleration.

Helwys had two successors at Spitalfields who both contributed to the cause of religious liberty. Leonard Buscher adduced that a ruler who kills heretics is putting souls in danger of hell-fire whom God might yet wish to redeem. John Murton's unique contribution to the debate was to face up honestly to the problem of how blasphemy should be handled. He demonstrated that the death-penalty for blasphemy was an Old Testament precedent which was superseded by Christ's coming. Christ now reserved to himself the right to deal with such things, and the temporal power no longer had the right to punish this crime. 'No man for blaspheming Christ and his Gospel may be destroyed or afflicted by imprisonments, death, or calamity whatsoever.'

A legacy of the seventeenth-century Test and Corporation Acts was the number of irritating disabilities under which Dissenters found themselves throughout the eighteenth and early nineteenth centuries. In the 1770s several unsuccessful attempts were made to repeal these Acts. Robert Robinson was one of a number of Baptists who entered the debate. He made a trenchant presentation of the case for religious liberty in *Arcana* where he argued that the question was not 'What?' but 'Why?' the church believed as it did. 'Make religion what you will', he wrote, 'uniformity in it is not to be expected. Philosophy is a stranger to it and Christianity disowns it.' He pleaded for variety in expression of religious belief and the abolition of the Acts which required dissenting people to subscribe to all but four of the *Thirty-nine Articles* of the Church of England. The task of removing these laws from the statute books and the attempt to disestablish the Church of England fell to the Nonconformists of the nineteenth century, who succeeded in persuading first Whig and later Liberal politicians to repeal the repressive statutes but did not achieve disestablishment.

BAPTISTS AND THE LIBERATION SOCIETY

Religious liberty was a constantly recurring theme in the nineteenth century and Baptists played a full part in the various societies which sought to remedy such grievances. **J.P. Mursell** of Leicester was one such Victorian Baptist minister who actively campaigned with Edward Miall, a Congregational minister, to secure the disestablishment of the Church of England by the formation in 1844 of the Anti-State Church Association. This body became in 1853 the Society for the Liberation of the Church from State Patronage and Control, or the Liberation Society.

J.P. Mursell.

Church Rates were a particular problem for Dissenters. They disliked paying the church rates, which could be levied in any parish by a decision of a majority of the parishioners and then used for maintaining the fabric of the parish church. Marriages could be celebrated only by Church of England clergy. Burials in a churchyard had to be conducted according to the *Book of Common Prayer* funeral service. The vast majority of charitable and educational endowments were in the gift of the Church of England. The taking of degrees at the universities of Oxford and Cambridge remained closed to Dissenters, who were allowed to matriculate but not to graduate. The failure to remedy these grievances, plus a growing sense of the power of Victorian Dissent, or Nonconformity, led to a head-on clash in the mid-nineteenth century.

THREE INFLUENTIAL SUPPORTERS

The extent of Baptist involvement in the Liberation Society is illustrated by the fact that three leading Baptist ministers were active supporters. **John Clifford**, minister at Westbourne Park, Paddington, for fifty years, was a supporter of the Society. In 1870, for example, he opened a discussion at one of the meetings on 'the union of Church and State, viewed in the light of present circumstances'. In 1902 he became President of the Society, stating that he had:

> the strongest desire to do what I can to promote a movement absolutely vital to the progress of real religion, to the uplifting and consecration of the State, and to the welfare, spiritual and ethical, of the people of England.

Charles Haddon Spurgeon was identified with the Liberation Society throughout most of his life, and regularly had the Annual Meetings at the Metropolitan Tabernacle. Addressing the Society in 1866 he urged his hearers not to be afraid of being called 'political Dissenters'.

Alexander Maclaren.

The slow coach and the fast train.
A cartoon from Spurgeon's time.

> **TO THINK ABOUT . . .**
> What do you think Spurgeon meant by the term 'political Dissenters'? Is there a role for them today?

Even the quiet and retiring **Alexander McLaren**, the great Baptist preacher in Manchester, was a member of the Society from the days when Edward Miall, his neighbour in Southampton, encouraged him to join. When McLaren was President of the Baptist Union in 1901, he apologised to the Secretary of the Liberation Society for non-attendance at the Society's Spring Meeting. He claimed to have been a supporter for many years and assured the meeting that the Baptist Union would be fully supportive of the Liberation Society's objectives.

OPPOSITION TO THE CORN LAWS

After the abolition of slavery in the British Empire by the 1833 Act, slavery remained in the American South. In 1835 Baptist ministers F.A. Cox and James Hoby were sent by the British Baptists to make a 'friendly expostulation' with American Baptists about slavery in the South, but it was unsuccessful. They believed that the Corn Laws, which were actually designed to protect English agriculture from foreign competition, helped to maintain the American slavery system. Americans argued that:

> if England desires America to be freed from slavery, England must receive the products of our free labour instead of the products of our slaves. Let then every abolitionist consider that view and strive in every lawful way to open your ports to the corn of our country which grows upon free soil, and is cultivated by free men.

To struggle against the Corn Laws was, for Baptists, to continue the battle against slavery and for religious freedom and human dignity.

The list of the Baptist members of the Anti-Corn Law League was almost a Victorian *Who's Who* of the denomination. William Brock of Norwich and Bloomsbury, Benjamin Evans of Scarborough, and J.H. Hinton of Reading were all supporters of the League, as was Thomas Price, editor of the *Eclectic Review* and personal friend of William Knibb. When Cobden called a meeting in Manchester in 1841 to urge that the Corn Laws were opposed to God's law, the Scriptures and Christ, 650 ministers were present. Of these, 182 were Baptists (more than would attend a Baptist Union Assembly for several years yet). The main speaker after Cobden was J.E. Giles, Baptist minister in Leeds and a known Chartist sympathiser.

Religious liberty and human freedom have been essential principles of Baptists, arising from their understanding of the Gospel. As H. Wheeler Robinson once described it:

> There is, in fact, an unachieved liberty *within* faith as well as *for* faith, and its best safeguard is found in the dominating principle of Milton's *Areopagitica*: 'Give me liberty to know, to utter, and to argue freely according to conscience, above all liberties'.

Such liberty involves risks which Baptists must be prepared to face honestly. This was stated finely at the Baptist World Alliance Congress in Atlanta in 1939.

> No man, no government nor religious institution, religious or civil, social or economic, has the right to dictate how a person may worship God or whether he shall worship no God at all. In the

William Brock.

continuance of our consistent Baptist practice we are imperatively constrained again to insist upon the full maintenance of religious liberty for every man of every faith and no faith.

TO THINK ABOUT . . .

How in practice is it possible to square this central tenet of Baptist principle [religious liberty] with the equally central call to vigorous evangelism?

ORIGINS OF THE BAPTIST UNION

PRESSURES TO CENTRALIZE

As the nineteenth century progressed the importance of a national statement of Baptist views demanded a formal organisation of some kind. Baptists were not alone in this, for among Nonconformists in general there was a growing self-awareness. Methodism in its three manifestations, Wesleyan, Primitive and New Connexion, had a reasonable level of national organisation, as did the Society of Friends (Quakers) through its annual London Meetings. Congregationalists became caught up in these centralising pressures and eventually created a voluntary union of churches to meet the national situation. Some Presbyterian and many Old

General Baptists moved over into Unitarianism. However, evangelicals united in a common opposition to the growing restoration of Roman Catholic emphases, through the Tractarian movement in the Anglican Church.

For Baptists, this movement towards a national organisation sprang from the demands of overseas missionary support. It was following a London-based meeting in 1812, where sermons were preached in aid of the Baptist Missionary Society, that a group of ministers met in Carter Lane chapel. They were concerned with 'the promotion of the cause of Christ in general, and the interests of the denomination in particular with a primary view to the encouragement and support of the Baptist Mission.'

They met again in 1813. They were all Particular Baptists who still accepted the doctrine of the 1689 *Confession of Faith*. John Rippon was a prime mover in the formation of the Baptist Union and recognised that it could have a wider place in the life of the British churches. He hoped its annual Assembly would consider 'whatever relates to the real issues of the denomination at home or abroad'. The constitution stated that the Baptist Union's first task was the support of 'our missions'. In its origin the Union was a voluntary fund-raising arm of the Missionary Society. Any attempt to superintend or guide the life and work of local churches, or to impose anything on their faith and order was specifically disclaimed. The original title of the organisation was 'The General Meeting of the Particular (or Calvinistic) Baptist Denomination' and this remained so until 1873 when it became the Baptist Union of Great Britain and Ireland. By then, however, it was known by the brief title, The Baptist Union.

TO THINK ABOUT . . .

How successfully do you think that over the years the Baptist Union has maintained a balance between honouring the independency of local churches and furthering the interdependence and corporate strength of the Union's life?

Not surprisingly one of the first treasurers of the infant organisation was Mr Burls, the then treasurer of the Baptist Missionary Society. The Baptist Union was run from the homes of its secretariat until 1849, when it rented rooms in the Mission House at Moorgate. Baptist Church House was opened in 1903. The Union recommended the forming of 'Auxiliary Societies in aid of the Mission', as well as collections for other Baptist philanthropic and educational interests.

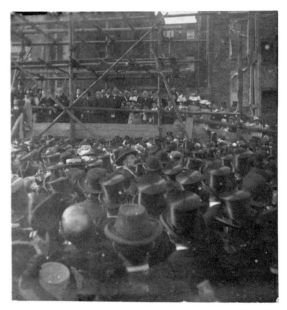

Laying Foundation Stone of Baptist Church House.

RE-ORGANISATION AND DEVELOPMENT

The Union was re-organised in 1832. It was felt sufficient to describe it as a union of Baptist ministers and churches 'who agree in the sentiments usually denominated evangelical'. This opened the door to co-operation with the New Connexion General Baptists. Some Baptists felt that to set aside the 1689 *Confession of Faith* was a false move, and so the more rigidly Calvinist Baptist churches set about forming Strict and Particular Baptist Associations.

The purpose of the Union was to encourage growing denominational awareness and mutual help between ministers and churches. It was to 'promote unity of exertion in whatever may best serve the cause of Christ in general and the interests of the Baptist denomination in particular'. To this end it was agreed to collect 'accurate statistical information' from the denomination's churches, societies, colleges and institutions, both in Britain and abroad. To encourage this process an annual report of the proceedings of the Union and the state of the denomination would be published. Although a modest enough beginning, the process helped the struggling Union to grow. Joseph Belcher, minister at Chelsea, produced a statistical survey which demonstrated that the denomination in England had trebled in size since 1790. It revealed considerable denominational strength in the West of the country, growth in Yorkshire, but very little progress in London.

Between 1832 and 1873 the Union struggled to find its place in Baptist life. Under the firm leadership of Edward Steane, from Camberwell, and J.H. Hinton, from Devonshire Square, its work gradually developed. The graph of Baptist numerical growth dipped slightly at the end of the 1840s but was on an upward curve in the next two decades.

In 1855 *The Freeman* appeared. It was a weekly Baptist newspaper and one of the fore-runners of

Edward Steane, Secretary of the Union 1835–1882.

today's *Baptist Times*. The paper was launched by a Leeds printer at the behest of the Revd Dr Benjamin Evans of Scarborough and was soon a considerable influence among Baptists nationwide. In the same period the Stepney College for training Baptist ministers moved from the East End to Regent's Park in London, to be closer to the new London University.

UNITY WITH DIVERSITY

In 1863 J.H. Hinton was aged 72, and he reflected on the state of the Union from its Presidential chair, albeit pessimistically:

> Denominational union among Baptists has been slow in manifestation, and difficult of cultivation . . . The Baptist denomination, while in name *one*, is in *fact* many . . . it is divided into two by a difference of doctrinal sentiment, some churches holding the Calvinistic system, some the Arminian . . . Of these two bodies the larger, or the Particular Baptists, is itself divided by a doctrinal diversity, according as the Calvinistic system has been found capable of being modified into two forms, which have been called High and Moderate Calvinism . . . The Particular Baptist body is further divided by a practical diversity on the subject of communion. It contains churches which restrict fellowship at the Lord's Table to persons who have made profession of their faith by Baptism, and churches who admit to Communion professed believers in Jesus, although unbaptised. These are called respectively Open-Communionists and Strict-Communionists . . . We have then six parties.

TO THINK ABOUT . . .

You may feel that Hinton's presidential pronouncement has a contemporary ring about it. Is diversity a strength or a weakness of the denomination today?

Hinton, though cautious about the Union's future and usefulness, had himself contributed significantly to its increasing usefulness, and the work grew rapidly in the next thirty years.

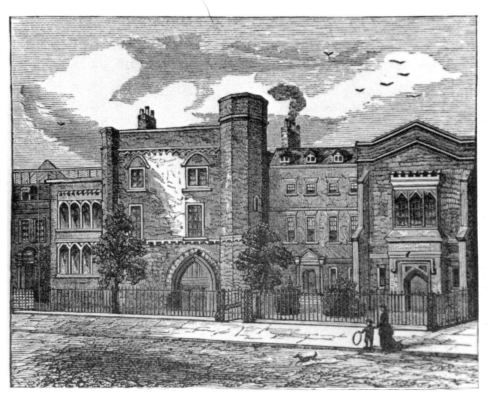

Stepney College before its demolition in 1856.

NINETEENTH–CENTURY BAPTISTS IN THE NORTH

CHARLES WILLIAMS OF ACCRINGTON

In the north of England, Charles Williams of Accrington became a superb builder of the denomination. Williams was liberal in temperament, methodical in conduct, evangelical in experience, Baptist by conviction and professional in training. He represented a new, and hitherto unknown, type of minister. When Williams was called to the Accrington Baptist Church, whose previous pastor had been a Strict Baptist, there was a breach in the Association. A Strict Baptist Association was formed in 1860. By 1876 Williams had won it back into fellowship with the Lancashire and Cheshire Association. In doing so, he secured the adjustment of the Association's churches to evangelism as a vital way of life for Baptist churches.

Charles Williams.

From 1876 onwards aggressive evangelism, church extension and the advance of God's kingdom became paramount. During a long ministry at Accrington, Williams led the church from a membership of 224 in 1850 to 625 in 1901. A new chapel was built in 1874; a Day School with 1575 children attending was opened in 1894; and at its height there was a Sunday School where 1154 children were taught each week by 133 teachers.

TO THINK ABOUT . . .
Consider the following examples of Baptist church architecture from different historical periods. What do the varying styles say about attitudes to worship and mission prevailing at the time? What does the architecture say about how the churches saw their place within society?

Cannon Street Baptist Church, Accrington.

Tetbury Baptist Church.

Mare Street Chapel, Hackney.

*Thatcham Baptist
Church, Newbury.*

*North Springfield Baptist
Church, Chelmsford.*

Williams was a great advocate of the Baptist Union. He was its President in 1886, and for many years he helped J.H. Millard, Secretary after Hinton, to develop the Union's role. He was responsible for establishing a Pastors' Income Augmentation Fund which within five years was distributing £1500 a year to augment the lowest paid ministers. In 1875 Williams took responsibility for raising an Annuity Fund for sick and aged pastors and their dependants, and by 1877 he raised capital of £50,000. If this was not sufficient, he was also fully involved in Association life, being the Secretary of the Lancashire and Cheshire Association for eight years from 1871. He epitomized Victorian evangelical Dissent and was a Baptist whose leadership inspired many in the Union. He said of himself:

> I profess to be a denominationalist. I hope to God I may never be a sectarian. I love the Baptists, as well I may, but I love them more for what I see of Christ in them than I do because they are Baptists; and when I see Christ in others I try to love them equally well, because the love of Jesus demands that we love all alike.

TO THINK ABOUT . . .
Does Charles Williams offer here an acceptable and useful model of the value and limits of denominational allegiance?

Personal example, theology, Nonconformity at its best, political or social affairs were all subject to one grand end as far as Charles Williams was concerned: that all people might discover a deeper faith in Christ and in the Bible. It was not only highly capable ministers but also churches in this period which showed great vigour and concern with the social application of the Gospel.

INDEPENDENCY AND MISSION AT BACUP

Just across the hills from Accrington is the Rossendale Valley in which there had been Baptist work since the late seventeenth century. In Bacup, at the head of the Valley, there was

Baptist industrialists built chapels for their workers.

one Baptist church in 1820, but by the end of the century there were nine. In Lancashire the fierce independency of local Baptist congregations was evident at every turn.

Following personal differences in the Ebenezer Baptist Church in 1821, a new church was formed just across the town square at Irwell Terrace. There were doctrinal disagreements at Irwell Terrace in 1854, which led to the formation of Zion Baptist Church, and in 1900 a dispute over the doctrine of 'conditional immortality' led to the formation of Mount Olivet.

The Valley was the centre of the newly industrialised cotton trade and the source of the River Irwell, just above the town, which provided good water for dyeing and at first the power which turned the mill machinery. At the Irwell Springs Print and Dye Works the small village of Weir developed. It was here that the local dye works owner, out of his own personal funds, provided Doals Baptist Chapel for his workers, as well as supporting the Ebenezer congregation. Mr Shepherd, another local Baptist industrialist, gave £850 to build a chapel and Sunday School for the workers living around his Whitworth Mill, along the road towards Rochdale. The chapel community was decimated during the cotton famine of the 1860s, but in 1887 Mr Shepherd provided a further £1700 towards the cost of enlarged premises.

The Waterbarn Baptist Church was commenced in 1838 at Orchard Hill, Stacksteads, to the south of Bacup, when members of the Irwell Terrace church living in the area gathered for worship in a local house. The chapel and schoolrooms were built in due course at a cost of £2000, a 'penny' day school opened and, under the remarkable leadership of the Revd John Howe from 1851–1887, the church grew quickly.

At his farewell he noted that during those years he had baptised 428 members, and of these, 70 were young people who had all been baptised in 1869. He recalled the contribution of Robert o' th' Moss, one of the so-called 'Deign Layrocks', a company of Christian musicians and preachers. Robert would ascend the pulpit, give out the first hymn, then descend to the singing pew where he had carefully placed his violin-cello, start the tune, conduct the hymn, then re-ascend the pulpit and continue the service. He would bring his lunch with him, whiling away the time by playing his 'cello until it was time for the next service.

He remembered with affection one of his deacons, James Cox, a printer and bookseller who had come to Stacksteads from Haddenham in Cambridgeshire about 1848. He was an educational pioneer in Day and Sunday Schools. It was he who carried on the 'Penny Day School' for 25 years and taught nearly 200 adults to read and write at his weekly night school. He started the Mutual Improvement Society, where on three nights a week he taught a class of 24 men reading, writing, arithmetic, dictation, essay writing and biblical instruction, all of which, states the Fifth Annual Report, 'creates mutual love towards one another, a love which cannot be obtained at the ale-bench, or the gambling table, or the foot race, or the theatre, where young men may be trained up to all sorts of infamy and wickedness.'

> **TO THINK ABOUT...**
> Should the time come again when a local Baptist church is the cultural and recreational centre for its members?

There were also others in the church of distinctive character and considerable spirituality; people like Henry Howorth who lived up on the hill and 'would always take the prayer meeting if they would put him down for a moonlight night'.

A group of out-of-work cotton spinners came to Bacup from Heptonstall Slack, Yorkshire, in 1852. They were seven families of the General Baptist persuasion and, as in Bacup they were all Particular Baptist churches, they formed their own church and built a chapel in 1872.

Bacup was typical of towns across the United Kingdom where the industrial revolution brought many people together for work. Baptist churches were strongly independent and they multiplied because of industrial growth, personal and doctrinal disputes, and also

Henry Howarth 'would always take the prayer meeting if they put him down for a moon-light night'.

because several of the churches had a genuine concern to meet the spiritual and social needs of the people.

BURNLEY – A MICROCOSM OF BAPTIST LIFE

Burnley, to the north of Accrington, presents a similar pattern of Baptist independency and growth. In 1801 it had a population of around 4000. Fifty years later it had become 20,000 and by the end of the century it was just short of 100,000. An obscure Lancashire hamlet had become a significant manufacturing town. Burnley Baptists originated in the work of Dan Taylor, of the New Connexion of General Baptists, and the Ebenezer Chapel in Colne Road was opened in 1787.

The small village of Sabden, just outside Burnley, also had Baptist work begun as the nineteenth century opened. It was founded by John and James Bury who owned the calico-print works there. Their care of the work force was remarked on by Richard Cobden, when he was working there, as a light to the surrounding countryside. This village cause founded the Padiham Church in 1840.

Sion Baptist Church was started by the Colne Road members in 1828, when a Sunday School was formed. In 1831 a chapel was built and in 1884 a complete new suite of Sunday School buildings was erected.

Aenon, Burnley, was begun in another part of the fast growing town in 1852, and it was in this chapel that the historic decision was taken in 1891 to merge with the Particular Baptists in the Baptist Union. Aenon itself started new work in a smithy in the High Street in 1884 and this became the Broughton Street Baptist Church with its own chapel in 1892.

Even C.H. Spurgeon had a hand in Baptist advance in Burnley. After correspondence between some Burnley Baptists and himself, he sent C.W. Oldring, from the 'Pastor's College' to begin a new work in what was to become the Mount Pleasant Baptist Church.

There were also in Burnley, unusually, three so-called 'Scotch Baptist' churches at Haggate, Angle Street and Brierfield. They were Baptists who maintained a Presbyterian church order, Calvinistic doctrine, and had an ordained lay eldership for leaders.

In this microcosm of Baptist life in the nineteenth century there is ample evidence of the vitality of the independent churches as they sought to meet the challenge of the new age. The evangelistic task of the church was tackled aggressively through a wide range of educational and social programmes, in a fearless and buoyant spirit that was typical of the age.

TO THINK ABOUT . . .
Looking back over this brief description of nineteenth-century Baptist life in the North, do you detect any parallels with Baptist life and witness today? Are there any features of the description which you feel could be applied usefully to the present?

UNIT 9

Clifford, Spurgeon and Christian Authority

JOHN CLIFFORD

The leader of the New Connexion of General Baptists in the nineteenth century was John Clifford, whose life spanned almost a century. Clifford was the son of a factory worker and was born at Sawley, Derbyshire. By the age of twelve he was working in the local lace factory. Seven years later he entered the New Connexion College to train for the ministry and at twenty-two he settled in London as the minister at Praed Street, Paddington.

John Clifford.

His thirst for knowledge was insatiable, and a condition of his acceptance at Praed Street was that the church allowed him to continue his studies. In those early years he took degrees in London University in Arts, Science and Law, but the studies never interfered with his commitment to the pastoral and evangelistic needs of the church. In his first year 73 people joined the membership. In 1877 the chapel was enlarged and took a new name, Westbourne Park, where Clifford ministered until 1915.

His interpretation of evangelicalism was Arminian, his appreciation of the new Biblical scholarship acute, and his adherence to the New Testament and its idea of the church unshakeable. He opposed blind conservatism and repudiated the antagonism between science and religion which was beginning to be so troublesome in this period. It was Clifford who took the New Connexion fully into the Baptist Union in 1891. He was twice President of the Baptist Union, the first President of the Baptist World Alliance in 1905, and President of the National Free Church Council. He was made a Companion of Honour in 1921.

He was the 'uncrowned King' of militant Nonconformity. He epitomized the Nonconformist Conscience and this resulted in attacks on his moral character in *Punch* and other weekly journals.

He was an unrivalled platform speaker, an outspoken supporter of the Liberal Party in politics, and always entirely Christo-centric in his outlook. He never tired of saying, 'Our first business is to make men see Christ.' Closely identified with the working classes in Paddington, he was an unashamed member of the Fabian Society.

Parsons in the Pulpit.
From a series of cartoons caricaturing Clifford's pulpit influence.

At the height of his powers in 1880, Clifford edited a book, *The English Baptists*, in which he commented:

> There has been advance of all kinds, all along the line, during the last quarter of a century, and most notably since the advent of the prodigious influence of the Revd Charles Haddon Spurgeon. He is the most pronounced Baptist force of the last quarter of a century. His works are as abundant as his position is unique. The enthusiasm of the great Evangelical Revival appears in him; and the strong passion for 'saving souls', characteristic of White-field, is supreme. But he has at the same time the organising skill of a Wesley, and is the centre of a splendid system of energetic and evangelistic beneficence. Theologically, he claims to stand by Calvin: but he will leave Calvin, and all his theologies to bring a man to Christ, and to extend the Kingdom of the Lord Jesus . . . 'Spurgeon's men' are going all over the planet; and the number of church members represented at the last Conference of the Spurgeon's section of the Baptists, reached a total of 44,505, i.e. nearly a sixth of the whole denomination.

An advert for the Building Society set up by Clifford and illustrating one aspect of his concern to improve conditions for people.

CHARLES HADDON SPURGEON

SPURGEON'S EARLY YEARS

There can be no understanding of nineteenth-century Baptist life without a knowledge of Spurgeon. Born in 1834 at Kelvedon, Essex, into the family of a Congregational minister, the first of ten children, he was largely brought up by his grandparents, his grandfather also being a Congregational minister. As a child he read Puritan writings like Richard Baxter's *Call to the Unconverted* and Philip Doddridge's *Rise and Progress of Religion in the Soul* (1745). He was converted through the ministry of a Methodist lay-preacher when one Sunday snow forced the young Spurgeon unexpectedly into a local chapel.

Spurgeon was baptised in his early teens at Isleham Ferry in Cambridgeshire, about eight miles from his Newmarket home. He went to work in a school in Cambridge and it was there he joined the St Andrew's Street Baptist Church

Isleham Ferry.

lively preaching soon filled the chapel each Sunday.

At his recognition service (he did not favour ordination), Spurgeon said:

> I am not ashamed to avow myself a Calvinist, although I claim to be a Calvinist according to Calvin rather than after the modern fashion. I do not hesitate to take the name Baptist . . . but if I am asked to say what is my creed, I think I must reply, 'It is Jesus Christ' . . . who is the sum and substance of the Gospel, who is in himself all theology, the incarnation of every precious truth, the all-glorious embodiment of the way, the truth and the life.

as a Sunday School teacher. He began preaching in his mid-teens and was appointed pastor at Waterbeach, Cambridgeshire, when only seventeen.

In November 1853, he was invited to preach at New Park Street, Southwark, in the city of London. He preached, was invited to accept the pastorate, and at the age of twenty became the minister soon known in London as 'the boy preacher'. He was an orator and an elocutionist, dramatic to the finger-tips, whose imaginative,

The New Park Street Chapel was soon replaced with the Metropolitan Tabernacle, which could seat five thousand people and was usually full each Sunday during Spurgeon's ministry which lasted till 1892.

SPURGEON'S WIDESPREAD INFLUENCE

Spurgeon was a great philanthropist who encouraged others in their work, people like John Groom working for disabled people and

Waterbeach Chapel, 1851, Spurgeon's first pastorate.

Metropolitan Tabernacle.

Charles Montacute who worked in London for forty years among destitute slum children. Spurgeon's particular concern for children was reflected in his founding of the Stockwell orphanage, which eventually became Spurgeon's Homes, now Spurgeon's Child Care.

Ten years later he began a Colportage Society which took books, pamphlets and tracts to people around the country and offered a personal ministry of care to the sick and the bereaved. There were soon fifty men doing this work with an annual turnover of £3000 from sales. Spurgeon was himself a prolific writer, publishing well over a hundred books, and each week his Sunday morning sermons were printed and sold throughout the country for a penny each.

Spurgeon contributed to Baptist national awareness in a number of ways. He was first and foremost, for over forty years, one of London's greatest and most popular preachers. This drew thousands of new members into Baptist churches, not only at the Metropolitan Tabernacle but nationwide. When in 1856 he founded the 'Pastor's College', now Spurgeon's College, he contributed significantly to the growth of the denomination. In the College many men, often from the working classes and who possessed ministerial gifts, were encouraged to become better equipped for the work of Christian ministry. With the help of these new ministers, Spurgeon was responsible for founding many new churches, most of them in London and the Home Counties.

> ### TO THINK ABOUT . . .
> **Why do leaders and pastors of Baptist churches come rarely today from the so-called working classes?**

When a new cause started, the Trust Deeds were drawn up by his lawyers at the Tabernacle. As the work achieved independence the property was invested in individual trustees, appointed by the new church itself. In a letter written to one such church at its opening, Spurgeon expressed his own understanding of being Baptist in Victorian London. 'Cherish full sympathy with the great denominational movements and seek association with sister churches that you may take your part in the work to be done.'

Spurgeon threw the denominational principle of believer's baptism into the arena of public debate with other evangelicals in the newly formed Evangelical Alliance in 1865. He made an out-right attack on infant baptism, especially as it was expressed in the rites and ceremonies of the Anglican *Book of Common Prayer*. By 1875, William Landels, minister at Regent's Park and President of the Baptist Union that year, rejoiced that baptism, 'our distinctive principle' was recognised as 'the very essence of Christianity'.

Spurgeon, Brock and Landels were three leading ministers in the formation of the London Baptist Association in 1865. It had as one of its primary objectives the formation of at least one new Baptist church each year. Spurgeon was active in his support of this part of the programme. At the opening of the new London Baptist Association chapel at Haven Green, Ealing, in 1881, which had been sponsored during his year of office by the Association President, John Clifford. Spurgeon preached at one service and Clifford at the other.

William Landels.

Charles Spurgeon baptizing at the Metropolitan Tabernacle.

DENOMINATIONAL CONTROVERSY

Charles Stovel.

THE ROOTS OF CONTROVERSY

It was in 1873, at a meeting of the Baptist Union Council, that Charles Stovel, a prominent member since 1832, successfully moved that there be a further change in the Baptist Union's Constitution. It was proposed that a Declaration of Principle replace all previous formulations.

> In this Union it is fully recognised that every separate church has liberty to interpret and administer the laws of Christ, and that immersion of believers is the only Christian baptism.

Liberty thus asserted, really Victorian individualism run riot, was seen as the guarantee of the total autonomy of local churches. Doctrinal statements were unfashionable and the *Confessions* of the previous 250 years were set on one side. Open or closed membership and communion issues were put into the background and Baptist unity was founded on a mode of baptism solely. The mood was reflected in a comment by John Clifford:

> Our conception of baptism is altering . . . stronger emphasis is being everywhere given to the relation of the believing soul to Christ, rather than its relation to church order. We feel it to be one form of expressing the loyalty of the soul to Christ.

TO THINK ABOUT . . .
Does Clifford's analysis of the trend in his day apply in our own age? If so, what factors contribute to an impatience with church order?

In some Baptist pulpits of the period there was a move towards Romanticism which expressed itself in a fashion for quoting poetry, specially Wordsworth, and in the elevation of feeling at the expense of doctrine. The embodiment of

Brimstone and Treacle.
From a cartoonist contemporary with Spurgeon

aesthetic and cultural influences was S.A. Tipple, the Baptist minister at Upper Norwood, a mile or so from Spurgeon's private residence.

> The services at Central Hill started at five past eleven to allow the train to arrive with the more influential members of the congregation from the West End: the church was closed for the summer when the minister was not there . . . The tone of Tipple's mysticism may perhaps be indicated from the following titles (in a book of prayers): 'Union Amidst Many Differences in Prayer and Praise' . . . 'The Intimate God, Whom Seeking to Express in Our Creeds, We Leave Ever Unexpressed', a delicate statement of the superiority of spiritual over credal religion; 'Through All and In All', a summing up of Tipple's concern to see the universality of God: there is no word more frequent in the title of his prayers than the word 'all'. (J.H.Y. Briggs, 'Image and Appearance', *Baptist Quarterly*, Vol. 23, *p*26.)

TO THINK ABOUT . . .

In what ways do you think contemporary worship patterns are shaped by cultural influences?

In April 1887 Spurgeon attacked such aesthetic preaching in his church magazine, *The Sword and Trowel.*

> Those who hold the eternal verities of salvation and yet do not see all that we believe and embrace, are by no means the object of our opposition: our warfare is with men who are giving up the atoning sacrifice, denying the inspiration of Holy Scripture, and casting slurs upon justification by faith: we care far more for the central evangelical truths than we do for Calvinism as a system.

Spurgeon also led Baptist reaction against the Biblical criticism which dominated this period. He saw the change to the Baptist Union's basis in 1873 as a final repudiation of doctrinal unity among the churches and urged the adoption of the Evangelical Alliance's credal statement.

He was increasingly unsympathetic towards the ministers in the Baptist Union who accepted the results of Biblical criticism. Typical of such ministers would be Richard Glover of Tyndale, Bristol, who was frankly interested in Darwin's researches and did not see why that barred him from keeping company with the New Testament. F.W. Gotch, Principal at Bristol Baptist College, was one whose modern critical approach was recognized by his appointment to the translation panel of those producing the 1884 Revised Version of the Bible.

'DOWNGRADE'

The denomination was clearly surprised by the public controversy which followed the publication of two unsigned articles in Spurgeon's magazine in the spring of 1887, under the title 'Downgrade'. They were written by Baptist minister Robert Shindler and attacked the Arminianism of the General Baptists. In August, September and October 1887 Spurgeon wrote three further signed articles on the issue. They contained pointed references to certain ministers, not named, whose beliefs were 'no

F.W. Gotch.

more Christianity than chalk was cheese', who 'derided Scripture', who 'degraded the Holy Spirit into an influence' and who turned 'the resurrection into a myth'. Yet Spurgeon claimed that in the Baptist Union, 'these enemies of our faith expect us to call them brethren and maintain a confederacy with them.'

On October 25, 1887 Spurgeon wrote to the Baptist Union Secretary, Samuel Harris Booth, resigning and complaining that these 'so-called Christian Unions . . . begin to look like Confederacies in Evil'. The news made national headlines; a special meeting of the Council was called, and in January 1888 Booth, the Union's President (John Clifford) and a Council member, James Culross (President of Bristol Baptist College) met Spurgeon privately, but to no avail. The resignation was accepted and a vote of censure was passed on Spurgeon for making allegations against individuals whom he repeatedly refused to name.

It fell to John Clifford to handle this matter in the Assembly meeting of 1888. In the morning

Samuel Harris Booth.

his Presidential address, titled *The Great Forty Years: The Primitive Christian Faith, its real substance and best defence*, had been masterly. It made clear how he would handle the business of the afternoon, for the address had as its thesis that 'the history of Christianity is the history of controversy', which he illustrated from the New Testament. 'The evils of controversy are all temporary and its benefits are all permanent', he argued. He concluded by addressing the 'modern questions' which faced young people.

> We shall not save or help them by the clashing of our creeds . . . Worse than useless will it be for us to ban thinking and denounce enquiry . . . [The divine vocation is to be] steadfastly resting on the FACTS, joyously experiencing the FORCES, clearly teaching and powerfully embodying the IDEAS of the Great Forty Years of the Christianity of Jesus Christ.

TO THINK ABOUT . . .
How do you respond to Clifford's statements?
Do they have any relevance for Baptists now?

At the afternoon session a Declaratory Statement of Faith was read and approved by the Assembly, which affirmed that the Union is:

> an association of churches and ministers, professing not only to believe the facts and doctrines of the Gospel, but to have undergone the spiritual change expressed or implied in them, [a change which is] the fundamental principle of our church life.

It then listed and briefly explained six facts and doctrines commonly believed by the Union's churches. They were

- the divine inspiration of Scripture,
- the fallen and sinful state of man,
- the person and work of Jesus Christ,
- justification by faith,
- the work of the Holy Spirit,
- the resurrection and judgement at the Last Day.

THE AFTERMATH OF THE CONTROVERSY

The Baptist Union survived both the theological reductionism which characterised the nineteenth century and the withdrawal of Spurgeon from its

Charles Haddon Spurgeon.

ranks. For Spurgeon the immediate safety of those who love the Gospel was:

> in the isolation of independency, tempered by the love of the Spirit of Christ which binds us all to the faithful in Christ Jesus . . . [where] we think the lovers of the Gospel will for the present find their immediate safety.

Such isolation was soon tempered for Spurgeon by his membership of the Surrey Baptist Association.

Ministers who supported Spurgeon, many of them trained at the Pastor's College, realised that such isolation was impossible for them. As Ernest Payne noted:

> The pastor of the Metropolitan Tabernacle might speak like this. For the minister of the average Baptist church the situation was different. The Augmentation and Annuity Funds, Home Mission and the Board of Introduction were drawing together and supplementing the resources of the individual churches, carrying out tasks they could not otherwise fulfil. The necessity of union had to be balanced against any desire for complete uniformity of doctrine. (*The Baptist Union – A Short History*, p142–3.)

The churches, as well as the leaders of the Baptist Union, were determined to maintain the corporate life which had been established. Despite changing ways of thought and expression, all believed the fundamental loyalty of the denomination was to evangelical Christianity. The Baptist Union emerged from 'Downgrade' shaken but not shattered.

> *TO THINK ABOUT . . .*
> **Does Payne's argument carry weight? On what issues would you find it no longer possible to walk in fellowship with other Baptists?**

PARTICULAR AND GENERAL BAPTISTS UNITE

'Starting from different theological and geographical centres, fed and nourished on a different theological diet,' General and Particular Baptists came together, said John Clifford, 'slowly, shyly and surely.' A further moderating of Calvinism among the Particular Baptists, the growth of open-communion in both bodies, and working together over thirty years on the common platform of the Baptist Union, made possible the formal uniting in 1891.

The Union left far behind the outdated eighteenth-century methods which it inherited in 1813, and in 1832 re-organised itself in such a way that Baptist ministers and churches recognised the potential of union for furthering the mission of the churches in a rapidly expanding industrial society. The churches realised the necessity of permanent officers if the Union was to succeed. Samuel Harris Booth served as the first permanent Secretary from 1883 to 1898. Both wings of the denomination saw the Baptist Union as providing a place for working together and getting to know each other. The Presidential Chair of the Union became a place for leaders in both denominations to provide innovative and imaginative leadership.

What actually happened in 1891 was the dissolution of the General Baptist Association and the redistribution of its member churches among existing Particular Baptist Associations. In fact, this was not too difficult an exercise since many already shared in local matters. The two missionary societies united and special arrangements were made for uniting funds held by the various trust bodies. The final meeting of the General Baptist Association Assembly took place in Aenon Chapel, Burnley, where after a four-hour debate the resolution in favour of amalgamation with the Baptist Union was carried. The Baptist Union was now ready for a considerable expansion of its role as the national body representing mainstream Baptist churches.

HAVEN GREEN BAPTIST CHAPEL, LONDON

One such General Baptist church, which had its origins in the work of the London Baptist Association in 1881, was Haven Green, Ealing. Planted by the London Baptist Association as part of its programme of advance in these years, it was founded under the leadership of John Clifford. C.H. Spurgeon preached at its opening, and Mr John Barran, MP for Leeds, presided at the welcome tea, commending the 'aggressive church work' of the Association and its wisdom in responding to the recently published rail traffic returns for West London suburbs.

> **TO THINK ABOUT . . .**
> **What social factors in your community lend themselves to potential church planting.**

Charles Clark.
By permission of Haven Green Baptist Church

Haven Green Baptist Church, Ealing.
By permission

CHARLES CLARK (1882–1887)

In 1882 Charles Clark became the first minister on an annual salary of £500 p.a. He was a Londoner with great personal charisma, having begun as a successful 'street preacher' in the East End. After ministerial training in London, and two years at Maze Pond Chapel, London, he went for three years to Broadmead, Bristol, where 'he did great work in reviving and inspiring with fresh courage and hope what was a declining congregation'. He left Bristol for Australia, where he ministered in Melbourne for eight years. He returned to London, aged forty-three, and was appointed to Haven Green. With his wife Jane, a brilliant musician who frequently played the organ at worship services, Charles Clark brought eloquence, breadth of experience, and popularity to his new task.

When Clark left in 1887, the church secretary wrote:

As a pastor and lecturer he is remembered with hearty regard and admiring satisfaction. It is chiefly as a lecturer that he is known beyond the bounds of Baptist churches. He rendered Dickens with marvellous power, and made scenes painted by that master live and move before his audience. Many have confessed they never reached the soul of Dickens' work till they listened to his representations, with their deep pathos and rollicking fun, irresistible humour and tender humanity.

Haven Green church at this time had many large Victorian families who rented pews so all could be seated together in worship. In fact, 'pew rents' were the secret of financial stability for the infant church. In 1884 the nine deacons each rented a family pew, jointly mustering sixty adults and children, all usually present each Sunday.

TO THINK ABOUT . . .

This may seem anachronistic to us, but in what forms are cliquishness and social differences expressed in our churches today?

Thomas Adey.
By permission of Haven Green Baptist Church

W. THOMAS ADEY (1888–1892)

By 1887, however, church income was not matching the costs of paying the minister and re-paying the building debt. A motion was proposed and carried to cut the minister's stipend to £300 p.a., which not surprisingly led to his resignation in June that year. The problem was that those who rented pews far exceeded membership. The membership only slowly rose to 100 by 1887, but there were 300 pew rents coming in. An average of twenty-seven members attended the monthly church meetings during Mr Clark's ministry. When in 1888 an invitation was given to Revd W. Thomas Adey to become minister, fifteen members were present and a further forty-nine postal votes were accepted. Adey had held pastorates in Leeds and Scarborough before London. For the previous two years he had been working in a predominantly Jewish area of London, seeking unsuccessfully to revive the Commercial Street Baptist Church.

Adey changed the church committee, which had originated the Haven Green cause, into an elected diaconate; passed all business through the church meeting; and kept a careful scrutiny of all the church funds. In 1889 there were two 'missions' in the church which resulted in thirty-two new members that year and twenty more the next. There was a doubling of the number of those subscribing to pew rents. Then the minister of the newly opened Presbyterian chapel began to 'poach' the pew renters from Haven Green. By 1892 the gains were wiped out and Haven Green was struggling to survive.

EVAN THOMAS (1893–1914)

Adey was forced to resign and in 1893 was followed by the Revd Evan Thomas, formerly of Mare Street, Hackney, who began what was to be a ministry of over twenty years. At the height of his ministerial powers, Thomas was noted as a 'poet preacher' with Celtic fire and mystical depth, a lover of liberty and personal friend of David Lloyd-George, MP, who could often be found worshipping at the church.

HAVEN GREEN'S LIFE GLIMPSED THROUGH ITS RECORDS

A Typical Year – 1895

The Annual Report of the church for 1895 gives some idea of a typical large Baptist suburban church of the period. There was the **Country Ministers' Aid Society** which had as its object provision for those who work 'in out-of-the-way places, where the church is small and the stipend poor'. A parcel with forty-five pieces of warm clothing had been sent to a pastor with eight children who was known by Evan Thomas to be deserving of such support. The Society meetings were held alternate Thursdays, from 3.30 pm to 7 pm, with tea provided at 5 pm.

The **Haven Green Dorcas Society** was formed 'for the benefit of families', and these families in the poorer districts of Ealing were visited by the women members of the Society. Each meeting, was opened with a reading from Scripture and, prayers for blessing on the workers. Then followed the work of making various garments; about 300 each year.

The **Mothers' Meeting** met between 2.30 pm and 4 pm. Members paid in towards the cost of coal, clothing and blankets, saving towards the heavy costs of future winter needs. To every shilling, up to five shillings saved, twopence was added. On the coal club, women who paid a shilling a week for twenty-one weeks, were given a five shillings bonus.

The **Haven Green District Visiting Society** comprised twenty women who regularly visited in the area. They persuaded some visited to sign and keep the Temperance Pledge, others to attend the Christian Endeavour held in private homes, and some to come regularly to Sunday worship. They distributed gifts of children's clothing, dolls, papers and magazines, and coal tickets.

Cottage Meetings were held for prayer and Bible study in seven homes, with a gross attendance of 900 for the year, and on occasion these were turned into evangelistic meetings. The Christian Endeavour had ninety-six active members; the minister's Bible Class for Young People had a weekly attendance of 150. The Sunday School had 200 scholars in regular attendance divided into twenty classes, with a weekly preparation class for Sunday School Teachers.

TO THINK ABOUT...
What might a future historian note as some significant features of your church's life and mission?

The Influence of Richard Lewis

From 1884 to 1916 the church secretary was Richard Lewis, a Fellow of the Royal Microscopical Society, who had been educated in Colchester in the same class as James Spurgeon, Charles Haddon's younger brother. He was intrigued with science, and lectured on it in his spare time to the students at the Exeter Buildings Ragged School, once his daily

The Haven Green Dorcas Society.

business commitments were over. For many years he wrote astronomical notes for the *Bible Class Magazine*.

He was regular in worship at Haven Green, both morning and evening, and at the mid-week service. As church secretary he kept very careful records. Against Miss Fudge, whose number on the church roll was 667, Lewis wrote successively: 'Went away 1897 and left no address – efforts to trace not successful – subsequently returned and married no. 669.' Members who left without formal transfer to another church had 'deserted to . . .' put against their entry. Lewis' wife was active in the Ministers' Aid Society, ran the Saturday night prayer meeting in their home and regularly entertained visitors. It was to her that Bessie Lean, Evan Thomas' Deaconness for eighteen years, reported each week. Mr and Mrs Richard Lewis were not untypical of those who worshipped and worked in a Baptist church at the end of the nineteenth century.

Haven Green came into being at the height of the Downgrade controversy, and it was firmly aligned with John Clifford, but the dispute does not seem to have left any mark on the congregation. The church joined the Baptist Union from 1881 onwards and remained firmly committed to it over the years.

THE BAPTIST UNION AND CHRISTIAN AUTHORITY

Various addresses at the Baptist Union meetings which followed 'Downgrade' reveal a growing concern to explain the way in which, as the Revd R.H. Roberts put it in his 1892 address from the Chair, working ministers might relate to the challenge of the new approach to Scripture.

> We have been urged of late to interrogate the Scriptures without any *a priori* assumption as to what an inspired book ought to be . . . To do this it is necessary to rid ourselves of all presumptions from any quarter – such as, e.g. the persuasion that miracles are impossible . . . [Taking 2 Peter 1: 20–21, from the recently published Revised Version, Roberts argued that it was people who were inspired; but that their inspiration came from God, for they were men] moved (borne along or carried) by the Holy Ghost . . . We grow bold enough to affirm that the real author of prophetic Scripture is the Holy Spirit. [At the best] human language is only an imperfect vehicle for infinite thought. As God fulfils Himself in many ways, so truth fulfils itself through many minds, in many forms of speech.

In 1889 Dr J.W. Todd was invited to give an Assembly address on High Biblical Criticism. In 1894 'The spirit in which we should regard the present phases of Biblical Criticism' was the title of a speech by the Revd S. Vincent. In 1909 it was H.G. Wood who spoke on the 'Criticism of the Gospel' and J.T. Marshall who addressed the Assembly on the 'Permanent Value of the Old Testament and Gospel'.

In statements issued after 1888, the Baptist Union itself firmly asserted the centrality of the Scriptures. In that year, replying to the Archbishop of Canterbury's letter concerning fuller organic Christian unity, the Union agreed that: 'The supreme authority of Holy Scripture in matters of religious faith and duty is a cardinal principle underlying our Church organization and individual life'. This scriptural emphasis led to the assertion in the same letter of the importance of 'non-sacerdotal religion', baptism and church government.

The Baptist Union Assembly in 1918 approved a doctrinal basis for the projected Federal Council of Evangelical Free Churches which contained the following statement about the Bible:

> The Scriptures, delivered through men moved by the Holy Ghost, record and interpret the revelation of redemption, and contain the sure Word of God concerning our salvation and all things necessary thereto. Of this we are convinced by the witness of the Holy Spirit in the hearts of men to and with the Word; and this Spirit thus speaking from the Scriptures to believers and to the Church, is the supreme Authority by which all opinions in religion are finally to be judged.

SCRIPTURE OR CREED?

The reply of Baptists to the *Lambeth Appeal*, 1920, clearly established the priority of Scripture over creed. 'The Scriptures in and through which the Spirit of God speaks' ran the reply, 'possess for us supreme and unique authority. While we recognize the historic value of ancient creeds, we cannot give them a place of authority comparable with that of the Scriptures.'

E.A. Payne

Dr E.A. Payne gave an address to the Baptist World Alliance Congress in Latin America in 1960, entitled 'Our Appeal to the Scriptures'. He claimed the appeal was five-fold in character:

- Our appeal is to the Scriptures;
- to the Scriptures as a whole; and
- to the living Word of God enshrined in and conveyed by the written word.
- This Scripture is authenticated to us by the Holy Spirit at work within our own minds and hearts.
- Our appeal is to the Lord Jesus Christ made known to us in and through the Scripture.

Dr Payne reminded his audience of words of Hans Denck: 'He who thinks he can be made truly righteous by means of a Book is ascribing to the dead letter what belongs to the Spirit.'

H. Wheeler Robinson

The problem which is at the heart of all matters relating to the Scripture is that of Authority. Where is authority to be found in the Christian religion? One Baptist who gave considerable thought to this in the present century was Dr H. Wheeler Robinson, Principal of Regent's Park College, Oxford.

H. Wheeler Robinson.
By permission of Regent's Park College.

Robinson, in a paper read at Oxford in 1942, began with the fact that in religion there must be revelation. He established that there are three media of revelation. There is history, the events of the early Christian tradition which are interpreted as the mighty acts of God and so become the foundation facts of Christianity. Next there is the social medium, the corporate organisation and fellowship of the Church. Finally there is the medium of the individual, because every form of the Christian faith demands some kind of personal response from its adherents.

Robinson said that while many Baptists were still content with a direct and simple appeal to the authority of the Scripture, an increasing number were becoming aware that the answer was not quite so easy. While Biblical criticism and the historical method had removed many ancient difficulties in the text, it raised new problems, the most important of which was in the realm of authority. As Baptists escape from obscurantism in regard to Biblical interpretation, they are delivered into the entanglements of subjectivity. The problem presents itself in terms of the competing claims of the 'Jesus of History' and the 'Christ of experience'.

Robinson concluded that the subjective and objective aspects of authority must not be held in isolation. Consciousness always includes both, though the emphasis may now fall on one side, now on the other.

> God is really known, notwithstanding the inevitable symbolism of all human thought and language, in the Bible, the tradition of the Christian community, the individual consciousness, and He is known in all these three realms by the intrinsic truth of the revelation, not by any claims which it makes for itself. To this intricate truth there is an intuitive response of personal faith. In all three realms the Holy Spirit is active partner and director. (E.A. Payne, *Henry Wheeler Robinson*, Nisbet, *p*178.)

TO THINK ABOUT . . .
For Baptists to maintain the authority of Scripture is one thing, but who is to interpret it?

AUTHORITY AND THE HOLY SPIRIT

That final reference to the Holy Spirit takes us into a consideration of Wheeler Robinson's book *The Christian Experience of the Holy Spirit*. He dealt specifically with matters relating to the Spirit and the Bible in chapter seven.

He began by remarking that the Bible, open before the 'plain man', makes a double impression – that it is both like and unlike any other book he has ever read. The literary and historical method of study pushes the whole problem of inspiration back to an understanding of the prophetic consciousness.

> Behind the literature there is history; within the history there are men who believe or are represented as believing that they are 'inspired' . . . The issue as to the reality and the nature of

inspiration of Scripture turns at last on the issue as to the inspiration of the prophetic consciousness – in other words on a particular case of the fellowship of Spirit and spirit.

God's knowledge is mediated in and through religious experience, and this is as crucial for inspiration as it is for the doctrines of Incarnation, Church and Sacraments. God has made human experience the medium of his revelation. God is revealed, of course, because he is there. 'But He is there in the midst of human experience, and the revelation is *wholly* through that medium, not in the creation of the record alone, but also in the original form of the experience.' (*p*148.)

Robinson developed the idea of the Bible as an organism – almost as the fruit of the Spirit in Christian experience:

> The authority of Scripture finds expression through the record of a rich and varied and extensive religious experience, within which we may discern the activity of God . . . (*p*153.)

Scripture reflects the actual experience of men who were inspired; their inspiration was by God's Spirit. It is important to recognize that revelation was mediated.

In *The Pattern of the Church* (1961), edited by Alec Gilmore, Stephen Winward wrote:

> The word proclaimed and written is the vital link between the Christ of yesterday and the Christ of today, and the essential medium of his continuing ministry to the Church and in the world. In the primary sense, of course, the word of God is not the medium of Christ's ministry: it is Jesus Christ himself . . . But in the secondary sense, the word of God was the *verbal* testimony of the eyewitnesses and their companions to Christ the incarnate word . . . In a tertiary sense, the word of God is the *written* testimony of the apostles and their companions to the incarnate word. (*p*65.)

The authority of Scripture and its inspiration depend on the mediation through human experience. Christian experience testifies to the fact that the guidance of God does not come to a passive mind, but that God's revelation is a supernatural enrichment of an active mind.

In the Bible we have the record of a transforming self-disclosure of God's ultimate reality to the personal spirit of men. The unique quality of Scripture derives from the fact that it deals with a unique God, a unique Person, and a unique community of faith. In that sense, no other book can supersede the Scriptures. The Scriptures both reveal God and reprove man, but it is Christ alone who through his Spirit creates a new person in Christ, and renews a human soul.

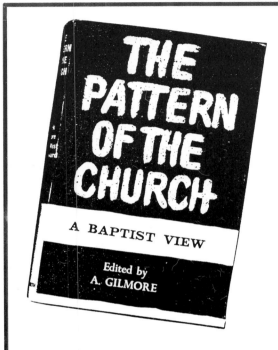

The book edited by Alec Gilmore was carefully sub-titled 'A Baptist View'.

You may like to use the space below to summarise your 'view' of the church, the authority of Scripture and the relationship between the two. The Baptist Union's reply to the Archbishop of Canterbury's letter, quoted on page 140, linked these same two issues.

UNIT 10

Denominationalism: Has it a Future?

EMERGENCE OF THE FREE CHURCHES

The last decade of the nineteenth century was marked by the emergence and rapid success of the Free Church Council movement. Evangelical Nonconformists united in action against clericalism and the rising tide of secularism. Local groups met regularly to plan a variety of activities which included united evangelistic campaigns, temperance demonstrations and school board election campaigns.

Each year from 1892 there was a national Congress whose resolutions were the embodiment of the Nonconformist Conscience. They were a force in politics which the Government of the day ignored at its peril.

> **TO THINK ABOUT . . .**
> **Should Nonconformists today be identified, as they were one hundred years ago, with the legitimate aspirations of the poor? Why do you respond as you do?**

The co-operation experienced in the Free Church Councils encouraged moves towards unity between the Free Churches, and there was a movement towards what W.T. Stead called the 'Civic Church', a non-credal organisation which dealt with all aspects of poverty. Social concern and ecclesiastical reconciliation were the dual objectives of the first Free Church Congresses, each providing stimulation to the other.

At the local level it was the social issues which dominated the scene. In the *Christian World* (December 13, 1894, *p*931) G.H. James, a Nottingham Baptist minister, wrote that his local Free Church Council:

> hoped to focus the convictions of their churches on the great social, moral and non-partisan political questions, such as the drink system, the opium traffic, gambling, peace and war, sanitation,

capital and labour, and the religious alienation of the masses.

United evangelistic action was a prime objective, as in Bradford, for example, where the town was divided into Free Church 'parishes' for the purpose of house-to-house visitation.

A new brand of churchmanship appeared which originated in the mind of Charles Berry, a Congregational minister. He claimed that the churches represented in the National Free Church Council were in a partnership he described as 'Scriptural Catholicism', and were the only genuine 'High Churchmen in England today'. It was an attempt to move from the negativism of the old title, 'Nonconformist', towards the positive affirmation of the inter-denominational nature of Free Churches. Among Baptists this idea was affirmed by J.G. Greenhough in a Baptist Union Assembly address in 1895, when he urged that 'Dissenter' be dropped in favour of 'Free Churchman'.

> **TO THINK ABOUT . . .**
> **How willing are you to abandon the names of 'Dissenter' and 'Nonconformist' in favour of 'Free Church' man or woman?**

These moves towards unity between the English Free Churches as the twentieth century opened put increasing pressure on Baptists to reconsider their understanding of the church, while yet remaining loyal to the congregational principle of the church as a gathered fellowship of believers.

One early challenge was a statement issued by the Lambeth Conference in 1881, which gave the basis on which Anglicans would consider any form of united church. These were the centrality of the Scriptures, baptism and the

Lord's Supper, the historic episcopate, and the Apostles' Creed as the baptismal confession and the Nicene Creed as the sufficient statement of the Christian Faith. The reply of Baptists to this was made under the stress of the Downgrade controversy, and although the need for organic union among Christians was accepted, the Baptist Assembly felt that a sacrifice of principle was being asked which they could not make.

The growing pressures for Free Church unity before the First World War were considerable, but it was out of that crucible of suffering and change that in 1918 J.H. Shakespeare, the Secretary of the Baptist Union, wrote *The Churches at the Cross Roads*. The book marked a watershed in the work of Shakespeare who had been appointed the Baptist Union's Secretary in 1898. To understand its context and effect it is necessary to outline Shakespeare's life and work prior to that date.

> **TO THINK ABOUT . . .**
> **What factors would either urge you to seek or discourage you from seeking closer unity between the English Free Churches?**

JOHN HOWARD SHAKESPEARE

J.H. Shakespeare.

The power of the man is well illustrated by this personal account of a meeting with Shakespeare which Ernest A. Payne, himself to be a future Secretary of the Baptist Union, had as a young boy.

Even a boy could not fail to be impressed. One of my own earliest memories of him belongs to the time of the First World War, when his powers and influence were at their height. My mother had taken me to a meeting in north-east London at which Shakespeare was one of the speakers. I remember nothing of the meeting itself, but on the way home we found Shakespeare on the same electric tram. It happened . . . my mother could claim personal acquaintance with Mrs Shakespeare's family. As the tram rattled its way up the Lea Bridge Road I received an ineffaceable impression of a rare and almost majestic personality who seemed to dwarf his physical surroundings. On several occasions I saw him on the platform of the Baptist Union, usually looking grave, pale and worn, but always commanding. When his book, *The Churches at the Cross Roads*, appeared, I was swept off my feet by its eloquent plea for Christian unity and eagerly entered for an essay competition based upon it. (R.W. Thomson (ed.), *Baptists Who Made History*, p127.)

Shakespeare was a pathfinder for the Baptists and an ecclesiastical administrator of the first order, who by powerful directive leadership drew Baptists together in the opening decades of the twentieth century and gave shape, purpose and hope to the national Baptist family. When he was elected as Secretary of the Baptist Union he told the Assembly:

If in any way I can promote the extension of our churches in the towns, quicken the denominational conscience to play its part in the national life – that part which its past history and the present opportunity demand – and if I can . . . lessen the burden of the humblest village minister, I shall have my reward.

Shortly afterwards he outlined his proposals to a Committee of the Union and one of its senior members asked in a voice tinged with incredulity, 'And is that *all* that you propose?'

TO THINK ABOUT . . .

If Shakespeare were making that statement today, what part in the national life, demanded by past history and present opportunities, might he expect Baptist churches to play?

SHAKESPEARE'S VARIED INTERESTS

The Three Funds

In the twenty-six crowded years of his tenure of office, Shakespeare raised three tremendous funds by which the Union was able to implement his vision for the churches. The **Twentieth Century Fund** was the first, and it provided the capital to purchase and build Baptist Church House, at 4, Southampton Row, London, and also helped with the erection of

seventy-five new churches in England. It was also used to establish the Scholarship Fund of the Union which gave able ministers opportunities for further training.

The **Sustentation Fund** provided a resource for dealing with the very difficult matter of ministerial recognition, pastoral oversight for small village and inner-city churches, and the easement of difficult situations arising from ministerial removal and settlement. It was at this stage that the denomination

Baptist Church House, London, which incorporated the original Kingsgate Baptist Church.

accepted the appointment of ten General Superintendents as agents of the Baptist Union, who would be 'pastors to the pastors' and forward the evangelistic policies of the Union. The final fund raised was the **Baptist United Fund**, shared by the Union and the Baptist Missionary Society, which relieved the resources of both, as both had suffered the results of the changing value of money consequent upon the First World War.

The Baptist Times

With the help of his brother, Shakespeare established *The Baptist Times* as the official weekly journal of the Baptist Union, a position it held until the 1960s when it became entirely independent.

Denominational Administration

He supervised the various departments which were set up within the framework of the Union – a Baptist Women's League, a Young People's Department, a Lay Preachers' Federation – and developed carefully the work of the Superintendents' Board. The Baptist family had arrived as a denomination in England with new leadership, new headquarters, a new weekly

newspaper, and new funds to be administered for the benefit of ministers and churches through the Superintendency and the agencies of the Union.

Baptist World Alliance

In 1905 Shakespeare was responsible for organising in London the first ever meeting of the newly created Baptist World Alliance and was one of its first Secretaries.

Chaplains

He had friends in Government, and in the First World War he persuaded Lord Kitchener to appoint Baptist, Congregational and Primitive Methodist chaplains to the armed forces. In support of these chaplains he established the United Army, Navy and Air Force Board.

The Role of Women

Shakespeare gave considerable support to the proper place of women within the Baptist Union.

Shakespeare wrote:

> I regard the liberation of women from the bonds of prejudice . . . as the most helpful feature of our time. Only at its peril can the Church make itself the last ditch of prejudice in this respect or forget that its problems will best be solved by men and women working together. (*pp*10, 12.)

TO THINK ABOUT . . .
Is 'the liberation of women from the bonds of prejudice' a marked feature of Baptist life in our own time?

The first woman member of Council, Mrs Stockford, from Portsmouth, was elected in 1894, although women had spoken at Assembly before then. Mrs Edward Medley addressed the Spring Assembly 1889 on 'Young Women's Guild work' and in the autumn Mrs Dawson spoke about 'Women's Work in the Church'.

In 1891 at Manchester two single women spoke, Dr Ellen Farrer on 'Women's work among the sick poor' and Miss Edith Angus on 'Women's

Sisters of the People. A group of early Baptist Deaconesses.

work in connection with the Social Condition of the Poor'. These addresses were not only the seeds of the Deaconess movement, which began in London when a number of women with nursing training devoted themselves to visiting and social work, but they had their roots in Baptist womens' missionary concerns during the previous generation. Missionary wives in India had been working in the closely guarded homes of Hindu women, called the Zenana, since 1867. In 1892 two women doctors, Ellen Farrer and Edith Brown, began 25 years of medical work amongst such women in India. Dr Brown's name is associated with the Lhudiana medical college in Vellore, which she founded for the training of Indian women as doctors and nurses.

> ### TO THINK ABOUT . . .
> It is said that women outnumber men in our Baptist churches by three to one. What conclusions do you draw from this and in what ways might it influence future development?

Free Church Identity

Shakespeare was deeply committed to the idea of a united Free Church in England, but the National Council of Evangelical Free Churches had failed to achieve that objective which seemed realisable in the 1890s. This was not a final goal, nor an ideal solution, as far as Shakespeare was concerned, but an intermediate step aimed at a reconciliation of autonomy with co-operation, liberty with order and unity with diversity. Free Church union depended on a shared understanding of Christian faith, and Shakespeare welcomed, as 'catholic, evangelical and positive', the Declaratory Statement agreed among the Free Churches, and which he had helped to write. He looked for a situation after the War when there would be one Free Church in every village in England, when all Free Church ministers would receive common training, and when commonly appointed Home Mission Superintendents would 'go with apostolic zeal through the land to cheer, to advise and to perfect in every parish the organization for bringing religion to the homes of the people'. He believed once the War was over the days of denominationalism would be numbered and that there was nothing more pathetic or useless than clinging to dead issues, worn-out methods and antiquated programmes.

> ### TO THINK ABOUT . . .
> Was Shakespeare's dream of Free Church unity groundless and misguided or was he a prophet before his time?

THE FAILURE OF DENOMINATIONALISM

Shakespeare had spent two decades giving denominational shape to the Baptist family in Britain, but during and after the First World War its impact was such that he could no longer see a solely denominational pattern as relevant to the changes which war brought about in society. 'No one could ever regard me as an indifferent Baptist' he wrote, 'I plan and toil for the church of my own faith, that when the grand festival of union comes she may be led to the altar in radiant beauty, a bride anyone may be proud to have.'

> ### TO THINK ABOUT . . .
> **Over seventy years later the Church in this country is still 'no longer at the centre of the stage', still largely disregarded.**
>
> **What aspects of Shakespeare's agenda focus the needs of the Church in England now?**

SHAKESPEARE ARGUES HIS CASE

The Churches at the Cross Roads (1918) considered

- the failure of the churches to unite in face of growing oppostion,
- the quickening pace of life, with its consequent demands on nervous energy,
- and the awakening of a social conscience, determined to secure a better change for the poor, the weak and disinherited.

Shakespeare knew that the Church was no longer at the centre of the stage. It was not so much beset as disregarded. He recognised that the new age needed a Church whose 'supreme function . . . is to know God, and to make its idea of God operative in human lives' (*p*18). The Church:

> must know God, with depths of humility and penitence, it must know Him for itself, not by tradition or in a creed, but with a vital, penetrating knowledge which dominates its worship, thought and activity, if it is to make its distinctive impression upon the world . . . The true objective of the Church is to establish the Kingdom of God in the world. [The question is whether the Church can find a] vital fund of spiritual creative energy for the immense new needs of the years which lie before it? (*p*22.)

The Church's place in the new order would depend on the strength and passion of the conviction at its heart. It must be ready to risk all, to venture everything on God. The Church must understand the attitude and temper of the age, look through its eyes, speak its vocabulary, wear the garb of the new age. It would not count for much unless it took its part in solving the ills of society and, particularly, transcended a narrow nationalism. Shakespeare wrote:

> Christianity is the religion of love and fellowship [but] organised Christianity does not strike the world in quite this way . . . The churches place that which is divisive and distinctive in the very forefront. Their glory is apparently not in that which unites them to one another, but in that which separates them. The names do not witness to Christ but to some historical controversy. (*pp*41, 43.)

> ### TO THINK ABOUT . . .
> **Have Christians and Christian churches been wrong in drawing attention to issues which divided them?**

The gains of denominationalism were few in Shakespeare's view. In separation, a special emphasis was put on truth that had been obscured, forgotten or denied. Among the Free Churches, there was the strength of piety. Sometimes, even, the painful divisions of Free Churches had added to the sacrificial activities of organised Christianity.

The losses were obvious. The radical numerical decline in the churches indicated that the denominations were bleeding to death. The divisions among the Free Churches were diverting energies from the spiritual to the material, with a consequent failure to secure the Church's goal. Denominationalism, in fact, no longer commended itself to the members of the churches or their adherents.

The Free Churches:

> have reached a stage in the religious life of this country when, if they are simply a denomination and not a united Church, they are doomed. (p102.)

WHAT KIND OF UNITY?

For Shakespeare the unity of the Church meant 'the different parts of the body working together in complete harmony of means and ends without any collision or frustration of the life force, each organ fulfilling its function and answering to its own type' (p104). He was convinced that continuing Free Church division would be disastrous. 'Unrelieved denominationalism will involve inevitable and increasing loss'. (p117.)

Reunion without the Church of England was unthinkable to Shakespeare. 'It is no use concealing my conviction that reunion will never come to pass except upon the basis of episcopacy. I did not think so once, but that was simply because I did not understand it.' (p178.) That sentence Shakespeare found costly in the remaining years of his Secretaryship at the Union. He had felt a profound change in the air, and was not afraid to frame it in words and actions. He concluded his book:

> I passionately desire the goal of Church Unity, but it is an issue I can leave with God . . . It is impossible – but the Church is always called to impossible tasks and there is no other national outlook for the world or the Church.' (p212.)

Baptists had given a cautious welcome to the Archbishop of Canterbury's invitation to consider the possibility of corporate reunion on the basis of the so-called Lambeth Quadrilateral. Baptists were present at the World Missionary Conference (1910) and early in 1914 the Baptist Union Council expressed its willingness to share in a proposed World Faith and Order Con-ference. The Union was also represented at a series of unofficial Anglican–Free Church conferences held in Oxford between 1918 and 1920.

The *Appeal to All Christian People* issued by the 1920 Lambeth Conference marked a new stage in church relations in Britain. Shakespeare was correct – the Anglicans made it clear in a series of joint conferences held between 1921 and 1925 that they would regard a direct link with the episcopal succession of the past as essential to a united Church. Shakespeare was ready for this. John Clifford and particularly Dr T.R. Glover were definitely not.

> ### TO THINK ABOUT . . .
> **On which side of this debate would you have been and why?**

CHALLENGE FROM T.R. GLOVER

Shakespeare had moved far beyond the rank and file of the Baptist family in this book, and he failed to take the denomination with him. The influential layman, Dr T.R. Glover, a classics fellow of St John's College, Cambridge, and the university's Public Orator, led the denominational opposition through a resolution carried at the Assembly in April 1919 which noted:

> If the price of Ecclesiastical Reunion be the acceptance of episcopacy, in its historical sense or in some non-historical sense, with the implied necessity of regularizing our ministry by episcopal ordination or re-ordination, the Baptists of this country . . . elect to stand by the priesthood of all believers and God's right to call and consecrate whom He will and how He will.'

Shakespeare told Assembly delegates: 'In leading this movement I have no intention of stampeding the Baptist denomination or doing anything dishonourable . . . I am not at the crossroads. I have chosen my path and I shall follow it.'

Glover wrote a splendid defence of the Free Churches in a series of articles in *The British Weekly* which were then published under the title *The Free Churches and Reunion* and it carried a commendatory preface, written by the veteran John Clifford who, after a long silence, finally declared himself against the Secretary of the Union. In the Assembly of 1921 Shakespeare secured the Archbishop of Canterbury to address the delegates on the *Lambeth Appeal to All Christian People* which invited other English churches to unite on an episcopal basis. But it did not convince the delegates.

At this stage Shakespeare's health gave way and he did little more as Secretary of the Union, suffering a cerebral haemorrhage in March 1925. He resigned his office and eventually died in 1928.

One appointment he did manage to keep was for the Baptist World Alliance meetings in Stockholm in 1923, when he preached at a special service arranged in the Cathedral by Archbishop Söderblom. His text was 'No man having put his hand to the plough and looking back is fit for the

Terrot Reaveley Glover.

The Shakespeare Room in the former Baptist Church House in London.

Kingdom of God.' The sermon opens with the necessity of the ploughman to stay at his task despite every distraction, and it is clearly autobiographical.

> It is hard work to be God's ploughman and endure . . . to maintain the first enthusiasm, the early devotion, sincerity of heart, purity of motive, unbroken courage and undimmed zeal . . . he must go straight and keep his eye fixed on the goal . . . The shadows lengthen and he is weary, but he must press on . . . All around as far as the eye can see, is the bare field. Not even the tiniest blade of wheat is above the surface. But the ploughman labours on . . .

Whatever else is said of Shakespeare's ecumenical vision, it must always be placed in the context of his deepest conviction that the task of the Church is to win the world to God, and his deep desire that the Baptist family might be best equipped for this task nationally and locally. He was without doubt the most formative influence on Baptists in the present century and he wrestled with the twin tasks of mission and unity which still demand Baptist commitment.

TO THINK ABOUT . . .

What is your view of the contention that the world would be more likely won to God if the Church was united?

MELBOURN E. AUBREY

M.E. Aubrey.

M.E. Aubrey succeeded Shakespeare in 1925 and held office until 1951. During this time he sought to steer Baptists away from a pre-occupation with ecumenism (although he was mindful of ecumenical developments) to a greater sense of relatedness within the Baptist family and a willingness to evangelise in a post-Christian society where the denomination was in serious decline. The aftermath of World War I and the trauma of World War II demanded much of Aubrey. He provided steady, if unsensational, leadership and sought a closer co-operation between churches in the Associations and in the work of the Union.

The son of a Welsh Baptist minister, Aubrey trained first at Cardiff Baptist College, then at Mansfield College, Oxford. His first post was as co-pastor with the renowned P.T. Thomson in Leicester, and then for twelve years he was minister at St Andrew's St Church, Cambridge. T.R. Glover was involved in Aubrey's election to the Secretaryship of the Baptist Union. He came to the post when the denomination was in evident and serious numerical and spiritual decline. Awkward ecclesiastical and domestic issues in a time of recurrent crises in international and public affairs called for courage, wisdom and inspirational powers of a high order.

Soon after coming to office Aubrey successfully raised a capital sum of £300,000 for the purpose of reorganising comprehensively the Superannuation Funds of the Union. It was launched in 1926, the year of the National Strike, and it underlined a growing sense of unity amongst Baptist ministers in their care for each other. It tied the churches and ministers more deeply into the programme of the Union, since only accredited ministers in Union affiliated churches qualified for benefits under the scheme.

ECUMENICAL AND DOMESTIC CONCERNS

Strong reaction to the ecumenical issue was reflected in the 1926 Assembly theme, 'The Faith of the Baptists', and the Union President's keynote address, entitled 'Protestant of Protestants'. It was itself part of the Baptist reply to the 1920 Anglican originated Lambeth Appeal, and echoed the Union's Council decision that English Baptists would not be represented at the Lausanne Faith and Order Conference in 1927. A decade later an *Outline of a Re-union Scheme* was published which was the result of conversations between Anglicans and the Federal Council of Evangelical Free Churches. Three Baptists were on the Free Church team, including Aubrey, but the proposals received no significant support. Neither were Baptists prepared to join in a scheme of Union which was proposed between Presbyterians, Congregationalists and Baptists. However, there was Baptist participation in the Oxford Conference on Church, Community and State in 1937.

Within the Baptist Union Aubrey began to consolidate certain aspects of Baptist work with the provision of full-time support staff, specifically for Youth and Women's work. In 1934 new lay leadership joined the officers of the Baptist Union when Gordon G. Fairbairn became the solicitor and Arnold S. Clark the treasurer. It was a team which supported Aubrey until his retirement.

Aubrey addressed the evident numerical decline with a variety of aggressive evangelistic programmes. In 1932 there was the Discipleship Campaign, which challenged every Baptist church member to win one new convert for the local church. A Baptist Union Evangelist was appointed from 1935 to 1938 to spearhead evangelistic outreach into the new towns and estates being built in the thirties. There was the Forward Movement, which linked a national appeal for funds to an evangelistic programme within the churches of the Union, which was a financial success but did no more than stay the decline among the churches.

TO THINK ABOUT . . .

To what extent do you think evangelistic programmes organised and promoted from the Union can be successful and fruitful?

THEOLOGICAL DEBATE

Theological tensions continued to surface during Aubrey's period in office. In 1932, both Dr A.C. Underwood, then Principal of Rawdon Baptist College, and Dr H. Wheeler Robinson, of Regent's Park College, Oxford, came in for public criticism for the teaching they gave within the colleges. During the Discipleship Campaign, T.R. Glover had been asked to prepare a supporting study pamphlet for use in the churches, called *Fundamentals*. The adequacy of the section on the atonement was challenged by the pastor of the Metropolitan Tabernacle, H. Tydeman Chilvers, and echoes of 'Downgrade' were heard by some within the denomination. Glover had no intention of offending and it was agreed by both parties that another pamphlet, dealing specifically with the substitutionary understanding of the atonement, be prepared and sent out with Glover's pamphlet. Such episodes are evidence of the sensitivity which Aubrey needed in his leadership role as Secretary of the Union.

SHARED HEADQUARTERS WITH THE BMS

Another domestic tension arose in the late 1930s when there was a possibility that the Baptist Missionary Society might quit Furnival Street to make way for new Government Offices on the site.

The Society officers raised the possibility of a

The Mission House, Furnival Street, 1870–1940.

new joint headquarters in London for the Society and the Union. The Union's leadership did not wish to leave Church House but gave serious consideration to the proposal on the understanding that some measure of integration between the two bodies be agreed prior to the purchase of the new site. It was agreed that Publications, Youth and Women's programmes would be united in the new premises, but beyond this there was considerable resistance from the Society. It was agreed in 1936 that the work of the Society and the Union should be carried on in the same new building in Russell Square. Despite approval being given by the executive bodies of both Society and Union the proposal was defeated at the 1938 Assembly and it was not until 1988 that the proposal came to fruition in the agreement to purchase a new joint headquarters at Didcot, Oxfordshire.

TO THINK ABOUT . . .
What opportunities for furthering our mission at home and abroad are offered by the move of the Union's and the Society's headquarters to Didcot?

Baptist House, Didcot.

Council Chamber – Baptist Church House, London.

DISRUPTION AND CO-OPERATION DURING THE WAR

The effects of war on church life in Britain during 1939–45 were much more extensive than they had been during 1914–18. Men and women were both conscripted into the armed services; the whole population was affected by evacuation programmes which emptied city churches overnight and filled small village chapels to overflowing; church buildings were requisitioned and evening services were cancelled because of inability to meet the 'black-out' requirements. There was also disruption to the central denominational planning. The Society moved to High Wycombe for safety at the start of the hostilities, then moved back to Furnival Street, only to be bombed out, ending back in Kettering where the Society had begun in 1792! The Union remained in Church House and suffered considerable disruption, including the loss of its upper floor by enemy action.

Ecumenical co-operation continued throughout the War. It was in 1941 that a delegation met the Secretary of State for Education, R.A. Butler, and laid down agreed principles about religious education in schools acceptable to all the churches which were embodied in the 1944 Education Act. A month later, at a meeting in Baptist Church House, Free Church interests, represented in the National Free Church Council and the Federal Council of Free Churches, united after a decade of protracted argument, to become the Free Church Federal Council. In the same building in 1942 the British Council of Churches was formed, with William Temple, the new Archbishop of Canterbury, as the first President of a body which united the mainstream Protestant churches in Britain in a programme of growing co-operation.

THE HOME WORK FUND

It was after the War that Aubrey and the Revd Grey Griffiths produced a major plan for the reorganisation of Baptist finances. They proposed a unified appeal by the Union within the churches and Associations which was to be called the Home Work Fund. The funds would meet all central and local needs which were currently appealed for individually within the constituency. Apart from the gifts received from personal members of the Union and affiliation fees from churches, all monies received would be credited to one fund to meet the Union's administration costs and to make grants to ministers of churches in need of help. From the total raised by each Association a quarter would be returned each year to the Associations to finance the local work of the churches. This radical plan changed the denominational pattern of work, giving much needed flexibility and freedom to the Union's staff under Aubrey's leadership.

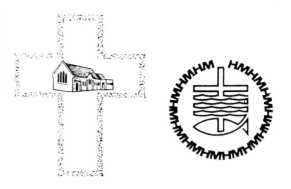

The original logo for the Home Work Fund, with alongside the current Home Mission logo.

> ## TO THINK ABOUT . . .
> To your knowledge, what are some of the undoubted benefits for the Kingdom of Christ which have come from the Home Work Fund (now Home Mission)?

Before retiring, Aubrey made one more concerted effort to address the continuing decline of the denomination through the 'Baptist Advance' programme launched in 1949. He travelled widely throughout the Baptist constituency, encouraging churches in programmes of renewal and evangelistic activity. At the end of his Secretaryship the Assembly recorded its appreciation of his faith, courage and resolution, his fervent evangelistic zeal and deep concern for the spiritual health of the churches, and noted appreciatively his many-sided public and religious services. He was followed in 1951 by Ernest A. Payne.

UNIT 11

Baptists in mid-Century

ERNEST A. PAYNE'S LEADERSHIP

The Baptist Union moved into the 1950s under the careful leadership of Ernest A. Payne who had grown up in London at The Downs, Clapton. His meeting with Shakespeare has already been recounted. After study at Regent's Park College, then housed in London, he was fully intending to go overseas to India with the Baptist Missionary Society. This was not to be, however, and he went to his first and only local pastorate at Bugbrooke, in Northamptonshire.

E.A. Payne.

After a few years he was called to be the Young People's Secretary of the BMS. He served in that capacity and later as editor of the Society until he was called back to Regent's Park College, now in Oxford, to serve as tutor in Church History. He wrote a wide range of Baptist missionary books, including *The Growth of the World Church* which set the missionary story in its widest possible church setting. He also reflected continuously on Baptist history and wrote the seminal study, already referred to, *The Fellowship of Believers*. This sought to provide a proper context for Baptist life and thought, especially in respect of the nature of the church and its ministry. He came to the post of General Secretary with much hesitation but was widely recognised as the person most suited to the task which faced the denomination in mid-century.

One of his first tasks was to be involved with the Golden Jubilee Congress of the Baptist World Alliance which had first met in London in 1905. It was at these meetings that British Baptists first became aware of the powers of a new American evangelist, who preached at the final gathering held in the Arsenal Football stadium, Dr Billy Graham. It established a lasting relationship which has been greatly used in the renewal of Baptist church life during the second half of the twentieth century.

Billy Graham.

The previous year Dr Payne had made a personal visit to the All Union Council of Evangelical Christians–Baptists in the Soviet Union and re-established contact with the Soviet Baptists who now numbered over 512,000 members throughout the various states. Nine Baptists came from the Soviet Union to the London Baptist World Alliance Congress, the first to be present since the 1928 Congress. At this period Dr Payne gave much time to strengthening European Baptist contacts in both East and West. Between 1955 and 1958 he established contacts with Baptists in Hungary, Poland and Czechoslovakia, who came with other European representatives to a European Baptist Federation gathering in Berlin in 1958.

Dr F.T. Lord and Dr E.A. Payne visiting Budapest Baptist Church.

> **TO THINK ABOUT . . .**
> How important a priority in our time should be the further strengthening of those links with Baptists in West and East Europe forged by Ernest Payne and others?

BAPTIST UNDERSTANDING OF THE CHURCH

In 1948 the Archbishop of Canterbury invited the Free Churches to take episcopacy into their system, to try it out for themselves. *Church Relations in England* (1951) was the resultant formal document. Baptists made it clear that they considered it fundamentally wrong to make inter-communion dependent on episcopacy, particulary in view of the unsubstantiated claims commonly made for the latter. Nonetheless, Baptists had been involved in the formation of the British Council of Churches in 1942. This was a useful forum for action in international and social matters.

In 1948 the British Baptists had been participants in the inauguration of the World Council of Churches, though the international community of Baptists had largely held back. It was in preparation for the Faith and Order Conference in Lund (1952) that the Baptist Union Council prepared a careful statement on *The Baptist Doctrine of the Church*. The opening paragraph stated:

> The origin of the Church is in the Gospel – in the mighty acts of God, the Incarnation, Ministry, Death, Resurrection and Ascension of our Lord and the Descent of the Holy Spirit. Thus it is the power of God in Christ which created the Church and which sustains it through the centuries. It is historically significant that Christ, at the outset of His ministry, 'chose twelve to be with Him' and gathered His people into a new community. In our judgement there is no evidence in the New Testament to show that He formally organised the Church, but He did create it. This 'New Israel', the expansion of which is recorded in the *Acts of the Apostles* and in the *Epistles*, is the heir to the 'Old Israel', yet it is marked by vital and significant differences. It is based upon the New Covenant; membership is not constituted by racial origins but by a personal allegiance; the ritual of temple and synagogue has given place to the ordinances of the Gospel and the national consciousness has widened to world horizons. The Messianic community was reborn by the events of the Gospel and is a 'new creation'. Therefore whilst there is an historical continuity with the Old Israel, Old Testament analogies do not determine the character and structure of the New Testament Church.

> **TO THINK ABOUT . . .**
> Why do you think there is in this statement a stress on the discontinuity between 'Old Israel' and the Church? Is it a stress you would also want to make?

During the 1940s Baptists gave considerable thought to the doctrine of the Church. Much of this is summed up in R.C. Walton's *The Gathered Community* (1946). He claimed the Church was more than a voluntary society. 'It is called into existence and its life maintained, not by the decision of man but by the will of God . . . The glory of the Church is a phrase without meaning unless we are thinking of the world Church.' He held it to be 'deeply significant that we do not eat our morsel alone, but in the company of believing men, and that we are not baptised privately but into the fellowship of the Church by our baptism into Christ . . . Baptism and the Lord's Supper are sacraments of the community; acts of God through the Church'. Walton called for 'a recovery of the high-churchmanship of the New Testament and seventeenth-century Baptists . . . A high-church man is one into whose consciousness has been ineffaceably burned a sense of the glory of the Church, and of the supreme privilege of being a member of its fellowship'.

> **TO THINK ABOUT . . .**
> How would you explain your position in relation to any tension between the individualism of the Gospel and the need to be a high-church man or woman?

NEW THOUGHT FROM TER-JUBILEE

As the fifties moved into the sixties Dr Payne constructed a wide-ranging programme of celebrations relating to the 150th anniversary of the founding of the Baptist Union. To set the scene he published in 1959 *The Baptist Union: A Short History*. The four-year celebrations produced a growing self-awareness among Baptists which resulted in discussions about the nature of the Church, its ministry and ordination, baptism, and the place of children in the Church, as well as marked liturgical renewal summed up in a denominationally formative book of *Orders and Prayers for Church Worship* (1960), written by Dr Payne and Stephen Winward, and the publication of *The Baptist Hymn Book* in 1962.

> **TO THINK ABOUT . . .**
> To what extent do you think that over the last one hundred years the denomination's life has been significantly influenced by key leaders? Does your answer please or disappoint you?

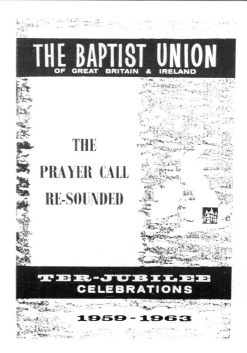

THE BAPTIST UNION OF GREAT BRITAIN & IRELAND

THE PRAYER CALL RE-SOUNDED

TER-JUBILEE CELEBRATIONS 1959-1963

The Prayer Call Re-Sounded *was one of a series of booklets on various themes, marking the Ter-Jubilee Celebrations.*

The Ter-Jubilee began with a renewing of the 1784 *Call to Prayer* which had been so important in the formation of the Baptist Missionary Society in 1792. It was proposed to raise £300,000 in the four years 1959–63 which would be used to help strengthen the ministerial training programmes of the Union and augment the needs of the Home Work Fund.

At the centre of the programme was a denominational conference held at the Swanwick Conference Centre. It considered the present state of the churches and suggested important matters which needed attention if Baptists were to move forward. Baptist independency must be faced with the Biblical and pragmatic grounds

The cover of Orders and Prayers for Church Worship, *together with a selection of further titles from the Ter-Jubilee series.*

TO THINK ABOUT . . .

What role do you think BU publications, such as study guides, books and booklets, should play in the denomination's life?

on which Baptist interdependency could rightly be established in the life of the Union. It was recognised that there could be considerable advantage in a re-alignment of Association boundaries. The possibility of churches grouping under one pastor to meet the need for proper pastoral oversight was canvassed widely. Alongside this went a demand for better programmes of lay training. It was suggested that the denomination must look at the present methods of ministerial settlement, the future of the deaconess group, and the recognition and ordination of potential ministers who were aged over 40. The Conference was one of the most important aspects of Dr Payne's Secretaryship, paving the way for future residential Assemblies, and opening up whole areas of denominational life to a positive re-assessment.

> ### *TO THINK ABOUT* . . .
> **If such a denominational conference was held today, which of the items mentioned above and which other items would you want considered?**

SEARCHING FOR UNITY

THE 1964 NOTTINGHAM CONFERENCE

When a special ecumenical conference organised by the British Council of Churches was called in 1964 at Nottingham, Baptists had been in some measure prepared for it by a small book from the Principal of Bristol Baptist College, published in 1962 against the exciting background of new ecumenical thinking amongst church leaders in Bristol. The Nottingham Conference issued a call to churches to covenant for unity by Easter Day 1980.

Dr Champion's book, *Baptists and Unity*, presented the 'hard facts of unity' which Baptists must ask their fellow Christians to consider, and, if the ecumenical conversation was to continue genuinely, those questions which other Christians would wish to pose to Baptists. He set the Baptist testimony to Church, ministry, worship and sacraments within the theological and religious causes of separation which gave rise to the Baptist churches. Baptist attitudes are thoroughly conditioned by history.

> Nonetheless, among Baptists there have always been men and churches willing to reach out hands to fellow Christians. In spite of important convictions and practices which Baptists have felt compelled to maintain and which have necessarily separated them from many Christians, a number of Baptists have always tried to overcome the separation and have cherished the vision of a church united in its witness to the Gospel, and its dependence upon the grace of God in Jesus Christ. (*p*21.)

Independence in regard to churches and individualism in regard to human persons are Baptist emphases which have made unity difficult.

Fellow Christians should listen to Baptists, for five reasons. Historical stability, geographical expansion, and numerical growth were three factors. The absence of a large section of the 30 million strong, worldwide Baptist community from the World Council of Churches was a fourth reason for listening intently to discover why so many Baptist Christians were outside the conversation. Finally there was a distinctive Baptist witness to valid and valuable theological emphases. Baptism and the significance of the individual, the gathered church, and religious liberty provided three such themes.

Champion believed Baptists must consider the place of infant baptism and children in the church; orders of ministry, specifically episcopacy; the nature of the Church and tradition. He continued:

> if Baptists are to venture along the way of Christian unity sharing with other Christians in this pilgrimage of faith, they will want the conversation to include four themes. They are the themes of evangelism, mission, freedom and fellowship. These are accepted by all Baptists for they are the characteristic themes of Baptist witness. These

four must be given proper place in any unity which Baptists could consider. (*Ibid*, p93.)

> **TO THINK ABOUT . . .**
> Do you agree with Dr Champion's analysis of the 'characteristic themes of Baptist witness'? What other themes would you want 'given proper place in any unity which Baptists could consider'?

THE RESPONSE OF THE BAPTIST UNION

The Baptist Union responded by publishing a Report, *Baptists and Unity* (1967). It concluded that Church Unity was an urgent, yet complex issue:

> whilst there is an undeniable spiritual unity binding together all believers to our Lord Jesus Christ and to one another, this needs to be given visible expression in a clearer and more unmistakable manner than at present.

Although so far no plan had been put forward in Britain for church unity to which Baptists could unitedly give assent, the close study of current negotiations was of great importance.

During the 1970s, when *The Ten Propositions* were issued for discussion, Baptists agreed to consider what 'covenanting together' might mean for the mainstream denominations, excluding the Roman Catholics. The Baptist Union Council felt unable to recommend the Propositions as a way forward for Baptists; and this reply was in accord with those from some of the other mainline denominations. However, this led to a growing participation in areas of local ecumenical experiment during the seventies, with almost one hundred local Baptist congregations engaged in such projects.

Baptists since the Second World War have had to face the growing ecumenical tension, as Christians together faced the pressures of national, cultural and religious diversity in a pluralist society. Baptists have been involved with other Christians more than ever before, yet there has been a reluctance to covenant together with other Christians in the ways suggested. This has been partly because of the Baptist love of liberty, both religious and civil. Yet fullness of life depends not only on liberty, but also on knowing when freely to surrender it.

> **TO THINK ABOUT . . .**
> Do you agree with that last sentence? What are the implications for Baptists in the 1990s?

THEOLOGICAL REFLECTION

NEW THINKING ON BAPTISM

One of the most widely read books on baptism in the twentieth century was **H. Wheeler Robinson's** small volume *Baptist Principles* (1925). It began by asserting that believer's baptism was a Gospel principle. This was 'central and fundamental enough to justify the existence of the denomination.' Believer's baptism emphasised 'the significance, the necessity and the individuality of conversion.' It makes central, unique and permanent the position of Scripture in the life of faith. Baptism carried with it an 'unmistakable definition of the Church, to which it is the door of entrance.'

(pp16 and 24.) Two chapters followed on the historical abandonment of believer's baptism by the Western Church and the various attempts to revive spiritual religion in the church prior to the Reformation.

> **TO THINK ABOUT . . .**
> Wheeler Robinson posed this question at the end of the second chapter: 'Can we defend our retention of Believers' Baptism on any other grounds than the authority of the New Testament?' How would you respond?

The final chapter looked at three contemporary issues: first, the catholicity of Christendom which comes through a conversion experience; second, the recovery of the New Testament emphasis on the Holy Spirit; and third, a deeper recognition of individual liberty of conscience. Believer's baptism, which was 'scripturally sound, psychologically true, and intellectually free,' was symbolically rich in meaning for Christians living in such times.

In 1946 **Robert C. Walton** had been concerned to re-state the traditional Baptist view of the Church. He sought to take back into Baptist thinking the word 'sacrament' which in Victorian times had been so offensive. He recognised that the material elements of water, or bread and wine, were 'instruments of the spiritual . . . and through them God acts and His grace is given.' (*The Gathered Community*, *p*158.) He wrote:

> Believer's baptism is the symbolic representation of the principle of the gathered church, whose members have each made their individual profession of faith . . . It is not, first of all, our act of obedience – an ordinance – but God's redemptive activity . . . There is indeed a corporate aspect to conversion. The convert lives with the Church and is influenced by its fellowship, preaching and life before he enters the Church. Before baptism, as in baptism, God deals with the soul through the holy community. (*p*163 ff.)

Henry Cook replied to Walton in a volume called *What Baptists Stand For* (1947), which was widely used in the denomination for twenty years. In it he attacked very strongly the use of the word 'sacrament' and pleaded for a return to 'ordinance.' But Walton's book had caught the imagination of some younger ministers who produced a series of major books on baptism.

TO THINK ABOUT . . .
Why do you prefer either the term 'sacrament' or 'ordinance' with reference to baptism and the Lord's Supper?

Alec Gilmore edited *Christian Baptism* (1961), which surveyed the Biblical and historical questions afresh, and urged Baptists to ground the doctrine of believer's baptism in the very nature of the Gospel, recognising it has more to say about the doctrine of the Church than it has about personal witness. It was a plea to reinstate the Godward aspects of baptism.

One of the most thorough-going reviews of the New Testament teaching on baptism was published in 1962 by **George Beasley-Murray**, *Baptism in the New Testament*. He stated that baptism could not be viewed as purely a symbolic rite, and to do so was out of harmony with the New Testament. Baptism:

> is the divinely appointed rendezvous of grace for faith . . . Faith is needful before baptism, to receive what God bestows; and after baptism in order to abide in grace so freely given and to work out by that grace what God has wrought within (*p*273 f).

Baptism in the New Testament is of the Holy Spirit and is into the Church. It is a Church act but it is effective by the Spirit. Therefore baptism is about hope because in Christ the believer receives assurance that his future is safe in Christ.

Beasley-Murray looked for a reform in baptismal discipline in the paedo-baptist communities; insisted that there must be an end to regarding re-baptism as blasphemy; and urged the oneness of baptism, confirmation, and first communion. To fellow-Baptists he commended the open-membership principle which allowed for tender consciences, asked for better pre- and post-baptismal training, and insisted that baptism and membership must go together.

TO THINK ABOUT . . .
Is Beasley-Murray right to insist that baptism and membership must go together? Why do you respond as you do?

THE LORD'S SUPPER

In the present century there is still a duality of thought among Baptists on this issue. In 1937 an open communion group put their point in these terms:

> We do not conceive ourselves to be at liberty to lay down any . . . requirements as a condition of access to the Holy Communion when it is observed by us. For our invitation, nay our duty . . . to admit our fellow believers to the Table of our Lord is based upon and presupposes not oneness of membership in one visible organisation but oneness of membership in Christ, and we do not think ourselves at liberty to assert that another is not in Christ merely because he has not been baptised either at all or according to our understanding of the rite. (R.L. Child, ed; *The Lord's Supper: A Baptist Statement*, London, 1951, *p*31.)

The closed communionists put their position thus:

> To us the Holy Communion is a Church ordinance to be partaken of by Church members. We see no evidence in the New Testament of any being admitted to Holy Communion who were not Church members and baptised as believers . . . holding that baptism of believers is New Testament baptism, we cannot admit to membership or to communion any but those who have been baptised on profession of belief . . . We are honouring both ordinances by observing them in the place and order that He himself gave them. We deny the right of any person or institution to cancel what Christ established . . . To us Open Communion and Open Membership are in principle the same, and are serious departures from the practice of the primitive Church. (*ibid, pp*31–32.)

> **TO THINK ABOUT . . .**
> **For what reasons do you take sides with one or other of these positions?**

In the late 1950s and the 1960s there was a considerable shift in Baptist understanding of the Lord's Supper. **R.C. Walton** began the process in 1946, when he wrote:

> Many Baptists will be content to see in the Lord's Supper no more than the act of remembrance and

an expression of the Church's fellowship . . . this seems altogether too limited an interpretation to do justice to the New Testament evidence and the convictions of Christendom. The Lord's Supper is also a means of grace and the Real Presence of Christ is manifested therein. To interpret the Supper as a memorial feast and no more is to reduce it to a method of auto-suggestion. Sacraments are not only symbols: they are also instruments. They tell the truth and convey the grace. They speak, but they speak with power . . . Divine power does not come from the bread and wine, but from God alone, though mediated through bread and wine. (*Op. cit., p*170.)

Henry Cook argued strongly for the use of the word 'ordinance' rather than 'sacrament' on the basis that the Lord's Supper and baptism are the only two acts ordained by Christ. Yet he was prepared to say that they are not only 'enjoined upon us by Christ but that they become to the man of faith an actual means of grace.' (*Op. cit., p*71.) He understood that the bread and wine:

> being symbolic of facts that constitute the heart of the Gospel, arouse in the believing soul such feelings of awe and love and prayer that God is able by His Spirit to communicate Himself in a vitalising and enriching experience of His grace and power . . . they make an appeal to the soul on behalf of God, and according to the response of believing faith there comes the flooding in of the tide of grace.' (*Ibid, p*71–72.)

Robert Child's *Report* (1951), repudiated 'bare memorialism' and claimed that the Supper, 'to the believing recipient', is not only 'commemorative but also communicative.' The Supper is:

> truly a means of grace, but not, be it noted, a means of special grace. The grace is that of our Lord Jesus Christ, and differs in no respect from that which is given through the preaching of the Word, or in prayer, or in other ways. (*Op. cit., pp*19–20.)

The Supper is a service of remembrance which also embodies a proclamation of the Gospel. 'Its actions and words become to us "the outward and visible sign of an inward and spiritual grace" – even the grace of Christ given and received through costly personal encounter with Him.' (*Ibid, p*22.) The idea of sacrifice, Christ's first, then ours, can be used in this context, as can the idea of a 'covenant-rite'. There is in the act a 'perpetual renewing of the Lord's covenant with His people, and so of our covenant with Him and with one another.' The Supper is set within time and eternity:

remembering those who have 'fallen asleep in Christ' we should affirm afresh that God is not the God of the dead but of the living, and that all live unto Him. In this way, the service will be a true 'communion of the saints' . . . (*Ibid, pp24–26.*)

THE THEOLOGY OF THE SACRAMENTS

An Approach to the Theology of the Sacraments (1956), by **Neville Clark,** considered the New Testament material relating to both the sacraments and urged the need for a synthesis which related the understanding of baptism and the Lord's Supper.

The discussion of baptism in terms of the presence and gift of the Holy Spirit, and of the eucharist in terms of presence and gift of the risen Christ may be traditional, but it is rather blatantly bad theology.

He suggested a broader canvas. The theology of the sacraments must be set within 'the whole-ness of the Christian faith.' (*p73.*)

In an important discussion of remembrance Clark commented:

For us, 'remembrance' means the recapturing of the 'memory' of an event, a transportation in thought back to the moment of its occurrence. There is the almost inevitable suggestion of the mental recollection of something or someone in fact absent. But in Hebrew and Greek the words indicate a 'sense of re-calling or re-presenting before God an event in the past so that it becomes living, powerful and operative.' Therefore, when disciples 'do this' it will bring the crucified Christ

out of the past into the present in an active role for believers. (*Ibid, pp62–63.*)

When Clark contributed to *The Pattern of the Church* he reiterated the relatedness of baptism and the Supper.

If the unrepeatability of baptism stands in corres-pondence to the *ephapax* of redemption and speaks of a passage from death to life already accom-plished, the continual repetition of eucharist mirrors the tension of the 'already' and the 'not yet', affirms the parousia as both 'presence' and 'coming', and witnesses to the ceaseless struggle within the Church between the new creation and the passing fashions of this sinful age.'
(*p95.*)

In **Stephen Winward**'s *The Reformation of our Worship* (1963), the emphasis is on embodied worship.

In the eucharist Christ is present, and the saving event is contemporary and operative. For where Christ is present, there also is his immortal sacri-fice . . .The eucharist is a sacrifice because *the sacrifice is present.* It is this eternally valid and contemporary sacrifice that we 'spread forth' in the sacramental signs and tokens.' (*p48.*)

Clark and Winward emphasised the effective and real presence of Christ in the sacrament. The sacraments are perpetually creative of the Church. It is in and through the sacraments that the Church is joined to the ascended humanity of its Lord, and the connecting link is the work of the Holy Spirit.

This was a new development in Baptist thinking about the Lord's Supper.

Both are sacraments of the Church and extensions of the atonement; both are concerned with incor-poration into Christ, with death and resurrection;

both are made powerful by the operation of the Holy Spirit; both stand under the sign of the Cross; both are sacraments of inaugurated eschatology. Nevertheless, while the one has a reference which is primarily individual, the other has a reference which is primarily corporate and cosmic; and while one is concerned with beginnings, new birth, new creation, the other is concerned with growth, re-creation and a pilgrimage. (Clark, *An Approach to the Theology of the Sacraments*, p83.)

BAPTIST MINISTRY TODAY

The Baptist Union established a list of ministers whose training and proven ability would commend them to the constituent churches in the Union. There was a growing concern for the settlement of ministers and their financial situation. The Union introduced the Superintendency to care for churches and ministers in the constituency, though their role from the beginning has always been advisory. There remains a division of opinion in the denomination, some churches believing the Superintendency should advise about ministers, but that the local church remains free to follow or ignore the advice. Others claim that the church deployment of the ministry is a matter of concern to all the churches, and the advice of the Superintendency should be followed.

> **TO THINK ABOUT . . .**
> **What views do you have about the most appropriate role for Superintendents and on what basis do you hold to those views?**

DAKIN'S UNDERSTANDING OF MINISTRY

As late as 1944 the argument as to whether the ministry was to a local church or the whole Church was still being waged. Arthur Dakin expounded the former position in *The Baptist View of the Church and Ministry*.

Dakin argued that:

a Baptist minister is one who is actually doing to the full, the work of a minister in a Baptist Church . . . Baptists have no "order" of ministry in the sense that there is in the Church a class of men made distinctive by some special endowment of divine grace regarded as being confirmed by an ordination ceremony, or the laying on of hands, or in any other way. In actual practice the minister is given a standing different from that of ordinary members of the church, but this is . . . not in any sense [because of] some special grace or "holiness" not available to others (p42).

There is nothing in Baptist theory to prevent any lay person fulfilling ministerial functions provided he or she has the gifts and is properly appointed by the church so to do.

Dakin projected this basic idea to its logical conclusion when he wrote:

a Baptist minister is one who is closely related to one Baptist Church which has given him an invitation and over which he presides. He is a Baptist Minister (with emphasis on the word 'Baptist') partly in virtue of that relationship, and if that relationship were entirely to cease, leaving him with no church over which to preside, he would for the time being cease to be a Baptist minister, just as a deacon ceases to be a Baptist deacon when he gives up the office. (*Ibid*, p44.)

Among Baptists, declared Dakin:

ministry is defined in terms of the local community, and not in terms of a central authority or of an ideal whole. To give up this principle would be to alter profoundly the whole Baptist view both of church and ministry. (*Ibid*, p45.)

How does Dakin's view of a Baptist minister work in relationship to the universal Church?

About this there is no difficulty. Baptists believe that every true Baptist Church is an expression and part of the Church of God. Therefore every minister of a Baptist Church is, *ipso facto*, a minister of the Church of God. Only, in Baptist theory, he is not first a minister of the Church of God in some general way and then a minister of the Church at Corinth. Rather the situation is exactly the reverse, first a minister of the local church and then by reason of that a minister of the Church of God. (*Ibid*, *p*48.)

TO THINK ABOUT . . .

At what points do you agree with Dakin and with what aspects of his views would you take issue?

Significantly the Baptist Union Council statement on the Church (1948) did not support the Dakin view, and claimed that:

> Many among us hold that since the ministry is the gift of God to the Church, and the call to exercise the function of a minister comes from Him, a man who is called is not only a minister of a local Baptist church but also a minister of the whole Church of Jesus Christ.

A thoroughgoing theological solution has yet to be found that will find total acceptance among Baptists.

The Church has power to act against the minister if doctrinal error or immorality is evident in the minister's life. The work of preaching the Word is not confined to ministers, but others, also gifted and equipped by the Holy Spirit for the work, can be approved and called by the local church.

The 1948 statement established that the fundamental Baptist belief about the minister's status and authority remains unchanged. 'The minister's authority to exercise his office comes from the call of God in his personal experience' and after testing of the call and training, the minister is invited 'to exercise his gift in a particular sphere. His authority is therefore, from Christ through the believing community'.

WOMEN IN MINISTRY

The present situation for the ministry is different from that which our spiritual forebears knew. Not least is the growing place which women have in Baptist ministry. The first woman trained for ministry was Violet Hedger, who was ordained in 1926, and a steadily increasing number have followed. At first women provided help as deaconesses, moving

Margaret Jarman.

from the realm of social work into a more clearly defined ministerial function after 1945. Eventually it was agreed that the remaining deaconesses should all be given ministerial status, and the training of women for ministry would be undertaken through the usual ministerial procedures in Baptist colleges.

In 1987, the Revd Margaret Jarman, who had served in a variety of churches and denominational posts, was elected President of the Baptist Union, the first woman minister so to be honoured, although not the first woman to be President of the Assembly. Mrs Nell Alexander served as President during the years 1978–1979. There is a full discussion of women ministers in the contemporary life of Baptist churches and a historical review of their contribution in the *The Baptist Quarterly*, Vol. 31 for July and October 1986.

WIDER SPHERES OF MINISTRY

The growth of denominational organisations like the Baptist Union and the Missionary Society means that ministry today is sometimes exercised within a wider fellowship and a person so used remains a minister despite Dakin's plea otherwise. The growth of worldwide inter-denominational groups (World Council of Churches) and international alliances (Baptist World Alliance) have all contributed to the broader understanding of ministry. There are also a host of Christian organisations (Christian Aid is one, Tear Fund another) into which ministers as such are recruited. Such factors complicate the existing understanding of ministry and create new tensions.

At the beginning of the 1970s *Ministry Tomorrow* was published. It sought to look into the future and see what kind of ministry would be required in Baptist churches. It considered the call and recruitment of ministers, their selection, accreditation, ordination, probation and settlement. Many of its recommendations are now part of Baptist practice, and it was a significant contribution to the present Baptist understanding of Ministry.

While not an official policy statement of the Baptist Union, the discussion of the issues certainly affected the understanding of ministry in our churches. It re-iterated the fact that 'ministry exists to serve the Church and there-fore cannot be understood apart from it'. Having considered church and ministry in a changing world and the present crisis being confronted, the *Report* expressed certain basic convictions.

> We believe in the continuance of the local church, and of a 'professional' ministry that belongs to it . . . That experimental and specialist ministries will need development seems certain. But crucial to the health of the Church is that ministry which builds up the Body and equips the saints for their work of ministry in and to the world. The central requirement for a 'general practitioner' ministry remains. Such ministry essentially consists in the bringing of Word and sacraments to the People of God, the giving of pastoral oversight and service, and the representing of the whole Church to the local manifestation of it . . .' (*p7*).

The *Report* argued for a 'properly trained, supplementary ministry, equally esteemed and recognised, normally drawn from those earning their living in trades, professions and skills of society . . . who will work in partnership with the professional ministry, as associate ministers or members of a larger team' (*p7*).

TO THINK ABOUT . . .
What shifts in understanding of ministry have taken place among Baptists since *Ministry Tomorrow*? Are they shifts in thought and practice which you welcome?

POSTSCRIPT

STATISTICS

The present century has been one of great change. Statistics make that clear. In 1921 there were 3068 churches within the Baptist Union with a total membership of 442,000. In 1981 there were 2058 churches with a total member-ship of 170,000. There is no way of disguising a 57% decline in membership. Set in the context of population in the United Kingdom the decline is greater still. When the century opened the total population was about forty millions; now it is over fifty millions. The decline is even more serious in church Sunday Schools. In 1921 there were 518,000 scholars listed – in 1981,

157,000, a decline of 70%. A part of this statistic is the changing nature of congregations at worship. Formerly they included many more people than appeared on membership rolls of churches. Now congregations are much more restricted to members only, with a very tiny fraction of worshippers not being either members or regular adherents.

WORSHIP

In terms of worship there has been much change, and the liturgical concerns of the 1960s, embodied in E.A. Payne and S.F. Winward's *Orders and Prayers for Worship*, are now very much on the edge of Baptist life. Sunday Schools in the afternoons have been replaced almost entirely by Family Worship services where adults and children are in morning service together. The larger congregations were in the evening fifty years ago, but now the morning congregations have most worshippers, of whom the vast majority come only once a Sunday, not twice.

MINISTRY

Ministry was formerly understood to be a specific function of those ordained to ministry of Word and sacrament, which included the pastoral care of members and leading the church in its mission and service to the surrounding community. Now ministry is understood to be that of the whole church and 'the minister' is regarded as an enabler whose task is to encourage members to fulfil their ministry. Without doubt this has clouded Baptist understanding of the minister's role and diminished his or her place in the life of the church. There is a growing 'professionalism' among ministers today, manifest in their concern about housing, sabbaticals, pensions, time off, etc., which would surprise an earlier generation and probably cause them to remark upon it.

CHURCH RELATIONS

Relationships between churches, as expressed in Associations and Baptist Union, have become both more intricate and looser. The ties which bind Baptists together in the Union and the Missionary Society through the raising and sharing of common funds in Home Mission and World Mission concerns have brought many churches closer together. This has also been strengthened by growing ecumenical relationships.

But there has also been a riding loose to these relationships, especially where churches have moved into 'charismatic renewal' and established new styles of worship and leadership which sometimes move away from the 'congregational' understandings of the Baptist past. This has all contributed to the present concern to reflect on Baptist principles and practice in the search for a properly historic, yet new, Baptist identity.

CULTURAL INFLUENCES

Some important changes have come about in Baptist churches as they have responded to the spirit of the times. A reviewer of D.W. Bebbington's book, *The Nonconformist Conscience*, in the *Times Literary Supplement* (1982), ended thus: '. . . the nonconformist conscience belonged to an age which was distinguished for its faith, its lively provincialism and its optimistic individualism. It perished at the hands of those three ogres of 20th century Britain, secularism, suburbanism and socialism.' There is more to be said than this about the present situation for Baptists, but those words underline the conviction that some important changes in Baptist church life have come about through the pressures of a secular environment and without sufficient reflection as to whether such changes have been in conformity with the Gospel.

These studies are inevitably highly selective and must be read within the context of other Baptist History writing, both ancient and modern. They can only be an introduction to some of the basic issues which confront those who seek to be Baptist Christians today, but hopefully those who are able to learn from their past will not have to re-live too much of it!

BIBLIOGRAPHY
AND
SUGGESTIONS FOR FURTHER READING

Many of the books mentioned in this volume are not generally available, but those which are have an * against them and can best be obtained from the Treasurer, Baptist Historical Society, 148 Greenvale Road, Eltham, London SE9 1PQ.

LIBRARIES

The following Baptist and National Libraries are known to possess copies of volumes referred to, and local libraries should be able to secure them on loan.

The most comprehensive collection of British Baptist and Missionary materials will be found at The Angus Library, Regent's Park College, Oxford, OX1 2IB, which is open during normal working hours to bona-fide researchers but not for genealogical enquiries.

The Baptist Colleges at Bristol, Cardiff, Manchester and Spurgeon's, London, all possess considerable Baptist materials and are usually willing to provide books for study purposes.

British Library, Great Russell Street, London WC1B 3DG.

National Library of Wales, Aberystwyth, SY23 3BU.

John Rylands University Library of Manchester, Deansgate, Manchester M3 3EH.

Dr. Williams's Library, 14 Gordon Square, London WC1 – a library which possesses the largest collection of Nonconformist materials in England.

BIBLIOGRAPHIES

Starr, Edward C., ed. *A Baptist Bibliography: Being a Register of Printed Materials By and About Baptists*. (Judson Press, USA). This is a 26 volume mine of information on who wrote what and where it can be found.

Whitley, William T., ed. *A Baptist Bibliography*. 2 Vols. (London 1916–22).

JOURNAL

* *The Baptist Quarterly*, is a continuing journal of the Baptist Historical Society and through its cumulative indices many articles can be traced on specific issues in Baptist history.

BOOKS AND OTHER SECONDARY SOURCES

The following lists are divided between volumes concerned with Baptist History and those dealing with Baptist Principles and Doctrine. This is in some cases an artificial distinction, but is made for the convenience of readers.

BAPTIST HISTORY

*Bassett, T.M. *The Welsh Baptists* (Ilston House, Swansea, 1977).

*Bebbington, D.W. ed., *The Baptists in Scotland* (Glasgow, 1988).

——, *The Nonconformist Conscience* (London, 1982).

——, *Patterns in History* (IVP, 1979).

*Bowers, Faith, ed., *Who are the Baptists?* A project pack for those wishing to understand the elementary outline of Baptist History thought (Baptist Historical Society).

*Brown, Raymond, *The English Baptists in the 18th Century* (Baptist Historical Society 1986).

Burgess, W.H., *John Smyth, the Se-Baptist, Thomas Helwys, and the First Baptist Church in England* (James Clarke, 1911).

Carey, S.P., *William Carey* (London, 1923).

Crosby, Thomas, *The History of the English Baptists*, 4 vols (1738–40).

*Hayden, Roger, ed., *Baptist Union Documents 1948–1977* (Baptist Historical Society, 1980).

*Hayden, Roger, ed., *The Records of a Church of Christ in Bristol 1640–87* (Bristol Record Society 1974).

Himbury, D.M., *British Baptists: A Short History* (London 1962).

Ivimey, Joseph, *A History of the English Baptists* (London 1811–30).

Lord, F.T., *Achievement: A Short History of the Baptist Missionary Society, 1792–1942* (London, 1942).

Lord, F.T., *Baptist World Fellowship: A Short History of the Baptist World Alliance* (Nashville: Broadman Press, 1955).

Lovegrove, D.W., *Established Church, Sectarian People: Itinerancy and the Transformation of English Dissent 1780–1830* (Cambridge, 1988).

*Lumpkin, William L., ed., *Baptist Confessions of Faith* (Judson Press, USA, 1959).

*McBeth, H. Leon, *The Baptist Heritage: Four Centuries of Baptist Witness* (Broadman Press, USA, 1987).

*Moon, Norman S., *Education for Ministry: Bristol Baptist College, 1679–1979* (Bristol Baptist College, 1979).

Murray, D.B., *the First Hundred Years: The Baptist Union of Scotland* (Dundee, 1969).

Nuttall, G.F., *Visible Saints: The Congregational Way 1640–1660* (London 1957).

Payne, Ernest A., *The Baptist Union: A Short History* (London 1959).

——, *The Growth of the World Church* (London, 1955).

——, *The Free Church Tradition in the Life of England* (SCM 1944).

Spurgeon, Susannah, comp., *C.H. Spurgeon: Autobiography, 2 Vols.*, (The Banner of Truth Trust, 1981).

Underwood, A.C., *A History of the English Baptists* (London, 1947).

Watts, M.R., *The Dissenters* (Oxford, 1978).

*White, B.R. ed., *Association Records of the Particular Baptists of England, Wales and Ireland to 1660* (Baptist Historical Society 1974).

White, B.R., *The English Separatist Tradition* (Oxford, 1971).

*——, *The English Baptists of the 17th Century* (Baptist Historical Society 1983).

Whitley, W.T., *A History of British Baptists* (London, 1923).

——, *The Works of John Smyth, 2 Vols.* (Cambridge, 1915).

BAPTIST PRINCIPLES AND DOCTRINE

Beasley-Murray, George R., *Baptism in the New Testament* (London 1962).

——. *Baptism To-day and To-morrow* (London, 1966).

*Burnish, Raymond, *The Meaning of Baptism* (Alcuin Club Vol. 67, 1985).

Clark, N., *An Approach to the Theology of the Sacraments* (SCM, 1956).

Clements, K.W., ed., *Baptists in the Twentieth Century* (Baptist Historical Society 1983).

Cook, Henry, *What Baptists Stand For* (London, 1958).

Gilmore, A., ed., *Christian Baptism* (London 1959).

——, *The Pattern of the Church* (London, 1961).

Payne, Ernest A., *The Fellowship of Believers: Baptist Thought and Practice Yesterday and Today* (London, 1952 edition).

Robinson, H. Wheeler, *The Life and Faith of the Baptists* (London 1946).

Shakespeare, J.H., *The Churches at the Crossroads: A Study in Church Unity* (London, 1918).

Walton, R.C., *The Gathered Community* (London 1946).

White, R.E.O., *Invitation to Baptism* (London, 1962).

Winward, S.F., *The Reformation of our Worship* (London, 1964).

Select Index of Names